SECTION 1983 LITIGATION

IN A NUTSHELL

Third Edition

By

MICHAEL G. COLLINS
Robert Ainsworth Professor of Courts
and the Federal System
Tulane Law School

THOMSON

WEST

Mat #40403792

Nutshell Series, In a Nutshell, the Nutshell Logo and West Group are trademarks registered in the U.S. Patent and Trademark Office.

© West, a Thomson business, 1997, 2001
© 2006 Thomson/West
   610 Opperman Drive
   P.O. Box 64526
   St. Paul, MN 55164–0526
   1–800–328–9352

Printed in the United States of America

ISBN–13: 978–0–314–16325–7
ISBN–10: 0–314–16325–5

TEXT IS PRINTED ON 10% POST CONSUMER RECYCLED PAPER

for

Annie

*

PREFACE TO THE THIRD EDITION

This book is designed to provide a concise but complete introduction to the topic of litigation under 42 U.S.C. § 1983. As discussed in the introduction, the "section 1983" cause of action is the primary vehicle for redressing federal constitutional violations by state and local officials. Litigation under section 1983 continues to be robust. In addition, section 1983 has established itself as the focus of separate courses in law schools, and it is a major component in courses on federal courts, civil rights, and constitutional litigation. It is my hope that this book will provide law students, lawyers, judges, and their law clerks, with an introduction to and a better understanding of this topic.

Because much of what is difficult and interesting about § 1983 litigation has to do with issues of procedure, remedies, jurisdiction, and federal courts law, I have emphasized these issues. In addition, although § 1983 got its modern start in the civil rights revolution of the 1960's, it is for reasons explained in the text no longer exlusively a "civil rights" statute. It is for that reason that I have somwhat de-emphasized discussion of the substance of the various underlying constitutional rights that § 1983 can be used to enforce. I have also included a chapter on constitutional litigation against federal officials, even though such suits are not controlled by § 1983.

Although each of the chapters stands more or less on its own and can be read independently of the others, two caveats are in order. First, much of § 1983 litigation is an extended footnote to the decision in Monroe v. Pape (1961), discussed in Chapter 2. It would be difficult for someone new to the subject to get a feel for § 1983 without first understanding the impact of *Monroe* which is recounted in that Chapter. Second, the whole of § 1983 may actually be somewhat less daunting than the sum of its parts. That is, an understanding of any one of the particular topics that is the subject of a separate chapter might best be achieved by a complete rather than a selected reading of this book.

Finally, this Nutshell is not intended to be a sourcebook for cases and articles on § 1983 litigation so much as it is intended to provide a broad outline, primarily descriptive and partly critical. I have therefore focused primarily on Supreme Court decisions and have only occasionally made use of lower federal court decisions or decisions from the state courts. The field, moreover, is a rapidly changing one. Final interpretation of comparatively recent decisions and legislation in the area still lies in the future. But I have done what I can to alert the reader to potential problems on the horizon. I hope this modest effort is successful at what it attempts to do.

MICHAEL G. COLLINS

Charlottesville, VA
November, 2005

OUTLINE

Page

TABLE OF CASES

References are to Pages

A

B

C

D

E

F

G

H

TABLE OF CASES

I

J

K

L

M

O

P

Q

R

T

U

V

W

*

TABLE OF STATUTES

UNITED STATES

UNITED STATES CONSTITUTION

TABLE OF STATUTES

UNITED STATES CONSTITUTION

TABLE OF STATUTES

UNITED STATES CONSTITUTION

TABLE OF STATUTES

UNITED STATES CONSTITUTION

UNITED STATES CODE ANNOTATED

18 U.S.C.A.—Crimes and Criminal Procedure

TABLE OF STATUTES

UNITED STATES CODE ANNOTATED
20 U.S.C.A.—Education

28 U.S.C.A.—Judiciary and Judicial Procedure

TABLE OF STATUTES

UNITED STATES CODE ANNOTATED
28 U.S.C.A.—Judiciary and Judicial Procedure

L

TABLE OF STATUTES

UNITED STATES CODE ANNOTATED
42 U.S.C.A.—The Public Health and Welfare

47 U.S.C.A.—Telegraphs, Telephones, and Radiotelegraphs

STATUTES AT LARGE

TABLE OF STATUTES

POPULAR NAME ACTS

———

AMERICANS WITH DISABILITIES ACT

CIVIL RIGHTS ACT OF 1964

EDUCATION AMENDMENTS OF 1972

JUDICIARY ACT OF 1789

SOCIAL SECURITY ACT

*

TABLE OF FEDERAL RULES
OF CIVIL PROCEDURE

FEDERAL RULES OF CIVIL PROCEDURE

*

SECTION 1983 LITIGATION

IN A NUTSHELL

Third Edition

*

CHAPTER 1

INTRODUCTION

Section 1983 is the primary vehicle today for obtaining damages and equitable relief against state and local officials who violate the Constitution. In addition, the statute allows for certain kinds of relief against local governments, and it provides a remedy for violations of federal statutes by state and local actors. Section 1983 actions run the gamut from police abuse and prisoner's rights litigation, to claims for takings of property and challenges to state and local regulations on pre-emption grounds, to school desegregation and other institutional reform litigation. It makes up a burgeoning area of the law. Critics complain of a "flood" of litigation produced by § 1983, but others have doubted the flood's extent. But whoever is right, the number of filings under the statute remains impressive.

A. Historical Background

Section 1983 was a product of Reconstruction and the fundamental alterations in state-federal relations that accompanied it. Enacted in 1871, the statute enabled victims of unconstitutional state action to sue the wrongdoing "person" in an action at law or in equity. Only slightly modified from its

1

original version, the statute (currently codified at
42 U.S.C.A. § 1983) now provides in pertinent part:

§ 1983. Civil action for deprivation of rights

Every person who, under color of any statute,
ordinance, regulation, custom, or usage, of any
State or Territory or the District of Columbia,
subjects, or causes to be subjected, any citizen of
the United States or other person within the
jurisdiction thereof to the deprivation of any
rights, privileges, or immunities secured by the
Constitution and laws, shall be liable to the party
injured in an action at law, suit in equity, or
other proper proceeding for redress, except that
in any action brought against a judicial officer for
an act or omission taken in such officer's judicial
capacity, injunctive relief shall not be granted
unless a declaratory decree was violated or declaratory relief was unavailable. . . .

Background and context are important to understanding § 1983. Before the Civil War and Reconstruction, only a handful of constitutional provisions were directed at state and local governments,
as opposed to the federal government. For example,
states could not pass laws retroactively impairing
contractual obligations under the Contracts Clause
of the Constitution; they could not enact ex post
facto laws; and they could not enact legislation that
interfered with interstate commerce. In addition,
they were obliged to treat out-of-state citizens no
worse than their own with respect to certain impor-

tant rights, and they had to accord full faith and credit to the judicial decisions of other states. But significantly, the express provisions of the Bill of Rights were held to be inapplicable to the states. Barron v. Baltimore (1833). State courts and the common law were therefore the primary guardians against state and local governmental invasions of life, liberty, and property under the Constitution of 1787.

Reconstruction and its aftermath changed much of that. Between 1866 and 1870, three constitutional amendments were passed in rapid succession: the Thirteenth Amendment with its abolition of slavery; the Fourteenth Amendment with its Due Process and Equal Protection clauses (as well as its proscription against state infringement of the privileges and immunities of U.S. citizens); and the Fifteenth Amendment with its right to be free from racial discrimination in voting. In addition, many scholars argue that the Fourteenth Amendment's Privileges or Immunities Clause was designed to make the Bill of Rights applicable to the States wholesale, although the Supreme Court rejected such a reading early on. E.g., Hurtado v. California (1884). Each of the Reconstruction amendments gave Congress the express power to legislate to enforce it by "appropriate" legislation.

Congress quickly acted to enforce these amendments. In 1866, for example, Congress acted to enforce the Thirteenth Amendment and passed a civil rights statute that, among other things, guaranteed to all citizens the "same rights" as "white citizens" to engage in a host of activities, including the right to contract, to give evidence, to sue and be sued, and to hold and alienate property. The statute thus guaranteed that various rights of citizens held under state law—i.e., their "civil rights"—should be enforceable without regard to race. The 1866 Act also provided for the removal from state court to federal court of state-law causes of action when a litigant is "denied or cannot enforce" in the state courts the rights that were guaranteed in the Act. The Act also provided for federal prosecution of certain violations of the statute by persons acting under color of law and, more unusually, for federal enforcement of state criminal law when state court prosecution would have encountered a barrier outlawed by the Act. See Blyew v. United States (1872). In addition, in 1867, Congress enacted a habeas corpus statute that, for the first time, gave those held under state authority the ability to go to federal court to challenge the constitutionality of their detention.

Section 1983 came after this initial wave of federal civil rights legislation, and was designed to open up the federal courts by giving litigants a direct federal cause of action against those who, acting "under color of" law, deprived them of their constitutional rights. The statute was one feature—and perhaps the least controversial feature—of a larger statute popularly known as the Ku Klux Klan Act. Distinguished primarily by its provisions (now codified at 42 U.S.C.A. § 1985(3)) that purported to reach private conspiracies to deny persons equal protection of the laws and to deprive them of their constitutional rights, the overall statute was Congress's response to widespread resistance to Reconstruction in the South by private actors, and by state and local law enforcement officials, legislatures, and courts. Unlike the statutes that preceded it, § 1983 seemed to give private litigants a federal court remedy of first resort, rather than a remedy that would be available only in default of (or after) state process. And by providing a federal cause of action that could be brought in federal court, litigants would no longer be bound by the vagaries of state law.

Prior to the advent of § 1983, however, suits to redress official wrongdoing by state and local actors were hardly unheard of. But the manner in which such suits were litigated would eventually be transformed by § 1983. Prior to the statute, the only option for a victim of unconstitutional action was to sue the wrongdoing official for whatever common-law harm he had inflicted. For example, if an official enforcing a tax enacted in violation of the Contracts Clause or the Commerce Clause were to seize the taxpayer's property to recover the unpaid tax, the official (prior to § 1983) might be sued for conversion, or for trespass, or for return of the goods. The official might then claim in defense that his acts were authorized under the particular state statute that he was enforcing, and the taxpayer might reply that the statute was unconstitutional. If the taxpayer were correct, he could recover against the official in tort. Thus, the Constitution was not irrelevant or unenforced in those older tort actions. But the cause of action was not created by federal law. And, unless the parties were from different states (in which case the federal courts' diversity jurisdiction could be invoked—see below at § C), such suits would be litigated in state court, because Congress did not give the lower federal courts general federal question jurisdiction until 1875.

B. Early Interpretations

Almost immediately on arrival, however, § 1983 entered into a long period of dormancy. According to some estimates of reported cases, litigants invoked the statute fewer than two dozen times over the course of the 50 years following its 1871 enactment. The reasons for § 1983's dormancy are not entirely clear. The Reconstruction-era amendments with which § 1983 was associated were given a narrow interpretation not long after their ratification. Slaughter–House Cases (1873); Civil Rights Cases (1883). Perhaps, therefore, § 1983 was little used because the Bill of Rights remained inapplicable against the states until the Warren Court of the 1950's and '60's began in earnest the process of "selective incorporation" of such rights through the Fourteenth Amendment's Due Process Clause. And at first, those Bill of Rights provisions that were applicable against the states were litigated mostly in criminal contexts, and as a shield to punishment, not as a sword invoked by plaintiffs in civil litigation. But this "narrow constitutional interpretation" explanation for § 1983's dormancy is incomplete because it ignores the fact that there was vigorous enforcement of the Fourteenth Amendment's Due Process Clause against progressive regulatory efforts from the end of the nineteenth century and well into the 1930's. And in those "economic" or "substantive" due process cases, litigants for some reason did not invoke § 1983.

Perhaps § 1983 was little used because, for a long time, it was not clear whether actions of public officials that were not formally sanctioned by state law would amount to state action. This is true insofar as early decisions from the courts seemed to have trouble concluding that unauthorized, ad hoc violations of constitutional norms by individual officials could satisfy the state-action requirement of the Fourteenth Amendment. Barney v. New York (1904). Yet this "limited state action" explanation may ignore the complexity of constitutional decisions during this period, and it overlooks the fact that the Supreme Court concluded early in the last century that the state-action requirement of the Fourteenth Amendment could be met even when officials acted contrary to state law. Home Tel. & Tel. Co. v. Los Angeles (1913).

A more likely but less obvious explanation for § 1983's dormancy may lie in the fact that the Supreme Court narrowly construed the "rights, privileges, or immunities secured by the Constitution" to which § 1983 spoke. This somewhat obscure subset of constitutional rights involved "civil" rights that were said by the Court to be newly created or granted by the Constitution or laws. It did not include, for example, ordinary common-law liberty and property interests that "preexisted" the Constitution (and which were primarily "secured" by state law), but which the Constitution, through provisions such as the Due Process Clause, "protected" from governmental interference. Thus, liberty and property interests were thought of as primarily created and secured by state law, not by the Constitution (or § 1983). In Brawner v. Irvin (C.C.N.D. Ga. 1909), for example, a police chief brutally whipped an African–American woman allegedly because of her race. Section 1983 could not help her, said the federal trial court, because the rights she had been denied were not ones secured by the Constitution but by state law. The court also seemed to doubt whether the police chief's unauthorized behavior amounted to state action.

Interestingly, many of the protections in the Bill of Rights—at least prior to their incorporation against the states through the Due Process Clause of the Fourteenth Amendment—were apparently considered ones that were not newly created or granted by the Constitution, and thus were off-limits to § 1983. See Robertson v. Baldwin (1897) ("The law is perfectly well settled that the first 10 amendments to the Constitution, commonly known as the 'Bill of Rights,' were not intended to lay down any novel principles of government, but simply to embody certain guarantees and immunities that we had inherited from out English ancestors."). And for a while, in the early days of the incorporation process, there were suggestions that § 1983 would not reach deprivations of property at all, but only liberty—thus ensuring that § 1983 would not be used for many of the economic or substantive due process claims that were once, but are no longer in vogue. Hague v. CIO (1939) (Opinion of Stone, J.).

C. Constitutional Litigation Before § 1983

As a consequence, during the period of § 1983's dormancy and before the Supreme Court's decision in Monroe v. Pape (1961) (discussed in Chapter 2), litigants continued to employ the familiar tort model of litigation against state and local officials for their constitutional violations—especially when they acted under unconstitutional statutes. And, of course, federal issues could be raised defensively in state court enforcement proceedings. But not all such suits would be relegated to state court. Many more such suits than one might have supposed were brought into federal court both during the antebellum period and later, during the heyday of substantive due process—i.e., the late nineteenth and early twentieth centuries.

First of all, many regulatory challenges to unconstitutional state action during this period were undertaken by out-of-state businesses, trustees, and bondholders. Thus, diversity jurisdiction would be available for them. Even when federal constitutional grounds were unavailable, federal diversity courts would often apply "general law" principles to the

exclusion of state law (before the Court put a stop
to it in Erie R.R. Co. v. Tompkins (1938)), including
uniform principles of "general constitutional law."
E.g., Citizens' Savings & Loan Association v. Tope-
ka (1874). In addition, with the enactment of the
general federal question statute in 1875, litigants
were able to bring what today might be called
"implied rights of action" under the Constitution
against state officials, without having to resort to
§ 1983. While the bulk of these actions were essen-
tially tort suits for equitable relief, recent scholar-
ship has concluded that at least some of them were
for damages as well. E.g., Scott v. Donald (1897).
What is more, for a number of years after the
enactment of the general federal question statute, it
was possible for litigants to remove civil enforcement actions from state to federal court, solely on
the basis of a federal defense. New Orleans, M. & T.
R. Co. v. Mississippi (1880). Criminal actions triggering constitutional issues were, for the most part,
relegated to state court, although, after 1867, federal habeas corpus was available to challenge unconstitutional state action, especially action taken under color of unconstitutional state statutes.

Thus, the dormancy of § 1983 did not disable
victims of unconstitutional state action from obtaining a federal trial forum to resolve their disputes.
But the modern "civil rights" litigant was not much
in the picture before the constitutional revolution of
the New Deal and Warren Courts. More importantly, as discussed in the chapters that follow, § 1983
would eventually be given an interpretation that

would allow litigants to transcend state tort law as the basis for their claims, and would make clear that public officials, whether or not their actions were formally authorized, could be held individually accountable for their violations of the Constitution and the Bill of Rights. But the older tort-law model of official accountability remains in place for most state and local actors insofar as they may often still be sued under state law for their illegal acts. In addition, state tort law still plays an important role even in the interpretation of § 1983, as discussed in Chapters 2–4.

CHAPTER 2

MONROE AND THE MODERN § 1983 ACTION

Overview

Section 1983 enables persons whose constitutional rights have been violated to sue the wrongdoer personally for redress. In the typical case, liability will attach if (1) the defendant has acted "under color of" state law, and (2) the defendant's action deprived the plaintiff of some right, privilege, or immunity secured by the Constitution (or federal "laws"). That was the message of the Supreme Court's path-breaking decision in Monroe v. Pape (1961), a damages action brought to redress an unconstitutional police break-in of a private home.

Two aspects of the Court's decision in *Monroe* continue to govern § 1983 litigation. First, § 1983 does not require victims of unconstitutional state action to exhaust state remedies that might be available to them before bringing suit under § 1983. Second, an official can act "under color of" law within the meaning of § 1983 and be subject to personal liability under the statute, even when he violates state law and commits acts that state law would not authorize or sanction. Thus, most unconstitutional behavior of state actors taken in the course of employment can potentially subject them to personal liability under § 1983. Although private actors, in contrast to governmental actors, ordinarily cannot violate the Constitution because they do not engage in "state action," they sometimes may be liable under § 1983 when they act in concert with officials or when their acts are otherwise fairly attributable to the government. (A third conclusion of *Monroe*—that cities could never be sued under § 1983—has since been overturned and is the subject of Chapter 6.)

A. *Monroe* v. *Pape*: The (Re)birth of § 1983

The Supreme Court in *Monroe* concluded that a party injured by the unconstitutional action of police officers could sue the officers for damages in federal court under § 1983. Chicago police broke into Monroe's home in the early morning, routed him and his family from bed, made him stand naked in the living room, and ransacked the entire house. He was then arrested and taken to the police station where he was held for ten hours incommunicado, not allowed to call a lawyer, and not promptly arraigned. After his release, Monroe—who was not prosecuted—sued the individual police officers and the City of Chicago in federal court under 42 U.S.C.A. § 1983 for damages for the violation of his constitutional rights. He claimed that the break-in was an unreasonable search and seizure in violation of the Fourth Amendment, a provision whose guarantees had recently been "incorporated" against states through the Due Process Clause of the Fourteenth Amendment. Mapp v. Ohio (1961). He also claimed that his constitutional rights had been violated by his prolonged post-arrest detention.

Justice Douglas's opinion for the Court was significant in a number of respects. It dusted off § 1983 after a long period of relative disuse and indicated that governmental actors could be personally liable thereunder for the injuries they inflict when they violate a person's constitutional rights. "Section 1983," stated the Court, "should be read against the background of tort liability that makes a man responsible for the natural consequences of his actions." The Court achieved this goal of personal officer liability through two important rulings. First, it held that Monroe's § 1983 remedy was "supplemental" to any remedy that he might have under state law. He therefore did not need to exhaust available state remedies as a precondition to bringing suit in federal court under § 1983. Second, it held that the police officers' action was action "under color of " law within the meaning of § 1983, even if what they did also happened to be in violation of state law. Although these two aspects of *Monroe* are related to one another, they identify separate themes that have been played out in subsequent § 1983 litigation.

1. Exhaustion of State Remedies?

The conclusion that the federal remedy was supplementary to any state remedy meant that the plaintiff did not have to show that the state judicial system was unable or unwilling to remedy the injuries inflicted by the Chicago police. The fact that the plaintiff might have a viable state-law tort remedy was therefore irrelevant to Monroe's being able to invoke § 1983. Thus, to call the federal remedy under these circumstances "supplemental" may not be a terribly precise use of the word. But it is clear that the Court meant that the federal remedy was a remedy of first resort and not just a "backstop" remedy when the state court remedy was somehow inadequate or unavailable in a particular case.

(a) Legislative History and the Purposes of § 1983

The Court gave three reasons grounded in legislative history why a § 1983 remedy should be available without regard to the availability of state court remedies: (1) Section 1983 was enacted to redress unconstitutional laws; (2) it was enacted to provide a federal forum when there was no state court remedy on the books; and (3) it was enacted to supply a federal remedy when the state court remedy was available in theory but not in fact. Of course, nothing in the facts of *Monroe* suggested that the Illinois courts were unavailable either in theory or in fact to redress the police illegality in Monroe's case. And there was no allegation in the case that the police acted pursuant to any unconstitutional state laws.

To reach its conclusion that the availability of state remedies was irrelevant to the availability of a § 1983 remedy, the Court must have supposed there was yet another reason that § 1983 was passed: Congress must have concluded that, because the state court remedy was unavailable in theory or in fact in a sufficient number of cases (particularly in the Reconstruction South), the option of choosing the federal remedy should be available to the victim of official illegality in every case of constitutional deprivation. In effect, the decision with respect to the question of whether the state courts might be inadequate or inhospitable to the vindication of federal rights was left unreservedly to the victim in the individual case. After *Monroe*, therefore, those challenging unconstitutional state action need make no showing of state court inadequacy before they can invoke the federal remedy. But the result is probably not compelled even by the Court's own reading of the legislative history.

(b) The Constitutional Dimension of Official Illegality

Because the § 1983 remedy is a remedy of first resort without regard to the availability of state remedies, it gives the victim of official illegality the ability to recover for specifically *constitutional* injuries. State tort law might have also compensated the victim in *Monroe* based on assault, battery, intentional infliction of emotional distress, trespass, and perhaps other theories. But any possible overlap between the interests that tort law protected and the interests that the Constitution protected would be fortuitous—a point made by Justices Stewart and Harlan in their *Monroe* concurrence.

For example, in Katz v. United States (1967), the Supreme Court concluded that the Fourth Amendment protects reasonable expectations of privacy; the amendment could thus be invoked even when state trespass law was not violated. *Katz* was a case of governmental eavesdropping on a call from a phone booth in which the Fourth Amendment issue was raised by the defendant to suppress evidence from his overheard conversation. The Court concluded that whether or not such an act would be illegal under the applicable state or common law of torts, it was nevertheless a violation of the Fourth Amendment.

Analogously, the police raid in *Monroe* might have involved injuries to some interests that state tort law protected quite adequately. On the other hand, the raid might have involved injuries to interests that state tort law did not protect, but which the Fourth Amendment did, and for which the plaintiff could recover damages in his § 1983 action. For example, the reasonable expectations of privacy and dignitary interests safeguarded by the Fourth Amendment may have covered ground that state tort law did not. In addition, state tort law may have given only limited protection to non-physical injuries. Thus, state tort law would cover the constitutional dimension of official wrongdoing only in a hit-or-miss fashion. As interpreted in *Monroe*, therefore, § 1983 allowed victims of constitutional deprivations, upon proper proof, to recover for the uniquely constitutional dimension of their harms, quite apart from their tort-law dimension. Such recovery, however, would be subject to various levels of immunity of the officers sued. See Chapter 8.

Here too, however, it is at least open to question whether § 1983 was originally designed to provide anything other than recovery for traditional common law harms to life, liberty, and property, as opposed to harms more uniquely associated with a violation of the Constitution.

(c) Alternative Possibilities

One might have imagined a different approach to § 1983 from that taken in *Monroe*. As an alternative, one might posit a scheme in which it was necessary—before being able to invoke the federal § 1983 remedy—to exhaust or try out state remedies first. The litigant might then be allowed to return to federal trial court if meaningful relief were unavailable or inadequate under state law. Or, the plaintiff might be allowed to resort to federal trial court as an initial matter if she could show affirmatively in her individual case either that there was no judicial remedy available in the state courts (in theory or in fact) or that there was a problem of state court prejudice that could be established at the outset of litigation. This exhaustion/inadequacy of state process model was one that largely characterized the other civil rights statutes of the Reconstruction era that preceded § 1983, including pretrial habeas corpus and civil rights removal. *Monroe*, however, concluded that § 1983 adopted no such model.

One may question whether *Monroe*'s approach or the exhaustion approach is preferable, given the interests of the litigants, and the interests of state and local governments in policing their own officials and in the integrity of their judicial processes. *Monroe* allows the litigant to by-pass the state judiciary altogether, even when it is ready, willing and able to give relief, while the hypothetical exhaustion scheme gives the state courts the first shot at correcting their officers' illegality, if they are so inclined. But the exhaustion approach would also put the federal courts in the position of having to assess the adequacy of state court remedies on a case-by-case basis. Also, failing to give preclusive consequences (if that is what should occur after preliminary resort to state court process) to state court resolution of law and facts suggests a somewhat cavalier attitude toward finality and the accuracy of state court decisionmaking, especially in light of the full faith and credit statute (28 U.S.C.A. § 1738). See Chapter 14.

In at least some respects, therefore, an exhaustion regime can be as intrusive on state court prerogatives as *Monroe*'s no-exhaustion rule. Besides, unless the state courts also compensated the victim for the uniquely constitutional dimension of his injuries (above and beyond state tort law, as *Monroe* seems to call for), one could argue that the state remedy would be "inadequate" to that extent (although it is doubtful whether the Constitution itself mandates such recovery). But *Monroe*'s leaving the forum choice to the victim of official illegality avoids the case-by-case assessment of state court adequacy and other problems of intrusiveness that would attend an exhaustion rule, while moving much of the relevant inquiry from tort law to the Constitution.

2. "Under Color of" Law

(a) "Unauthorized" Official Illegality

The second significant aspect of the holding in *Monroe* dealt with whether a state or local officer was engaged in action "under color of" law for the purposes of § 1983 when that officer acted contrary to state or local law. A related question (see section 4, below) was whether such officials had engaged in "state action" for the purposes of the Fourteenth Amendment.

On the statutory (color-of-law) question the Court concluded that it was irrelevant that the officers' particular actions may not have been authorized or sanctioned by the City of Chicago in some formal sense. It was enough that the officers were performing their job (i.e., making an arrest and conducting a search) when they violated the Constitution. As to the state-action question, the Court appeared to indicate its answer long before in Home Tel. & Tel. Co. v. Los Angeles (1913), holding that the Fourteenth Amendment could be violated by those who exercised state or local governmental power and who happened to act contrary to the command of state law when doing so. State action, said the Court in *Home Tel. & Tel.,* includes the case "where an officer . . . in the exercise of the authority with which he is clothed misuses the power possessed to do a wrong forbidden by the Amendment." It therefore reaches an "abuse of power" by any person "who is the repository of state power." Even if the wrong committed by the official is not itself authorized by state law, "if the commission of the wrong is itself rendered possible or is efficiently aided by the statutory authority lodged in the wrongdoer," the state-action requirement is satisfied.

Of course, the fact that the illegal actions of the Chicago police may have been state action for Fourteenth Amendment purposes in *Monroe* did not necessarily mean that such action was also—as a matter of statutory interpretation—action "under color of" law for the purposes of § 1983. In other words, it might have been possible to say that the behavior of the Chicago police amounted to state action within the meaning of the Fourteenth Amendment, but that the 1871 Congress only wanted to reach action taken pursuant to, rather than contrary to state law.

But the *Monroe* Court read the less-than-clear legislative history of the statute as indicating that Congress meant to reach those who acted under the guise or pretense of lawful authority, and not just those who were acting pursuant to established law, custom, or policy. In so doing, the court reaffirmed its reading of similar color-of-law language in a criminal civil rights statute, 18 U.S.C.A. § 242, originally enacted along with § 1983. Screws v. United States (1945). There, the Court upheld federal prosecutions of state and local officials who "willfully" violated others' constitutional rights, even though the officials also happened to act contrary to state law. As a consequence of *Monroe*, therefore, an official can act under color of law even when she is acting contrary to it and can be personally liable in damages for her violations of the Constitution.

(b) Justice Frankfurter's Dissent

Justice Frankfurter filed an important dissent in *Monroe* in which he stated that an official could not be said to act "under color of" law unless he acted pursuant to some unconstitutional law or pursuant to some custom or policy having the force of law. He found it difficult to see how an officer could act under color of law when his acts were illegal under state law and the local judiciary system was prepared to remedy them. He argued that a federal trial court role was needed only when the wrongs of state and local officers were commanded by their government, or were otherwise "systemic" rather than "ad hoc." Although Justice Frankfurter was on the losing end of the decision in *Monroe*, his dissent suggested a viable counter-model for federal involvement in state and local governmental accountability. In addition, his concerns about systemic versus ad hoc illegality have been echoed by the current Supreme Court, both in the area of entity liability and in the area of Due Process violations not involving fundamental rights. See Chapters 3 and 6.

3. Municipal Liability

The *Monroe* Court also held that Chicago itself, as opposed to the individual police officers, was not suable at all. Here the Court was unanimous. Justice Douglas's opinion held that cities were not among the "persons" mentioned in § 1983 who could be sued. He read the Reconstruction Congress's rejection of a proposal called the Sherman Amendment—which would have made cities liable for their failures to protect against mob violence— as meaning that Congress did not want cities to be sued under any circumstances. This particular part of *Monroe,* however, was a holding from which the Court would later retreat, based on a reinterpretation of the same historical evidence. The topic of local governmental liability under § 1983 is taken up in Chapter 6.

B. Permutations on the No–Exhaustion Rule

1. State Administrative Remedies

Monroe made the federal remedy one of first resort when it held that state remedies did not need to be exhausted as a precondition to suit. Nevertheless, a number of lower courts had suggested after *Monroe* that exhaustion of state administrative remedies would be required, even if exhaustion of judicial remedies was not. The Supreme Court eventually held that no such requirement could be imposed consistent with the purposes of § 1983. Patsy v. Florida Bd. of Regents (1982).

In *Patsy*, the Court concluded that the legislative history of § 1983 indicated that Congress wanted to interpose the federal courts between the state— which had precipitated the injuries complained of—

and those who had been the victims of unconstitutional action. The Court rejected any requirement of administrative exhaustion despite the fact that, in other contexts, exhaustion of available administrative remedies is ordinarily a prerequisite to obtaining judicial relief. The Court also concluded that if Congress wanted to create an exhaustion requirement it could do so more expressly.

In fact, at the time of *Patsy*, Congress had expressly legislated an administrative exhaustion requirement for § 1983 suits involving adult prisoners. 42 U.S.C.A. § 1997e (current version at 42 U.S.C.A. § 1997e(a)). At that time, the provision required prisoners to exhaust avenues of administrative review within the prison system before proceeding with their § 1983 suits, at least when the prison's procedures complied with certain procedural standards promulgated by the U.S. Attorney General. Congress's enactment of such a provision led the *Patsy* Court to conclude that the § 1983 default rule was one that did not require exhaustion of either administrative or judicial remedies. (The prisoner-suit exhaustion requirements have changed somewhat since *Patsy*, but exhaustion is still the norm for suits challenging prison conditions. See section 3(b), below.)

2. State–Law "Notice of Claim" Requirements

Patsy's no-exhaustion rule was also partly responsible for the Court's conclusion that a state's pre-suit "notice of claim" requirement could not be applied to a § 1983 suit, even if the suit was filed in state court instead of federal court. Felder v. Casey (1988). Wisconsin's notice-of-claim provision required a party who intended to file suit against state or local officials or the entity for which they worked to notify the officers and the entity of the nature of the claim and the amount of damages sought, before filing suit. The Supreme Court concluded that there were a number of reasons why the statute could not be applied in a § 1983 action, including the fact that such a requirement would have been tantamount to a rule of exhaustion. If such a pre-suit notice-of-claim requirement could not be a precondition to a § 1983 action in state court, then it clearly would not be a precondition to a § 1983 suit brought in federal court.

3. Qualifications on the No–Exhaustion Rule

(a) Abstention and Related Doctrines

Although federal courts have adhered to *Monroe*'s and *Patsy*'s basic message, there are nevertheless a number of related principles, discussed elsewhere, that either delay or foreclose a § 1983 remedy by effectively requiring the § 1983 litigant to pursue state remedies in the first instance. For example, under the doctrine of equitable restraint associated with Younger v. Harris (1971), a § 1983 action may be dismissed when the § 1983 plaintiff is subject to an ongoing state court enforcement proceeding in which he can raise defensively the very constitutional question that forms the basis of his § 1983 complaint. Other abstention doctrines may require postponement or even dismissal of a § 1983 action. See Chapter 15. And, as discussed in Chapter 3, certain due process claims involving the deprivation of non-fundamental rights (unlike in *Monroe*) may be barred from federal court when the state provides adequate post-deprivation process.

In addition, various congressionally imposed barriers require the would-be § 1983 plaintiff challenging the constitutionality of state and local taxes or rates to proceed in the state courts. When there is a "plain, speedy and efficient" remedy in the state courts, these statutory provisions largely withdraw the jurisdiction of the federal courts. 28 U.S.C.A. §§ 1341–1342. And finally, preclusion rules may practically foreclose a federal § 1983 forum for the victim of unconstitutional action if he has already litigated (by force or by choice) the issues or claims that are the subject of his later tried § 1983 suit. See Chapter 14.

(b) Suits by Convicted Persons

As noted above, federal statutes sometimes require prisoners to exhaust their internal prison procedures before proceeding with a § 1983 suit in federal court over constitutional violations. Currently, prisoners must exhaust available administrative remedies in suits involving "prison conditions under [§ 1983] or any other federal law." 42 U.S.C.A. § 1997e(a). In addition, if suit is filed prior to exhaustion and the court determines that a claim, "on its face," is frivolous, is malicious, fails to state a claim, or seeks to recover from an immune official, it may be dismissed outright, without first requiring exhaustion. Id. at § 1997e(c)(2). The exhaustion requirement for prisoner cases is discussed further in Chapter 16.

In addition, in Preiser v. Rodriguez (1973), the Court held that a prisoner with a § 1983 claim for injunctive relief will be forced to pursue avenues of relief under habeas corpus instead, at least when the relief sought challenges the fact of or duration of the prisoner's confinement (as opposed, for example, to the conditions of his confinement). A prisoner seeking return of lost "good-time" credits today would therefore be obliged to sue in habeas instead of § 1983. See Chapter 16.

What is more, the Supreme Court has imposed a separate quasi-exhaustion rule on certain § 1983 suits brought by those who have been convicted. In Heck v. Humphrey (1994), the Court concluded that a litigant could not proceed with his § 1983 damages action when the constitutional questions in that suit, if resolved favorably to the claimant, would necessarily undermine the validity of his prior conviction. For example, if a party convicted of a crime later learns that officials selected him for prosecution on a constitutionally impermissible basis, he could not proceed immediately with his § 1983 suit seeking damages for the officials' unconstitutional actions. Such a party would first have to explore state remedies, including both judicial and administrative ones such as executive pardon, or have the federal questions raised and favorably resolved on federal habeas corpus. Along with habeas corpus, and the prisoner-suit exhaustion requirement under § 1983, *Heck* is taken up in detail in Chapter 16.

(c) Takings of Property

Many § 1983 actions claiming that government has taken property for public use without just compensation also have an exhaustion-like requirement, in part because of the peculiar nature of the constitutional protection. The Constitution prohibits, not simply takings of property, but takings without just compensation. Thus, the Court has held that the constitutional violation in one sense is not complete or "ripe" until just compensation has first been denied. Williamson Cty. Regional Planning Comm'n v. Hamilton Bank (1985). *Williamson*'s rule means that even when there has been final state action regarding the application of state or local law to the plaintiff's property, his takings claim may not properly be brought in federal court before first resolving the question of compensation through state procedures. However, unlike the "as applied" challenge in a case such as *Williamson*, "facial" challenges to state or local governmental action on takings grounds are apparently ripe without any requirement to first seek compensation. "[Such] claims do 'not depend on the extent to which petitioners are deprived of the economic use of their particular pieces of property or the extent to which the particular petitioner's are compensated.'" San Remo Hotel v. San Francisco (2005) (quoting Yee v.

Escondido (1992)). Such facial claims therefore lack the sort of exhaustion requirement that attaches to "as applied" claims under *Williamson*. *Id.*

In the typical "as applied" challenge, there are state remedies available to assess what compensation is due to a person whose property has been taken for public use—either through procedures commenced by the state itself, such as condemnation, or procedures commenced by the property owner, such as inverse condemnation. While it is not possible to canvass here all of the permutations of state procedures that might be available, ordinarily efforts to secure just compensation must first be made before the takings claim will be available. Of course, completion of those same state processes may also make a suit appropriate for direct review in the Supreme Court. See Palazzolo v. Rhode Island (2001) (ruling on inverse condemnation proceeding alleging taking of property). And having to proceed first in state court under *Williamson* runs the risk that principles of issue preclusion arising from the state court proceeding could adversely impact the would-be federal litigant in his § 1983 action thereafter. *San Remo Hotel, supra* (refusing to carve out exception to ordinary rules of preclusion in takings claims). The result is that many as-applied takings claims may end up never seeing the inside of a federal trial court. The Catch–22 impact of *Williamson* plus *San Remo Hotel* recently prompted four members of the Court to suggest reconsideration of *Williamson*'s requirement of initial resort to state court in as-applied takings chal-

lenges, even when state court compensation mechanisms are available. See *San Remo Hotel, supra*
(Rehnquist, C.J., concurring in the judgment).

Of course, even under *Williamson*, if it can be
determined at the outset that adequate state remedies for compensation are lacking, a takings case
would still be ripe, and a federal § 1983 action
should be available in the first instance, without
having to repair initially to state court, so long as
the taking itself is otherwise final. Cf. Suitum v.
Tahoe Reg. Planning Agency (1997) (finding agency
action sufficiently "final" in federal court § 1983
takings case, even though property owner might
have (but did not) make application for transferable
development rights).

4. The Consequences of Exhausting State Remedies

Although § 1983 imposes no exhaustion of remedies requirement, that does not mean that a litigant
might not choose to pursue them anyway. But the
decision to do so may effectively foreclose the ability
later to obtain relief under § 1983 in federal court.
The main reason has to do with doctrines of preclusion. As discussed in full in Chapter 14, a litigant
who voluntarily pursues her state law claims in
state court while saving her federal § 1983 claim
for federal court may find herself barred from raising a § 1983 claim later because of rules against
claim splitting. Migra v. Warren City School Dist.
Bd. of Educ. (1984). Similarly, pursuing state judicial remedies or administrative remedies that are

judicial in nature may preclude a plaintiff from relitigating factual issues that were found adversely to her in a state administrative hearing. University of Tennessee v. Elliott (1986). Pursuing state remedies is therefore not only not required in most § 1983 litigation, it also may not even be desirable in some cases from the perspective of the would-be § 1983 plaintiff.

C. Permutations on "Color of" Law and "State Action"

1. The Relationship Between the Two

In any § 1983 action the statutory "under color of" law requirement and any applicable constitutional "state action" requirement both need to be satisfied. The state action requirement must be met before there can be a violation of the Fourteenth Amendment or most other constitutional provisions. The "color of law" requirement needs to be met in order to satisfy § 1983. Most times, the concepts completely overlap. For example, when a § 1983 action is brought against a state or local official for a violation of the Bill of Rights inflicted while carrying out his duties, the "state action" and "color of law" requirements typically collapse into one another, and both are satisfied. Lugar v. Edmondson Oil Co. (1982). State action by officials will almost always be action under color of law for purposes of § 1983, as in *Monroe*.

On the other hand, it is sometimes possible for an individual to act under color of law and yet *not* engage in state action. For example, a party may act pursuant to a state's common law or U.C.C. that allows him privately to enforce a lien or repossess a vehicle. He may thereby effect a seizure of property in a manner that might not comport with due process were the seizure being undertaken by a state official. The Court has held that such private actions, even if taken consistent with state law, ordinarily do not amount to "state action" absent the involvement of state officials in the seizure. Flagg Bros., Inc. v. Brooks (1978). Thus, no § 1983 action can be brought against the Repo Man because, as a private actor, he has not violated the Fourteenth Amendment. Thus, while all state action will amount to action under color of law, not all action under color of law will necessarily amount to state action. *Lugar, supra.*

2. Private Actors and State Action

The question of when ostensibly private actors can engage in "state action" is a question familiar to Constitutional Law. But the topic deserves brief mention here because so many § 1983 suits implicate violations of the Fourteenth Amendment, which is addresses only "state" behavior. Civil Rights Cases (1883). One traditional way in which private actors can engage in state action is by acting in concert with state or local officials. Dennis v. Sparks (1980). Thus, if the repossession or seizure described above was carried out with the assistance or accompaniment of state officials, or by first obtaining a writ of attachment from a state court, then the state action requirement would be satisfied (as would § 1983's color of law requirement). *Lugar, supra.* And a judgment creditor invoking a state's judgment-enforcement mechanisms pending appeal can become a state actor (and therefore act under color of law) for § 1983 purposes. Pennzoil Co. v. Texaco, Inc. (1987). The Supreme Court has also held that a private physician who treated inmates in a state prison engaged in state action and action under color of law when he acted with deliberate indifference to the medical needs of an inmate. West v. Atkins (1988).

But not all private parties in a contractual or cooperative relationship with the state engage in either state action or action under color of law simply because of that relationship. For example, the Court has held that even though a private school received virtually all of its funding from the state to educate "problem" students, its employment decisions were not thereby converted into state action. Rendell–Baker v. Kohn (1982). And the NCAA did not become a state actor when it decided to discipline a state university's basketball coach, even though the university had agreed contractually to abide by the NCAA's rulings. NCAA v. Tarkanian (1988).

However, more "symbiotic" relationships between the state and ostensibly private entities have sometimes resulted in a finding of state action. That, at least, was the explanation for the Court's conclusion in the 1960's that the race discrimination practiced by a private restaurant located in a state office building amounted to state action. Burton v. Wilmington Pkg. Auth. (1961); see also Brentwood Academy v. Tennessee Secondary School Athletic Ass'n (2001) (finding symbiotic relationship between state and ostensibly private high school athletic association). But even pervasive regulation will not convert the actions of a private utility company into state action, Jackson v. Metropolitan Edison Co. (1974); nor will the simple fact that a facility has a license from or is chartered to do business by the state. Moose Lodge No. 107 v. Irvis (1972). And although the Court long ago held that a nominally private company town that exercised many "public functions" could engage in state action, Marsh v. Alabama (1946), the suppression of free speech by a shopping mall is not actionable under § 1983 because the mall is still a private actor. Lloyd Corp. v. Tanner (1972).

The various decisions may be difficult to rationalize, but they all have a similar focus: To what extent can it fairly be said that the harm in question was facilitated because of the authority given by the state to a particular actor? Like all questions of causation, the state-action inquiry is a question of degree, and the conclusion represents a policy choice as to when it makes sense to attribute any particular behavior to the government. At the level of cause-in-fact, perhaps all private action is state action to the extent that government "permits" particular private activity by leaving it alone. On the other hand, failure to limit the concept of state action would obliterate the sphere of private ordering that is an important aspect of civil society. The

Court has therefore consistently required more active involvement by the state before finding that the constitutional state-action requirement has been satisfied. And its unwillingness to conclude that "state inaction" or non-regulation of certain private behavior implicates the Fourteenth Amendment reinforces its recognition elsewhere that the Constitution imposes few affirmative duties on government. See Chapter 4.

3.   State Actors and Private Action

In *Monroe,* the illegal acts of the Chicago police officers were not authorized by (and indeed violated) state law, but the officers were exercising general governmental power that they possessed. *Monroe* means that state officers act under color of law whenever they are carrying out tasks they ordinarily perform, as well as when their actions are "rendered possible or efficiently aided by the state authority" lodged in them. But *Monroe* does not stand for the proposition that any act of a state or local officer is state action and under color of law.

For example, not every act of an official while "on the job" is state action or action under color of law. If an on-duty police officer were to get into a fist fight with his brother-in-law over a family dispute, it is questionable whether he would be acting under color of law. On the other hand, even extraordinary deviations from acceptable practice may be considered under color of law if the harm was materially aided by the power and authority given by the state to a particular actor. For example, a number of lower courts have found off-duty police officers who continued to wear various trappings from their day jobs while on private security duty were engaging in action under color of law in certain encounters with private persons. E.g., Lusby v. T.G. & Y. Stores, Inc. (10th Cir.1984); see also Rossignol v. Voorhaar (4th Cir.2003) (holding that off-duty plain clothed deputy sheriff who bought up election-day newspapers critical of their candidate for statewide office acted under color of law). Accordingly, some *on*-the-job actions of public officials will not amount to state action, while some *off*-the-job actions will. See also Wudtke v. Davel (7th Cir.1997) (sexual assault of school teacher by school superintendent threatening adverse job action was under color of law).

Nevertheless, some officials do not act under color of law at all, according to the Supreme Court, even though they are salaried by the state and their challenged actions are undertaken in the scope of their employment. In Polk County v. Dodson (1981), the Court held that a full-time public defender did not act under color of law for purposes of § 1983 while she was representing an indigent defendant. The client alleged that the public defender had provided ineffective assistance of counsel in violation of the Sixth Amendment and sued her for damages and injunctive relief. The Court was unwilling to attribute the public defender's decisions to the state when her professional role was to represent her client against the state. The conclusion that the public defender's acts were not under color of law is questionable, however, and the case might better have been resolved on immunity grounds. But even a public defender can be liable under § 1983 if she acts in concert with other officials acting under color of law—for example, by conspiring with a judge or prosecutor to sell her client down the river. See Tower v. Glover (1984).

D.   The Constitutional Coverage of § 1983

1.   The Scope of Enforceable Duties

In addition to showing that a defendant acted under color of state law, a § 1983 plaintiff must also show that he was deprived of a right secured by the Constitution and laws. The constitutional deprivations redressable under § 1983 are potentially as broad as the Constitution itself. The statute speaks of the deprivation under color of law of "any rights, privileges or immunities secured by the Constitution and laws." Section 1983 readily covers violations of the Reconstruction-era amendments which the statute was ostensibly designed to enforce, including the Equal Protection Clause, the Due Process Clause, and those Bill of Rights provisions that have been incorporated against state action under the Due Process Clause.

But § 1983's coverage is not limited to such deprivations. The Supreme Court has also allowed § 1983 actions to redress "dormant" Commerce Clause violations—claims that state or local regulations discriminate against or unduly burden interstate commerce. Dennis v. Higgins (1991). In so doing it overruled without discussion older precedents which had plainly held that language like that in § 1983 would not cover such cases, even though such cases might arise under federal law. E.g., Bowman v. Chicago & N.W. Ry. Co. (1885). And lower courts have extended § 1983 to claims under Article IV's interstate Privileges and Immunities Clause which guarantees equality of treatment as between in-staters and out-of-staters with respect to certain rights. O'Reilly v. Board of Appeals (4th Cir.1991).

Lower courts have also concluded that a § 1983 action may be brought to redress a state or local government's retroactive impairment of the obligation of contracts, U.S. Const. art. I, § 10, cl. 1, despite unambiguous nineteenth century Supreme Court precedent to the contrary. Carter v. Greenhow (1885). The *Carter* decision, however, was made at a time when the Court believed that the rights, privileges, and immunities "secured" by the Constitution to which § 1983 referred made up a fairly narrow category of rights. In light of this, and in light of cases such as *Dennis, supra*, the continuing viability of *Carter* may be in some doubt. Finally, while § 1983 also covers Supremacy Clause violations, such federal pre-emption claims are most often treated as violations of federal "laws," not the "Constitution." (The availability of § 1983 for pre-emption claims and other violations of federal "laws" is discussed in Chapter 5.)

2. State of Mind and § 1983

Because § 1983 merely provides a cause of action for enforcing underlying constitutional (or statutory) guarantees, liability in each case will depend on establishing the elements needed to make out a breach of the relevant constitutional or statutory duty. Accordingly, § 1983 has no independent "state of mind" requirement of its own, apart from the underlying constitutional (or statutory) duty that is being enforced.

For example, proving a violation of the Equal Protection Clause ordinarily requires a showing of discriminatory "intent." Washington v. Davis (1976). If the § 1983 plaintiff is claiming a violation of one of the Bill of Rights provisions incorporated through the Due Process Clause, the relevant state of mind is the one for the particular right in question. Thus, for example, the Fourth Amendment bars searches and seizures that are "objectively" unreasonable. Graham v. Connor (1989). And the Eighth Amendment's ban on cruel and unusual punishment requires intentional acts taken with "deliberate indifference" to the rights of prisoners. Farmer v. Brennan (1994) (conditions of confinement); Estelle v. Gamble (1976). Still other constitutional provisions may have their own state of mind requirements. But as discussed in the next chapter, the relevant state of mind required for certain procedural and substantive Due Process deprivations is not fully resolved. And personal immunity doctrines may require that a plaintiff show an objectively "unreasonable" violation of the Constitution in order to obtain damages from individual officers. See Chapter 8.

sued or shown to be inadequate before a § 1983 action may be brought.

A. Fundamental Rights and "Substantive" Due Process

Some constitutional claims arising under the Fourteenth Amendment's Due Process Clause implicate Bill of Rights violations like the Fourth Amendment search and seizure violation in *Monroe*. These are rights that have been incorporated under the Due Process Clause and made applicable against the states. And *Monroe* stands for the proposition that state remedies are "irrelevant" to whether a § 1983 action can be brought to redress such deprivations. Zinermon v. Burch (1990).

By way of additional illustration, § 1983 has provided a remedy for violations of First Amendment rights respecting speech and religion. Eighth Amendment cruel and unusual punishment claims and other prisoner-rights actions have also been brought under § 1983. And, as noted in Chapter 2, violations of other constitutional provisions, including the Equal Protection Clause, the Commerce Clause, and Article IV's Privileges and Immunities Clause, may all be redressed under § 1983. In sum, complaints alleging violations of the Bill of Rights and most other (non-due process) provisions of the Constitution are immediately actionable in a § 1983 suit, without regard to state remedies.

In addition, some Fourteenth Amendment violations involve so-called "substantive due process" guarantees, such as the fundamental right to marry and certain rights respecting reproductive freedom. Roe v. Wade (1973). Deprivations of these rights can typically be redressed in a federal court § 1983 action just as can Bill of Rights guarantees. The existence of state remedial procedures that the plaintiff might initiate is irrelevant in these cases as well, because these rights represent areas in which the state is disabled from acting, "regardless of the fairness of . . . procedures" by which it acts. *Zinermon, supra.*

B. Other Rights and "Procedural" Due Process

Things become problematic when the liberty or property interests protected by the Due Process Clause that the plaintiff seeks to vindicate do not involve deprivation of an underlying fundamental right such as a Bill of Rights protection or a substantive due process right, but merely involve deprivation by a state or local actor of an otherwise non-fundamental, typically state-created right (such as an interest in property or contract). With respect to such non-fundamental rights, the Court has suggested that the Constitution may provide protection from governmental deprivation, but that the protection afforded by the Due Process Clause is generally procedural. Thus, when the deprivation of a common-law or state-created right is at issue, the Due Process Clause may require the state to provide some meaningful pre-or post-deprivation process in connection with the particular state deprivation of liberty or property. And if the state provides such process, a § 1983 action will be unavailable.

In Parratt v. Taylor (1981), the Court outlined these basic limits on the ability of § 1983 litigants to proceed in federal court in the first instance. A prisoner claimed that prison officials had deprived him of his property without due process of law when they lost certain mail-ordered hobby materials valued at $23.50. He sued the prison Warden and Hobby Manager of the prison in a § 1983 action seeking to recover the value of his lost property. He did so despite the fact that a state tort-claims procedure existed that would have remedied the loss in state court.

The Supreme Court concluded that the prisoner, who was seeking a post-deprivation remedy, could not go forward with his § 1983 suit, but must pursue his state remedies instead. The Court first distinguished *Monroe*, which stressed the non-necessity of pursuing state remedies, as having involved a Bill of Rights violation, whereas the prisoner's suit was based on the Fourteenth Amendment's Due Process Clause alone. Although even a negligent loss of the materials could, according to the *Parratt* Court, amount to a "deprivation" within the meaning of the Fourteenth Amendment (a position from which the Court would later retreat), it concluded that this deprivation was not "without due process of law," when the state was prepared to make good the loss through a post-deprivation state judicial proceeding. In short, the Court treated the prisoner's negligent loss as presenting only a procedural due process question, and the sole issue was whether state post-deprivation process was sufficient to remedy the loss.

While the Constitution has sometimes required *pre*-deprivation process before a person may be deprived of his property, those instances, said the *Parratt* Court, were ones in which the deprivation was "authorized by an established state procedure" and when it could be "predict[ed]" that wrongful deprivations might occur. In *Parratt*, it was all but impossible to predict the "random and unauthorized" behavior of the officials who had failed to follow established state procedures and who were responsible for the loss of the hobby kit. No meaningful pre-deprivation process would therefore have been possible. And in any event, the plaintiff was only seeking a post-deprivation remedy. Nevertheless, because the state could not take property without some meaningful opportunity to be heard, the state's providing of an after-the-fact hearing was required. And, the Court concluded, such a hearing was also sufficient to safeguard constitutional interests because the existence of the state's adequate post-deprivation remedy meant that the deprivation could not be said to have been without due process.

The *Parratt* Court noted that the state tort-claims procedure would not allow for a jury trial or punitive damages, and that it substituted state liability for individual liability. Although conceding that such procedures might not provide for all of the relief that a § 1983 action would have provided, it could still "fully compensate" the prisoner, and it therefore satisfied due process.

1. State of Mind and Due Process

(a) Intentional Deprivations

Parratt involved a "negligent" deprivation. But the *Parratt* principle of requiring initial resort to adequate state remedies was quickly applied to "intentional" deprivations of non-fundamental rights. Hudson v. Palmer (1984). Another prisoner-§ 1983 suit, *Hudson* involved the alleged intentional destruction of personal property by prison guards during an unannounced shakedown of the prisoner's cell. If such intentional conduct by state officials was "random and unauthorized," said the Supreme Court, pre-deprivation process would be as impractical as in the negligence context. Accordingly, even intentional deprivations of property would not violate the Due Process Clause when the state provided a meaningful post-deprivation procedure to make good the loss. Admitting that the guards' actions were "under color of" law, the Court nevertheless added that "the state's action is not complete until and unless it provides or refuses to provide a suitable post-deprivation remedy."

(b) Negligent Deprivations

Significantly, the Supreme Court backtracked from one of its subsidiary conclusions in *Parratt*, when it later held that the Due Process Clause was not violated by the merely negligent behavior of governmental officials. In a prison slip-and-fall case, the Court concluded that no "deprivation" within the meaning of the Due Process Clause can occur when only negligent conduct is involved. Daniels v. Williams (1986). Its rationale was that the Due Process Clause was addressed to "deliberate" decisions of government and focused on "abuse[s] of power," not the lack of due care. Thus, even though the prisoner apparently had no effective post-deprivation remedy in the state courts, "[w]hen a government official's act causing injury to life, liberty, or property is merely negligent, 'no procedure for compensation is constitutionally required.'" Id. This latter conclusion was driven home in a companion case, Davidson v. Cannon (1986), in which an inmate sued prison guards for their negligence in allowing him to be beaten by another prisoner. The Court made clear that even though there might be no effective post-deprivation remedy for the prisoner in *Davidson* because of an amalgam of state-law immunity doctrines, merely negligent acts did not trigger the Due Process Clause.

(c) Between Negligence and Intent

How much more culpability than mere negligence (but, perhaps, short of intent) would be enough to make out a due process violation in these settings was left unresolved. Later cases, discussed below, have continued to struggle with the issue. But it is important to note that the state-of-mind inquiry for due process is just that: a predicate for showing an unadorned due process violation. Other constitutional provisions will carry their own state of mind requirements in § 1983 litigation.

2.   Authorized versus Unauthorized Official Behavior

Parratt's resort-to-state-court-remedies rationale is limited to cases in which the due process deprivation is random and unauthorized. Of course, the deprivation in a search and seizure case such as *Monroe* was random and unauthorized as well, but according to the Court, such Bill of Rights cases may proceed immediately in federal court under § 1983 without regard to state remedies. *Zinermon, supra.* Thus, *Parratt*'s random-and-unauthorized limitation is generally relevant to due process deprivations of non-fundamental rights alone.

By contrast, when an official's deprivation of such non-fundamental rights is *not* random and unauthorized, but is pursuant to some "established state procedure" or is otherwise systemic, then the *Parratt* requirement of resort to post-deprivation state remedies is said to become inapplicable. *Zinermon, supra*; Logan v. Zimmerman Brush Co. (1982). When a deprivation is pursuant to established policy and is not random and unauthorized, "it is practical and feasible for the state to provide pre-deprivation process for the aggrieved party." Moore v. Board of Educ. (6th Cir.1998). If, however, the claim is that constitutionally required state pre-deprivation process was in place, but that state officials merely failed somehow to follow it, then the deprivation becomes effectively random and unauthorized, and state court post-deprivation remedies are all that the Constitution demands.

Of course, one might argue that—at some level— even the random and unauthorized activity of government officials is caused by "the system." This is especially true of acts of officials who have been delegated broad discretion in the manner in which they exercise their power. In Zinermon v. Burch (1990), for example, the § 1983 plaintiff sought damages, alleging that state officials had failed to assess properly whether he had "voluntarily" committed himself to a state mental health care facility. By an ordinary reading of the complaint, the plaintiff was alleging that the officials made an ad hoc, one-shot mistake in committing him. If so, then *Parratt* should have barred the § 1983 suit. But the Court read the complaint as stating a procedural due process challenge to the adequacy of the state's procedures themselves. Because such mistakes could be predicted to happen absent additional safeguards, the patient's (reconstituted) claim was that he had been denied constitutionally mandated predeprivation process. Consequently, *Parratt* did not bar the § 1983 suit for damages, and resort to postdeprivation state remedies was not required. Yet insofar as the "officials could have done more" argument can almost always be made, *Zinermon* came close to blurring the distinction between what is random and unauthorized (i.e., "ad hoc" illegality), and what is authorized (i.e., "systemic" illegality) for purposes of *Parratt*.

3. The Scope of Protected "Liberty" and "Property"

Although *Parratt* and its initial progeny all involved deprivations of property, its strictures have been held to apply to deprivations of liberty interests as well. *Zinermon, supra.* Again, however, the liberty interests to which the *Parratt* rationale applies are those that are not fundamental in the sense noted above. In other words, *Parratt* is inapplicable to claims implicating freedoms in the Bill of Rights as incorporated through the Fourteenth Amendment, and it is inapplicable to other fundamental rights covered by the rubric of "substantive" due process, such as rights relating to reproductive freedom. Deprivations of such rights remain actionable in the first instance in a federal court under § 1983. But state deprivations of even nonfundamental (i.e., state-created) liberty (as well as property) interests may require some kind of state-provided remedial process, whether it is pre-or post-deprivation. And if a litigant claims that the Constitution requires pre-deprivation process which the state did not provide, that question, too, may be heard in the first instance in a federal court § 1983 action.

Thus, in Ingraham v. Wright (1977), when a student brought a § 1983 damages action for a paddling that he received at the hands of the school principal, the Court rejected *on the merits* his claim that the Constitution required pre-deprivation process, or some kind of pre-paddling notice-and-hearing right. But the Court did not suggest that the

Due Process Clause was not implicated in the protection of the student's liberty interests in bodily integrity, even though, as the Court noted, those interests were "shaped largely by local law." Rather, the state's tort system provided an adequate safeguard for those liberty interests through the post-deprivation remedies that it provided. Although decided before *Parratt*, *Ingraham*'s logic seems to parallel that of *Parratt* and later cases.

A more difficult decision is Paul v. Davis (1976). There the Supreme Court turned back a § 1983 procedural due process challenge to a local official's defamatory posting of a notice that the § 1983 plaintiff was an active shoplifter. The plaintiff, who claimed injury to his good reputation, argued that he should have received pre-deprivation notice and a hearing before such a posting occurred. The Court disagreed. Although the Court may have assumed that the state's tort system would provide protection to reputational interests, it did not suggest that such a post hoc tort remedy was in any respect obligatory, as it arguably had for the liberty interests at issue in *Ingraham*. Instead of concluding that post-deprivation process under state tort law would satisfy the Due Process Clause by providing monetary damages for injury to reputation, the Court stated that no liberty or property interest within the meaning of the Due Process Clause had been implicated by the claimed deprivation.

The Court's expressed fear in *Paul* was that § 1983 should not become "a font of tort law" that would displace or parallel state remedies. But that fear could just as well have been addressed simply by concluding—as *Parratt* did—that the state's tort process was constitutionally adequate to remedy the particular deprivation; the Court did not need altogether to exclude state-created liberty or property interests in "reputation" from the protection of the Due Process Clause. Perhaps the Court meant to suggest that not all common-law liberty interests—such as those protected by defamation and libel law—warranted state remedial protection from official deprivation as a federal constitutional matter. But if so, then the Court has failed to develop a principle to explain why bodily integrity from an undeserved paddling by state officials, or destruction of hobby materials might warrant such protection, and damage to reputation by state officials does not.

Some lower courts succeeded in distinguishing *Paul* when § 1983 plaintiffs alleged something more than mere injury to reputation arising from a defendant official's speech. But in Siegert v. Gilley (1991), the Supreme Court reaffirmed *Paul*'s holding in the context of a constitutional action against a federal official, even when the plaintiff alleged that his job prospects (as well as his reputation) were harmed by a federal official's reckless falsehoods. Moreover, in the federal officer context, unlike in *Paul*, there is ordinarily no alternative state court action or any other tort claim available against either the wrongdoing federal official or the federal government for such defamation. See Chapter 17.

C. "Substantive" versus "Procedural" Due Process

The pleading incentives for § 1983 plaintiffs bent on a federal forum are clear. If it is possible to shoehorn one's deprivation of life, liberty, or property into one of the Bill of Rights guarantees, or otherwise successfully argue that there has been a deprivation of "substantive" due process, resort may be made immediately to the remedy provided by § 1983. Also, most non-due process substantive constitutional violations (such as a violation of the Equal Protection Clause) can be remedied in federal court in the first instance under § 1983. Absent such possibilities, however, there is only the procedural due process right that there be some pre-or post-deprivation process within the state court system to remedy the state's deprivation of non-fundamental liberty or property interests.

1. Construing "Fundamental" Rights

As just noted, many deprivations of liberty or property can be squeezed into the mold of a Bill of Rights deprivation, and thus be remediable in the federal courts in the first instance under § 1983. The Fourth Amendment's guarantee against unreasonable searches and seizures protects against many kinds of governmental invasions of person and property. For example, the Court has held that the use of deadly force to arrest implicates the

Fourth Amendment, and may therefore be challenged without having to exhaust state civil remedies. Tennessee v. Garner (1985). In Soldal v. Cook County (1992), the Court held that the (random and unauthorized) taking away of a mobile home by the police implicated not just due process issues, but an issue of unlawful seizure in violation of the Fourth Amendment. Hence, a § 1983 action could proceed immediately in federal court without the plaintiff's having to resort to post-deprivation state remedies. In short, the § 1983 plaintiff in *Soldal* was able to recast what would have been only a deprivation of an ordinary state-created property interest (meriting only after-the-fact, state procedural protection) into a Fourth Amendment search and seizure violation immediately actionable in federal court. See also Altman v. City of High Point (4th Cir.2003) (concluding that animal control officers' shooting of family's aggressively behaving pit bull running loose on the streets implicated a "seizure" of one's personal "effects" under the Fourth Amendment, although finding seizure reasonable).

Of course, not all deprivations of liberty or property can be brought within one of the Bill of Rights or found on the Court's short-list of fundamental rights protected by substantive due process. And not every deprivation of property can be bootstrapped into a "seizure" for purposes of the Fourth Amendment. See Chapter 4, § A, 1. If they could be, then far too many ad hoc deprivations of otherwise non-fundamental interests could be converted into deprivations meriting "substantive," not just "procedural" protection.

2.   From Torts to "Substantive" Due Process

A favorite way of avoiding *Parratt*'s requirement of resort to state post-deprivation process when non-fundamental rights have been invaded is for would-be § 1983 plaintiffs to try to bootstrap otherwise seemingly ordinary torts by officials into substantive due process violations (actionable under § 1983 without regard to state remedies). The Supreme Court has itself suggested that some official behavior may be so egregious—so "brutal" and "offensive to human dignity"—as to "shock the conscience" (Rochin v. California (1952)), and that such behavior can violate substantive due process norms, even when the Bill of Rights or other underlying fundamental rights are not implicated. E.g., Sacramento County v. Lewis (1998); Collins v. Harker Heights (1992).

But it is not clear what sort of behavior by law enforcement officials or other executive branch personnel will satisfy this seemingly high threshold of arbitrariness. Different courts have articulated the relevant showing differently in different settings. In addition, the Supreme Court has indicated its reluctance to expand the universe of substantive due process, and it clearly prefers to locate claims within the Bill of Rights when that is possible. *Lewis, supra.* The general issue is taken up in the next Chapter.

it is not altogether obvious why post-deprivation state remedies are relevant in some cases of official deprivation, but not in others. The official behavior challenged in both *Monroe* and in the *Parratt* line of cases was "random and unauthorized" and could not be "predicted." Yet immediate federal post-deprivation process is available in *Monroe*-type cases, and only state post-deprivation process is available in *Parratt*-type cases. Nor is it obvious why state action is "complete," and suit can be brought in federal court under § 1983 when the wrongdoing official is "done" with his victim in a case like *Monroe* (even though the state is prepared to make good the wrong), but state action is somehow *in*complete in a case like *Parratt* or *Hudson*, precisely because state remedies are available.

The frequent retort that claims that are relegated to state remedies under *Parratt* are merely ones for "procedural" as opposed to "substantive" due process only partially helps the analysis. What it does is describe the Court's conclusion: If a litigant is not allowed in the first instance to remedy a particular deprivation under § 1983 (without regard to state remedies), then all that the litigant may have is a procedural due process right to have her loss redressed by post-deprivation state process. But the two labels do not describe the deprivations. Surely the deprivations of which the prisoners complained in the hobby-materials, slip-and-fall, and beating cases were "substantive" in an important sense. And the fact that the Court effectively requires at least post-deprivation tort mechanisms to redress certain nonnegligent deprivations of liberty and property recognizes a measure of substantive, not just procedural, protection for these interests.

In any event, the Court's basic insight in *Parratt* is defensible. A constitutional violation potentially lurks behind any official deprivation of life, liberty, or property. Unless all such deprivations are to be made immediately actionable in federal court under § 1983, some formula for inclusion and exclusion has to be developed. That is arguably what the Court has tried to do in its refusal to fundamentalize all liberty interests, in its focus on systemic versus ad hoc deprivations, and in its creation of high barriers to finding "substantive" due process deprivations. Moreover, by leaving primarily to state court adjudication most ad hoc official deprivations of rights that take their primary shape from state law, the Court has arguably made a sensible institutional choice and also has prevented the trivialization of § 1983. Whether what the Court is doing is imposing a kind of exhaustion rule on some deprivations, or a rule of abstention, or simply a narrowing of the scope of due process, it is fundamentally making a choice about what sorts of official deprivations of life, liberty, and property should be remediable in federal court under § 1983 in the first instance. That, of course, was also what *Monroe* tried to do.

E. Constitutionally Compelled Remedies?

Finally, *Parratt* and its progeny do not purport to foreclose a federal court § 1983 action when mean-

CHAPTER 4

EXCESSIVE FORCE, PRIVATE VIOLENCE, AND § 1983

Overview

A claimed right to governmental protection from harm characterizes a host of § 1983 actions. Litigants—whether those in prison or those in "the free world"—often assert a right to be free from bodily harm, violence, and uses of excessive force at the hands of government officials and others. Of course, no specific constitutional provision identifies a generalized right to safety or to governmental protection from harm. But § 1983 will often supply a remedy for official violence—i.e., violence inflicted by governmental actors. Various provisions of the Constitution, especially the Fourth Amendment's prohibition on unreasonable searches and seizures and the Eighth Amendment's prohibition on cruel and unusual punishments, as well as the Due Process Clause, may offer a theory of recovery for official violence in different contexts. The Fourth Amendment would cover excessive force in the context of arrests, the Eighth Amendment would cover excessive force in the prison context, and the Due Process Clause could conceivably cover other contexts.

In addition, litigants sometimes assert a right to be protected by government from "private violence," i.e., violence inflicted by private actors. For example, a prisoner injured by another prisoner, a private citizen assaulted by a parolee, or a public high school student harassed at school by another student might all seek to hold state or local officials accountable for the failure to protect them. In these and related contexts, however, § 1983 provides only a limited remedy. Prisoners and those in the custody of the state have been able to claim minimum guarantees of safety and care, largely because they are not able to fend for themselves. But for those on the outside, the Supreme Court has been reluctant to find a constitutional guarantee of minimum levels of safety from harm or private violence, even in settings in which the government is seemingly actively involved.

A. Official Violence

1. Searches and Seizures

Remedies against the use of excessive force by law enforcement or other officials in the performance of their jobs were once the exclusive domain of state tort law. Now, many claims that officials used excessive force have become constitutionalized. For example, the use of such force incident to a stop, an arrest, or the search of an individual may constitute a violation of the Fourth Amendment's prohibition on unreasonable searches and seizures. For a time, some courts supposed that an unconstitutional use of force in such circumstances required a showing of behavior on the part of officials that was "malicious and sadistic." Johnson v. Glick (2d Cir.1973). But to establish a Fourth Amendment violation, there is no need for the victim of unconstitutional action to show such a level of grossness or egregiousness of behavior. Rather, the requirement is the one familiar to all Fourth Amendment claims: whether the officer's action was "reasonable" when judged by an objective standard in light of the facts and circumstances confronting the officer. Graham v. Connor (1989). In *Graham*, the Supreme Court made clear that the Fourth Amendment, not the Due Process Clause, is the source of constitutional protection from excessive force used incident to arrest.

Moreover, the Fourth Amendment's language of "searches and seizures" has some flexibility to it, even if it does not apply to every governmental interference with freedom of movement. California v. Hodari D. (1991). The use of deadly force to arrest, for example, would trigger a Fourth Amendment inquiry because such action implicates a "seizure" of the person. Tennessee v. Garner (1985). Thus, if an officer lacks probable cause to believe that a particular suspect poses a threat of serious physical harm to others or to the officer, use of deadly force would be unreasonable. As in all Fourth Amendment excessive-force § 1983 cases, the existence of a constitutional violation would turn on the facts of which the officer was aware and the objective reasonableness of the use of the level of force employed by the officer under the circumstances. Thus, for example, the fact that the suspect was unarmed would not be dispositive of the question whether the officer was reasonable in using deadly force if he reasonably believed that the suspect was armed. Sherrod v. Berry (7th Cir.1988). Even if the use of force was unreasonable and thus violative of the Fourth Amendment, however, the officer may still be immune from damages if he can show he acted in good faith—i.e., that he was not unreasonably unreasonable. Saucier v. Katz (2001). See Chapter 8.

Similarly, the deadly consequences of high-speed encounters with the police may, in some circumstances, implicate a search and seizure of the person pursued. In Brower v. Inyo County (1989), an individual in a stolen car was killed when he drove into a police roadblock. The Supreme Court found the Fourth Amendment to be implicated because the individual was stopped by the very mechanism the police had set up to stop motorists. Because the seizure took place "through means intentionally applied," the question was whether the particular seizure was reasonable under the circumstances. If, therefore, in a high-speed chase, officers intentionally swerved their patrol car into a fleeing suspect's car causing him to lose control and crash, there would likely be a seizure whose reasonableness would then be at issue. By contrast, if only a bystander was injured during the course of such a chase, or the fleeing suspect lost control on his own, no Fourth Amendment issue would arise. The only possibility for making a constitutional case out of such a scenario would be under the more problematic "substantive due process" rubric discussed below (at § 3) (discussing Sacramento County v. Lewis (1998)).

2. Cruel and Unusual Punishments

In addition, the "unnecessary and wanton" infliction of pain on prisoners by prison officials constitutes cruel and unusual punishment forbidden by the Eighth Amendment. The use of excessive physical force by officials upon those who are in custody pursuant to a judgment of conviction can, therefore, provide the basis for a § 1983 action in the appropriate case. Nevertheless, decisions of prison officials to use force are often made on the spur of the moment, under pressure, and without much chance for reflection. Prisoners must therefore show that the prison official used force "maliciously and sadistically" and for the very "purpose of causing harm" or with a "knowing willingness" that harm would occur. Whitley v. Albers (1986).

This heightened standard of purposeful conduct for establishing that the infliction of harm was unjustified therefore requires more than a showing of "reckless indifference" (or "objective unreasonableness") on the part of officials. In addition, in § 1983 cases involving the use of excessive force against prisoners, the absence of "serious" physical injury may be relevant to deciding whether the Eighth Amendment has been violated, but it will not automatically foreclose such a possibility. Hudson v. McMillian (1992). (Absent a showing of *some* "physical injury," however, a prisoner may not recover for mental or emotional injury under § 1983. 42 U.S.C.A. § 1997e(e).) In reasoning similar to that in *Graham, supra*, the Supreme Court in *Whitley* made clear that the Eighth Amendment, not the Due Process Clause, was the constitutional touchstone for acts of official violence inflicted on convicted persons. (It should be noted that most prisoner suits under § 1983 must contend with special restrictions, including an exhaustion requirement. See Chapter 16.)

3. "Substantive Due Process"

(a) The Argument of Last Resort

Nevertheless, not all uses of excessive force by government officials can be shoehorned into the rubrics of "cruel and unusual punishment" or "search and seizure." The former can be invoked only by those who have been subject to a conviction. Ingraham v. Wright (1977). Thus, the infliction of punishment in any other context—such as a principal's paddling of a public school student as in *Ingraham*, or a police officer's beating of a pre-trial detainee—is not covered by the Eighth Amendment. And while the concepts of "search" and "seizure" are flexible, the protection against unconstitutional searches and seizures arguably runs out at some point after a subject has been arrested and taken into the custody and control of law enforcement officials. The point at which it runs out, however, remains unclear. Albright v. Oliver (1994); id. (Ginsburg, J., concurring).

Consequently, some victims of official violence or excessive force will fall in the gap between the protections of the Fourth and Eighth Amendments. Pre-trial detainees, for example, who are in the post-arrest custody of the state, may be unable to take advantage of the Fourth Amendment; they are also not yet subject to a conviction, and thus are not able to take advantage of the Eighth Amendment. See Parrish v. Cleveland (4th Cir.2004). Yet, as a matter of the Due Process Clause, the state has no right to "punish" a pre-trial detainee prior to his conviction. Bell v. Wolfish (1979). Perhaps other provisions of the Bill of Rights will be implicated in particular contexts—for example, a beating to coerce a confession later used at trial might implicate the Fifth Amendment. See Chavez v. Martinez (2003). But within the gaps, uses of excessive force by government officials (whether on a pre-trial detainee, for example, or on a high school student) will be immediately actionable under § 1983 only if they are sufficiently egregious as to amount to what the Court has considered to be a substantive due process violation.

The Court, however, has stated its reluctance to look to or to expand the notion of substantive due process. "Where a particular amendment provides an explicit textual source of constitutional protection against a particular sort of government behavior, that Amendment, and not the more generalized notion of substantive due process, must be the guide for analyzing these claims." Sacramento County v. Lewis (1998); see also *Graham v. Connor, supra.* What is more, outside of a Bill of Rights violation or the violation of some other fundamental right, lies an area in which state tort law has a presumptive claim. Parratt v. Taylor (1981); *Ingraham, supra.* Section 1983 plaintiffs must therefore be able to convince a court why something that ordinarily would be merely tortious (and remediable in state court after-the-fact) is sufficiently outrageous to qualify as a substantive due process violation deserving of immediate access to the federal courts.

(b) Sacramento County v. Lewis

The Supreme Court grappled with these issues in connection with a § 1983 suit over an accidental death suffered by a motorcycle passenger arising from a high-speed chase with police. Sacramento County v. Lewis (1998). The Court focused on substantive due process instead of the Fourth Amendment because force had not been intentionally applied in order to cause the motorcyclist to stop. The *Lewis* Court concluded that a substantive due process violation could only be established by official behavior that "shocked the conscience." And such a showing could not be made by the passenger unless the officer's actions were motivated by "a purpose to cause harm unrelated to the legitimate object of arrest[ing]" the driver.

The Court rejected a lower standard of "deliberate or reckless indifference to life" that it had used in other contexts (such as inattention to the medical needs of pretrial detainees) because of the absence of any real deliberation in the high-speed chase context. Thus, the "much higher" standard that it applied resembled the one it applied in suits against prison officials for injuries inflicted in prison riots. Whitley v. Albers (1986). *Lewis* suggests generally that, whenever law enforcement or other behavior by executive branch officials is concerned and when no specific constitutional guarantee (apart from due process) is applicable, the arbitrariness sufficient to implicate due process must always shock the conscience. But whether "intent to harm" or "deliberate indifference" will be the measure will depend on context. And the greater the opportunity for deliberation, the more likely a standard resembling deliberate indifference will apply. E.g., Brown v. Nationsbank Corp. (5th Cir.1999) (concluding that officers who planned a sting operation that injured an innocent third-party had time for reflection and that whether they were deliberately indifferent to the risk of injury was the proper inquiry).

Interestingly, even the narrow opening for substantive due process allowed by the Court in *Lewis* was too much for Justice Scalia. Invoking (with apologies) the lyrics of songwriter Cole Porter, he chastised the majority for "resuscitat[ing] the ne plus ultra, the Napoleon Brandy, the Mahatma Ghandi, the Celophane subjectivity, th' ol' 'shocks the conscience' test." Lower courts, however, had been way out ahead of the Court in acknowledging substantive due process deprivations for particularly egregious behavior. E.g., Wudtke v. Davel (7th

Cir. 1997) (upholding, as substantive due process claim, complaint alleging extreme and outrageous acts of sexual harassment of public school teacher by public school superintendent). Given *Lewis*, many § 1983 plaintiffs may decide to go forward with a claim under the Bill of Rights along with a fall-back claim under substantive due process.

(c) *Chavez v. Martinez*

The Court may have confirmed such a strategy in *Chavez, supra*. There, the Court considered and rejected a Fifth Amendment damages claim against police officers for a confession extracted in violation of Miranda v. Arizona (1966). A four-member plurality held that because there was no criminal proceeding against the confessing party at which the confession was used, the Fifth Amendment's self-incrimination clause was not implicated. Two other Justices rejected a Fifth Amendment damages claim arguing that exclusion at trial was ordinarily a sufficient remedy. But these two Justices, along with three others, voted (unlike the plurality) to remand the case to consider whether substantive due process had been violated by the allegedly outrageous manner in which the confession was extracted. The decision is therefore in some tension with the rationale in *Graham v. Connor, supra*, which suggests that when there is an arguably applicable Bill of Rights provision, it should control, and not the more general analysis of substantive due process. A strict reading of *Graham* would indicate that a near miss under an otherwise relevant Bill of Rights provision should make a court reluctant to allow substantive due process to expand a protection that the arguably relevant Bill of Rights provision does not, in fact, provide.

B. Private Violence and Affirmative Governmental Duties

1. Custodial Settings

(a) Prisoners

Because of the Fourteenth Amendment's state-action requirement, private actors ordinarily cannot violate another person's due process rights or other Bill of Rights guarantees that are incorporated against state action under the Due Process Clause. But the Court has recognized that in some contexts—such as prisons—an incarcerated person may be constitutionally entitled to protection from violence at the hands of another prisoner (or even from himself). The Eighth Amendment's proscription against cruel and unusual punishment has therefore been held to impose affirmative duties on government to protect incarcerated persons from the violence of other private parties, not just from violence at the hands of state actors. Farmer v. Brennan (1994). The rationale is that, because of the deprivation of his liberty, a prisoner is unable to care for himself and protect himself in a way that those on the outside can.

For similar reasons, the Eighth Amendment has also been read as imposing an affirmative duty on government to provide for the "serious" medical needs of inmates and for other necessities. These, too, are items that the prisoner cannot provide for himself. The Supreme Court has held that "deliberate indifference" to those needs would violate the Eighth Amendment. Estelle v. Gamble (1976). The standard for such Eighth Amendment prison-condition suits, while high, is therefore less demanding than that for showing an Eighth Amendment excessive-force claim. E.g., *Whitley, supra.*

In an Eighth Amendment § 1983 action alleging prisoner-on-prisoner violence, suit is not brought against the wrongdoing private actor. Suit is brought against the prison officials or other state actors responsible for the failure to protect the prisoner from injury. Provided that the inmate can show that there was a substantial risk of serious harm arising from a particular setting, a prison official's "deliberate indifference" to that risk will violate the Eighth Amendment. So, for example, a prisoner who is sexually assaulted by his cellmate could sue the wrongdoing prison official under § 1983 for damages arising from the assault if he can show the deliberate indifference of the official in some relevant regard, such as in the assignment of cellmates.

The "deliberate indifference" standard in Eighth Amendment failure-to-protect cases is a subjective one (even though the inquiry in such cases into whether the risk of harm was sufficiently serious is "objective"). An officer will therefore not be liable for prisoner-on-prisoner violence unless the official disregarded a serious risk of which he was *actually* aware. *Farmer, supra.* An official would be liable in the assault described above, for example, only if he was aware of a risk of sexual assault by the new cellmate and consciously disregarded that risk. Unlike in other contexts in which the phrase "deliberate indifference" is sometimes given an "objective" reading, it is not sufficient in these failure-to-protect cases that an official disregarded a risk of which he *should have been* aware. Imposing liability on a prison official only when the risk of harm is one of which the official was actually aware, said the Court, was required by the Eighth Amendment's proscription on "punishment." Wilson v. Seiter (1991). Of course, if the private wrongdoing individual acts in concert with state officials, it may be possible to secure relief under § 1983 against the private party himself. See Chapter 2 (action under color of law) & Chapter 8 (official immunities).

As noted above, even when a prisoner succeeds in making out a claim under § 1983, a host of other requirements—unique to prisoner litigation—may limit or modify the prisoner's remedies or manner of proceeding. See The Prison Litigation Reform Act of 1995. Those limitations range from a showing of physical injury before being able to recover for mental or emotional injury, 42 U.S.C.A. § 1997e(e), to restrictions on recoverable attorney's fees, id. at (d)(1)-(4). There are also restrictions on the ability of prisoners to obtain prospective injunctive relief to remedy prison conditions under § 1983. See 18 U.S.C.A. § 3626(a)-(g); see generally Chapter 10 (equitable relief).

(b) Others in Custody

Because of their control by the state, involuntarily committed mental patients are also affirmatively entitled to services needed to ensure their " 'reasonable safety' from themselves and others." Youngberg v. Romeo (1982). There may also be certain guarantees respecting the conditions of confinement for pre-trial detainees and persons under arrest. But such guarantees of protection for non-prisoners are based, not on the Eighth Amendment, but on the Due Process Clause. Revere v. Massachusetts General Hospital (1983). It is not clear whether a subjective, deliberate-indifference standard similar to that in *Farmer* would apply to due-process-based failure-to-protect claims, such as in the pre-trial detainee context. But some lower courts have thought so, despite the arguably greater claim to protection from harm on the part of those who have not yet been convicted.

2. Non-custodial Settings

(a) Private Violence and the "Free World"

In DeShaney v. Winnebago County Dep't of Soc. Serv's (1989), the Supreme Court held that there is ordinarily no constitutional duty on the part of government to protect individuals in non-custodial settings from private violence. *DeShaney* involved a severe beating of a child by his father. Although social workers had been put on notice of likely past abuse, they did not take action to remove the child from the home until after he had been hit so badly that he suffered permanent brain damage and had lapsed into a coma. A § 1983 damages action was filed on the child's behalf by his mother alleging that, because officials were aware of the risk of harm to the child, it was a violation of the child's due process rights not to intervene.

The *DeShaney* Court concluded that "[n]othing in the language of the Due Process Clause itself requires the State to protect life, liberty, and property of its citizens against invasion by private actors." Instead, the Court viewed the Constitution's commands as consisting largely of "negative" limits on state action, "not as a guarantee of certain minimal levels of safety and security." These comments echoed the Court's conclusions in other areas that there is no fundamental right to various forms of "affirmative" governmental services at state expense, such as welfare or education. San Antonio Independent School Dist. v. Rodriguez (1973). Because the purpose of the Due Process Clause was to protect individuals from abuses of state and local officials, not from other private persons, the clause could not be invoked to remedy violence inflicted on a child by his father. Judge Posner earlier noted in Jackson v. Joliet (7th Cir.1983) that adopting a construction of due process that required affirmative governmental services would "turn the clause on its head. It would change it from a protection against coercion by state government to a command that the state use its taxing power to coerce some of its citizens to provide services to others."

Of course, in *DeShaney*, the state was not entirely uninvolved in the child-father relationship that was

at issue there. County officials had knowledge (or
should have known, according to the complaint) of
the violent relationship between Joshua DeShaney
and his father. By their earlier actions, officials had
in some measure undertaken to protect "poor Joshua" (Blackmun, J., dissenting). The plaintiff alleged
that the failure to protect him thereafter was an
abuse of power that "shocked the conscience" and
amounted to a substantive due process deprivation.
The Supreme Court disagreed and concluded that
no "special relationship," such as that involved
with state prisoners or involuntarily committed
mental patients who are under the guardianship of
the state, was involved. The nexus between the
state and the child-father relationship was held to
be insufficient to implicate the Due Process Clause,
in contrast to the nexus between the state and its
prisoners or its involuntarily committed mental patients.

(b) Parolee Violence

Prior to *DeShaney*, the Court had reached a similar decision, focusing more on questions of state
action and causation, in Martinez v. California
(1980). There, a parolee had killed a person after
being released by the state's parole board. Although
the case involved violence inflicted by one private
person on another, the victim's relatives brought a
§ 1983 suit claiming that the deprivation of the
victim's life violated due process because the parole
board had been derelict in its duty adequately to
screen and supervise the parolee, and in its failure

to warn the public of his release. The Supreme Court concluded that the relationship between the state's actions (the decision of the parole board) and the killing was "too remote."

But the Court was not clear whether the reason for dismissing the plaintiffs' § 1983 suit was because there had been no "state action," or because the state did not "cause" the deprivation, or because there had been no "right" of which the victim had been deprived that was secured by the Due Process Clause. In addition, *Martinez* was decided before the Court had made clear that official negligence (which arguably was all that was involved in the parole board's actions) could not trigger a due process violation. Daniels v. Williams (1986). Yet the decisions in *DeShaney* and *Martinez* expressed a similar sentiment not to hold public officials responsible under § 1983 for the actions of private persons absent a sufficiently tight nexus (and something well beyond a "but for" relationship) between the actions of public officials and the subsequent harms inflicted by private persons.

(c) Workplace Safety and Public Employees

The Court invoked *DeShaney* in Collins v. Harker Heights (1992), to reject a claim that a state was constitutionally required to protect the on-the-job safety of public employees. *Collins* was a § 1983 action brought of behalf of a city sanitation worker who was asphyxiated when he entered a manhole to unstop a sewer line. His wife claimed he had a substantive due process right to be free from unreasonable risks of harm in the workplace and that the city had been deliberately indifferent to the health and safety of its employees in its failure to train them about the dangers of noxious gasses.

The Court disagreed. *DeShaney*, stated the Court, stood for the principle that absent a state-imposed (i.e., involuntary) custodial setting, the state is under no affirmative obligation to spend its resources to protect individuals from harm. Minimum levels of safety and security in the workplace were not required by the Constitution, even in the context of public employment when the public-sector jobs thrust the employee in harm's way. Thus, even if the city was "deliberately indifferent" in its failure to train its employees, and although that indifference may have caused the particular deprivation, the deprivation itself was not of constitutional dimension. The decision in *Collins* is therefore likely to preclude § 1983 claims by persons who are not public employees who attempt to assert a due process right to safety in government buildings, public transportation, public housing, or similar government-run facilities.

3. The Limits of *DeShaney*

DeShaney itself allowed for the possibility that the state might be sufficiently involved in an act of private violence so as to implicate the Due Process Clause. The opinion assumed that a substantive duty to protect could exist, as in the prison setting, when there was a "special relationship" between the state and particular individuals; there is also language in the decision suggesting that constitutional liability might attach when the risk of danger from private violence was "state-created." In addition, *DeShaney* implicated a substantive due process claim and would therefore not control a claim under other constitutional rubrics, such as the Equal Protection Clause, or a claim for procedural due process.

(a) Special Relationships

Lower courts have wrestled with whether a "special relationship" like the custodial setting associated with prisoners or state mental patients could be found in other contexts. For example, the beating by a foster parent of a foster child might be distinguishable from *DeShaney* because of the state's role in the selection and supervision of the child's custodian. See, e.g., Nicini v. Morra (3d Cir.2000); Doe v. New York City Dep't of Soc. Serv's (2d Cir.1981) (pre-*DeShaney*).

On the other hand, a number of lower courts have concluded that public school boards and educational personnel ordinarily cannot be liable on a due process theory for the violence or sexual abuse inflicted by one student on another, even when school attendance is compulsory. E.g., D.R. v. Middle Bucks Area Vocational Technical School (3d Cir.1992); cf. Hasenfus v. LaJeunesse (1st Cir.1999) (concluding that particular failure to prevent public school suicide attempt did not "shock the conscience"). One court of appeals even went so far as to find that there was no "special relationship" for

§ 1983 purposes when a resident of a state school for the hearing-impaired sexually assaulted another resident on more than one occasion. Walton v. Alexander (5th Cir.1995). Although the limits on the freedom of school residents in *Walton* were not unlike those in mental institutions, the fact that the residency was voluntary was dispositive for the court. McKinney v. Irving Indep. Sch. Dist. (5th Cir.2002)("special relationship" exception "only arises when a person is involuntarily confined or otherwise restrained against his will pursuant to a governmental order or by the affirmative exercise of state power"); see also White v. Lemacks (11th Cir.1999) (concluding that nurses working in prison infirmary could not maintain § 1983 action for assault upon them by inmates, because nurses were not there involuntarily). In any event, even when such actions can survive *DeShaney*, they will violate due process only if they involve official behavior that is conscience shocking. And whether that will require a showing of "intent to harm" or something less, will depend on the need for quick action versus an opportunity for deliberation.

(b) State–Created Dangers

DeShaney also suggested that if the danger of harm from private violence is sufficiently "state-created" the Due Process Clause may be implicated. In one private violence case, Wood v. Ostrander (9th Cir.1989), a woman was raped in a high crime area after the police arrested her companion, impounded his car, and left her stranded. The Ninth Circuit concluded that § 1983 could provide a remedy for such a state-created danger. But other courts have ruled differently in analogous settings. For example, no liability under § 1983 attached when an intoxicated person was hit by a car after a police officer removed him from a from a nightclub, and left him at a gas station pay phone. Stevens v. City of Green Bay (7th Cir.1997). See also S.S. v. McMullen (8th Cir.2000) (refusing to distinguish *DeShaney* when child was released from state custody into abusive environment); Tucker v. Callahan (6th Cir.1989) (finding no police liability under § 1983 in watching the plaintiff be beaten by another, and taking no immediate action).

Cases such as *Wood*, like some of those involving "special relationships," suggest that perhaps *De-Shaney* may not be a categorical bar to holding officials accountable under § 1983 for otherwise private harms. As with the "state action" inquiry under the Fourteenth Amendment, the level of required involvement of the state is ultimately a question of degree. At some point, affirmative conduct on the part of the state that directly places individuals in danger, or heightens a specific known risk of harm, may suffice to trigger official accountability, whereas simple inaction or failure to aid in circumstances which the state was less immediately involved in creating typically will not.

(c) Non–Due Process Claims

Certain additional limits on the scope of *DeShaney* should also be noted. *DeShaney* was a substan-

tive due process case. The opinion itself noted that
an equal protection claim would not face similar
obstacles. If, for example, an official's failure to
protect a person from private violence was based on
impermissible considerations, such as race or gender, a § 1983 action might be available against the
official who acted or failed to act because of his
unlawful animus, *DeShaney* notwithstanding. Thus,
according to one lower court, a § 1983 plaintiff was
able to state a claim for relief when he alleged that
police officers—pursuant to a policy that discriminated against Native Americans—failed to conduct
a thorough search for the victim of a car wreck who
wandered from the scene and later died. Estate of
Amos v. City of Page (9th Cir.2001).

Similarly, some have attempted to recast their
DeShaney claim as one grounded in procedural due
process. In Town of Castle Rock v. Gonzales (2005),
a woman reported that her estranged husband was
violating a restraining order and had taken their
children, but her calls were ignored. The children
were eventually killed by the husband. She argued
that under state law, she had a property interest in
the enforcement of the restraining order and that
she had been deprived of this property interest in
violation of procedural due process. The Court disagreed with the lower federal courts as to the interpretation of state law and concluded that no such
property interest existed, thus defeating the plaintiff's claim. Nevertheless, the decision appeared to
assume that *DeShaney* did not prevent the effort to
recast the case as one involving procedural due

process—a strategy that might have been successful in other circumstances.

(d) Other Civil Rights Legislation

In addition, there may be other federal statutes that redress some kinds of private violence apart from § 1983. Such statutes are generally beyond the scope of this work, and are treated in detail in Harold S. Lewis, Jr. & Elizabeth J. Norman, Civil Rights Law and Practice (West Group 2001). But a few examples may serve to illustrate the difficulty of legislatively addressing private violations of the Constitution. The Violence Against Women Act of 1994, 42 U.S.C.A. § 13981, for example, makes both public and private parties liable under federal law for certain acts of gender-motivated violence perpetrated against women. But the Court has concluded that the Act cannot be upheld as a constitutional exercise of Congress's power to regulate interstate commerce, or its power under § 5 of the Fourteenth Amendment to enforce the Equal Protection Clause, at least insofar as violence by a private actor was concerned. U.S. v. Morrison (2000). Other civil rights statutes allow for recovery for certain class-based private conspiracies to deprive individuals of equal protection of the laws or that interfere with certain rights secured by the Constitution. E.g., 42 U.S.C.A. § 1985(3). But they have been justified against private action as enforcing the Thirteenth Amendment and the right to interstate travel— neither of which has a state action requirement. See Griffin v. Breckenridge (1971).

In addition, under Title IX of the 1972 Education Amendments to the 1964 Civil Rights Act, educational institutions funded by the federal government may be under an affirmative duty to protect students from sexually-motivated harassment whether it is inflicted by school employees or other students. But recovery is limited to situations in which responsible officials had actual knowledge of the employees' or students' harassment and were deliberately indifferent to it. Gebser v. Lago Vista Indep. Sch. Dist. (1998). This statute probably survives *Morrison, supra*, because the spending feature of Title IX avoids both the commerce clause and the § 5 concerns at issue in *Morrison*.

CHAPTER 5

ENFORCING RIGHTS UNDER FEDERAL "LAWS" THROUGH § 1983

Overview

Section 1983 provides a remedy for violations of rights secured by the "Constitution and laws" of the United States. The Court has read this language as providing not just a means to redress state and local officials' constitutional violations, but as providing a means to redress their violations of federal statutes as well. Moreover, the "statutory" scope of § 1983 includes (1) laws that may have little or nothing to do with traditional "civil rights" issues; (2) claims based on federal statutory pre-emption of state law; and (3) it may provide a private right of action even when the underlying federal law does not itself provide for one, either expressly or impliedly. Nevertheless, a § 1983 action will be unavailable to redress violations of federal statutes by those acting under color of law unless, in the underlying federal statute, Congress has unambiguously created judicially enforceable individual rights. In addition, even if the underlying statute does create such rights, § 1983 will be unavailable to enforce it if the statute has its own enforcement mechanisms from which it can be inferred that Congress meant to displace the § 1983 remedy.

A.   Statutory Violations and § 1983

In Maine v. Thiboutot (1980), Justice Brennan took what he called a plain-meaning approach to the wording of § 1983. The statute's language referred to "the deprivation of any rights, privileges, or immunities secured by the Constitution and laws." Writing for the Court, he concluded that § 1983 "means what it says" and that persons acting under color of law may be sued for their violations of rights under federal statutes, as well as for their violations of the Constitution. *Thiboutot* was a suit filed in state court against a state Commissioner of Human Services to recover welfare benefits withheld from the plaintiffs in violation of federal laws. In concluding that § 1983 allowed a remedy for the violation of federal statutory rights—in that case, to enforce compliance with provisions of the Social Security Act (SSA) on the part of participating states—the Court ratified a number of older decisions that had, without much discussion, allowed such claims. E.g., Rosado v. Wyman (1970). The Court was careful to note, however, that the SSA did not itself provide a private cause of action for its enforcement; instead, § 1983 supplied an express and independent one.

There were at least two potential objections to the Court's ruling, and both were made in dissent. First, it was arguable that § 1983's reference to "laws" only meant to refer to "civil rights" laws and other laws associated with the enforcement of the Reconstruction-era amendments with which § 1983 was itself historically linked. Section 1983's own specialized jurisdictional provision, 28 U.S.C.A. § 1343(3), referred only to violations of the Constitution and of laws "providing for equal rights." At the time of *Thiboutot*, there was an amount-in-controversy requirement for actions brought under the federal question statute, 28 U.S.C.A. § 1331, but not under § 1343(3). The Court's interpretation led to the odd result that there were some § 1983 claims that could not be brought in a federal court but only in a state court: namely, claims like the Thiboutots' that were for violations of non-"equal rights" statutes that could not clear the then-existing amount-in-controversy hurdle of § 1331 (and which, as statutory non-equal-rights claims, could not qualify for federal jurisdiction under § 1343(3)).

Second, the Court's reading of § 1983 meant that there was now an express right of action to enforce, as against public officials, the myriad federal statutes having to do with such diverse subjects as pollution, strip mining, wildlife conservation, migrant labor, and historic preservation. In addition, virtually all federal spending programs in which the states are participants, including Medicaid, public housing, and health care could potentially be enforced under § 1983. Many of those statutes did not allow for private enforcement but only for enforcement by federal officials or agencies. Thus, the

Court had effectively imputed to Congress an intent to have broader private enforcement of federal statutes when they were violated by state and local actors than when they were violated by private parties. In addition, the Court's holding arguably meant that § 1983 was implicitly passed, not just pursuant to congressional power under the Reconstruction amendments, but pursuant to all of the Article I powers that gave Congress the ability to regulate in these other areas.

B.   Exceptions to Statutory Enforcement Under § 1983

1.   Non-enforceable Rights

Despite the apparent direction of *Thiboutot*, § 1983 is not available for all federal statutory violations by those who act under color of law. Instead, the Supreme Court has concluded that a § 1983 remedy is available only if two conditions are met. First, the underlying federal statute must create enforceable rights in individuals. Second, Congress must not have substituted its own remedies for those under § 1983.

Although there was some post-*Thiboutot* uncertainty over the meaning of the first requirement, the Court attempted to clear things up in Gonzaga v. Doe (2002). *Gonzaga* concerned a student's § 1983 suit to remedy a private university's violation of the Family Educational Rights and Privacy Act of 1974 (FERPA), 20 U.S.C.A. § 1232g. FERPA is a federal spending statute that prohibits release of student records without consent; the statute provides for the cut-off of federal funds to a school not in substantial compliance. In *Gonzaga*, a student sued the university when it disclosed records of his sexual misconduct to state officials engaged in the certification of teachers in the state. Although the lower courts upheld the liability of the university under § 1983 for its violation of FERPA (including finding that the private university had acted under color of state law), the Supreme Court reversed.

The Court concluded that what is required for a statute to create enforceable rights is no different than what would be required under the Court's implied right of action decisions. Under those increasingly restrictive decisions, when a federal statute is silent about whether it may be privately enforced, the Court has insisted that the plaintiff show Congress's "unambiguous" intent to confer individual rights upon a class of beneficiaries of which plaintiff is a member. It is therefore not enough that a claim falls "within the general zone of interests that the statute is intended to protect." "Section 1983," said the Court, "provides a remedy only for the deprivation of 'rights,' not 'benefits' or 'interests' "; it provides a remedy only for "violation of rights not laws."

Because FERPA's text was not "phrased in terms of the persons benefited"—with language such as: "no person shall be subjected to" violations of FERPA—it could not meet the rigorous standard imported from the Court's implied right of action cases. Of course, for a court to find an implied right of action under a federal statute, the statute must also manifest an intent to create not just a private right *but also* a private remedy. This is where implied right of action analysis and congressional displacement analysis diverge. No such additional showing of an intent to create a private remedy has to be made by the § 1983 plaintiff; for him, it is § 1983 itself that supplies the remedy—but only if the underlying statute creates enforceable rights. Note, however, that if the underlying federal statute does evince an intent to create a private remedy, that may actually foreclose the § 1983 remedy under the "congressional displacement" theory, discussed below.

Gonzaga thus appeared to confirm the direction of a number of the Court's post-*Thiboutot* decisions that had stressed the need for plaintiffs to show that the underlying statute created individual rights before the statute could be enforced in an action under § 1983. For example, in Blessing v. Freestone (1997), the Court turned back efforts of a custodial parent to sue state officials under § 1983 for failing to comply with Title IV–D of the Social Security Act. The Act requires states to enforce child support agreements as part of a federal-state spending program. Instead of pointing to particular claims of individual right, however, the plaintiff in *Blessing* asserted a generalized "right to have the state substantially comply with Title IV–D in all respects." Conceding that the plaintiff might have some specific enforceable rights that § 1983 could arguably remedy—such as an individual right to recover state-collected child support—the *Blessing*

Court remanded the case for the plaintiff to fine tune her claim.

Similarly, in Suter v. Artist M. (1992), the Court rejected plaintiffs' efforts under § 1983 to compel state officials to undertake reasonable efforts to prevent removal of children from their own homes to foster homes, as called for by The Adoption Assistance and Child Welfare Act of 1980 (AACWA). Another congressional spending program, the AACWA allowed for federal reimbursement to states of the costs they incurred in administering certain foster-care and adoption services. But reimbursement was conditioned on a state's coming up with a "plan" through which it would undertake "reasonable" efforts "in each case" to prevent removal of children to foster homes. The Court held that individual rights to insist on such a plan had not been "unambiguously" conferred under the AACWA.

Suter stood in contrast to Wilder v. Virginia Hospital Ass'n (1990), where the Court allowed private health care providers to sue state officials under § 1983 in a challenge to the "reasonableness" of the rates by which they were reimbursed for treating Medicaid patients. As in *Suter*, the federal statute in question arguably required only that the state develop a reimbursement "plan," but not that the rates themselves be reasonable. Given the statutory care with which "reasonableness" was defined, however, the Court found that the statute created enforceable rights by imposing a substantive requirement that rates be judicially reviewable for their reasonableness at the behest of individuals, not simply that the state provide procedures that would help ensure reasonable rates.

2. Congressional Displacement

Second, even if a federal statute creates enforceable rights, a § 1983 remedy will be unavailable if Congress has displaced it. What it takes to displace the § 1983 remedy has undergone change over time as well. Soon after *Thiboutot*, the Court stated that if Congress has provided its own "elaborate" or "comprehensive enforcement mechanism," the Court will infer that Congress meant to displace any remedy under § 1983. Middlesex Cty. Sewerage Auth. v. National Sea Clammers Ass'n (1981). In *Sea Clammers*, the plaintiffs tried to avoid some of the many limitations on private enforcement of various federal environmental statutes by suing the defendant sewerage authority under § 1983 for dumping waste into the ocean in violation of those environmental statutes. Federal law allowed for the Environmental Protection Agency (EPA) to initiate proceedings to enforce the statutes, for judicial review of the EPA's action, and for citizen-suits for injunctive relief under limited circumstances. Consequently, the Court concluded that Congress had not only foreclosed most private rights of action under the statute against any violator, "but also that it intended to supplant any remedy that otherwise would be available under § 1983." Early post-*Sea Clammers* decisions seemed to suggest that the less Congress said about a remedy in a statute, the more likely § 1983 would be available to enforce it (although the lack of any remedy could just as easily suggest the absence of "unambiguous" intent to create enforceable rights). E.g., Wright v. City of Roanoke Redev. & Housing Auth. (1987) (allowing suit under § 1983 to remedy violation of federal regulations respecting overbilling for utilities in low-income public housing although statute lacked any reference to judicial enforcement).

But the Court has arguably toughened up this inquiry. To be sure, if a statute creates enforceable rights as called for by *Gonzaga*, it remains possible that a § 1983 action will be available to enforce it even when a private right of action would not, because of the lack of congressional intent to provide a private remedy within the underlying statute. But in City of Rancho Palos Verdes v. Abrams (2005), the Court made clear that the "enforceable rights" showing merely created only a "rebuttable presumption" that a § 1983 remedy would be available. *Rancho Palos Verdes* involved a federal court § 1983 suit for damages arising from a municipality's actions taken contrary to the Telecommunications Act of 1996 (TCA), 47 U.S.C.A. § 332(c)(7). The plaintiff alleged that the city denied him a conditional-use permit to have an antenna on his house for mobile phone relay services, in violation of limitations imposed by the TCA on local zoning authorities. He sought injunctive relief as provided for under the TCA (i.e., an order that the permit be granted), and he sought damages and attorney's fees under § 1983 for the violation of the TCA.

The Court assumed *arguendo* that the TCA created individually enforceable rights; the *Gonzaga* issue was therefore off the table and there was a
rebuttable presumption in favor of the plaintiff that
rights under the TCA were enforceable under
§ 1983. But the Court went on to say that the
presence of some private remedy in a statute itself
creates a nonconclusive but rebuttable "inference"
in favor of the defendant that the § 1983 remedy
has been displaced. Quoting from an earlier implied
right of action decision, Alexander v. Sandoval
(2001), the Court stated: "The express provision of
one method of enforcing a substantive rule suggests
that Congress intended to preclude others." The
Court also characterized the various cases in which
it had found no congressional displacement as ones
in which the underlying statute provided no private
enforcement mechanism at all, judicial or administrative. E.g., Livadas v. Bradshaw (1994) ("complete
absence of provision for relief from governmental
interference"); *Wilder, supra* ("The Medicaid Act
contains no ... provision for private judicial or
administrative enforcement").

The "ordinary inference" of displacement arising
from the presence of some private enforcement
mechanism could be overcome, said the *Rancho
Palos Verdes* Court, "by textual indication, express
or implicit, that the remedy is to complement, rather than supplant, § 1983." Such proof was wanting
in the TCA which added no remedies to § 1983's
and which limited relief vis à vis § 1983 which

would have allowed for damages and attorney's fees. The Court even went out of its way to note that the imposition of fees, not provided for in the TCA for violations of § 332(c)(7), would have a "particularly severe impact" on local governments for their "misapplication of a complex and novel statutory scheme."

The Court's reasoning makes it easier to find congressional displacement than initially suggested in either *Sea Clammers* or *Thiboutot*. Instead of insisting on a comprehensive enforcement scheme, the Court appears to take an *expressio unius* approach, itself an important feature of the Court's implied right of action cases. If Congress expresses one private remedy (in its statute), it is "indicative of" congressional intent to exclude other private remedies (such as § 1983). Thus, exclusion of a § 1983 remedy may now be "inferred from the statute's creation of a comprehensive enforcement scheme" (as in *Sea Clammers*), or "congressional intent may be found directly in the statute creating the right" (as in *Rancho Palos Verdes* in which the TCA provided for some private judicial enforcement). Taken in combination with *Gonzaga*, the *Rancho Palos Verdes* decision shows that both the "enforceable rights" and "congressional displacement" inquiries have now been greatly accommodated to the Court's implied right of action cases. The "and laws" wing of § 1983 has thereby been considerably narrowed, especially in the setting of congressional spending provisions.

C. Pre-emption and Supremacy Clause Claims

It might be supposed that a claim that state or local action was pre-empted by federal law presented a constitutional claim under § 1983 because such allegations implicate the Supremacy Clause. U.S. Const. art. VI, cl. 1. But the Court has held that pre-emption claims are actionable under § 1983 not because they present a violation of the Constitution, but only because they present violations of rights under federal "laws." Golden State Transit Corp. v. Los Angeles (1989).

At issue in *Golden State Transit* were the efforts by the City of Los Angeles to settle a local labor dispute—efforts that turned out to be pre-empted by the National Labor Relations Act (NLRA). The City had held up a taxicab company's franchise renewal by conditioning it on the company's resolution of an ongoing dispute that it was having with its taxicab union. In an initial round of litigation the Supreme Court held that the City's regulatory actions were pre-empted by the NLRA. On remand, the taxicab company sought damages from the City under § 1983 for the delay in obtaining the franchise. In concluding that the § 1983 suit could be maintained, the Court observed that "the Supremacy Clause, of its own force, does not create rights enforceable under § 1983," but rather that the Clause secured federal statutory rights when they came into conflict with state law. Thus, the cab company's pre-emption suit was founded on the

City's violation of federal labor laws and was therefore viable under *Thiboutot*.

The Court denied that a § 1983 action would be available "every time a federal rule of law preempts state regulatory authority." It stated that the question would turn on whether the federal statutory obligation is " 'sufficiently specific and definite' to be within 'the competence of the judiciary to enforce,' ... is intended to benefit the putative plaintiff and is not foreclosed 'by express provision or other specific evidence from the statute itself.' " *Golden State Transit, supra.* See also *Rancho Palos Verdes, supra* (finding municipality violated specific provision of 1996 Telecommunications Act limiting local regulatory authority, and assuming Act created enforceable rights).

In the absence of express congressional foreclosure from suit, however, it is hard to see how the party regulated by a state or local law or other governmental action that is pre-empted by federal law would not be able to clear the Court's rather low threshold in pre-emption claims for finding enforceable rights. If congressional pre-emption exists, it creates a zone of freedom from state or local regulation, and thus a "right" in favor of the regulated party to the absence of such regulation. Indeed, the Court has since stated that the § 1983 remedy in cases of federal pre-emption is "presumptive." Livadas v. Bradshaw (1994). And as *Golden State Transit* makes clear, damages as well as injunctive relief may be recovered in the proper case when governmental action is successfully challenged on pre-emption grounds. But *Rancho Palos Verdes* serves as a reminder that the § 1983 pre-emption remedy may itself be pre-empted by a comprehensive enforcement scheme or by the presence of some private remedy in the statute itself.

The most troublesome practical aspect of these pre-emption damages claims under § 1983 (as with dormant Commerce Clause claims) is that many of them involve economic challenges to the customs or policies of local governmental entities who are trying in good faith to regulate in areas of traditional local competence without running afoul of pre-emptive federal legislation. Local governments are not only monetarily liable for their customs and policies which violate the "Constitution and laws" under § 1983, they are strictly liable for those violations because they cannot claim good faith immunity. See Chapter 6. Plus, attorney's fee awards will attach to a successful plaintiff's claims for injunctive or monetary relief. And often the challengers are fairly well-heeled business concerns. See Nextel Partners, Inc. v. Kingston Township (3d Cir.2002) ("[P]laintiffs are often large corporations or affiliated entities whereas ... defendants are often small rural municipalities"). A similar point was made in *Rancho Palos Verdes, supra*.

As the rationale for individual officer immunities suggests, denial of good faith immunity from damages may result in overly cautious governmental action that comes up well shy of the permissible regulatory line. Ironically, the Court's rulings in certain of its pre-emption cases have meant that

Congress has not only created a zone from which state or local regulation is excluded, but a buffer zone even beyond that area, into which a rational local government should be reluctant to tread. No such problem was presented when the Court, pursuant to its former (pre-*Golden State*) practice, merely allowed for injunctive relief against pre-empted state laws, without reliance on § 1983. Shaw v. Delta Air Lines (1983) (approving implied equitable right of action directly under federal question statute, 28 U.S.C.A. § 1331, for pre-emption challenge to state law).

D. "And Treaties"?

Finally, brief mention should be made of the efforts of litigants to enforce treaties under § 1983 against state and local actors. The question whether treaties confer individual rights and are enforceable at the behest of individuals is an involved and disputed one at a more general level. But some lower courts have assumed that § 1983 provides an express right of action to enforce individual rights under treaties (when such rights exist) against persons acting under color of law, in the same manner that it provides a right of action against persons who violate rights under federal laws. E.g., Cree v. Waterbury (9th Cir.1996) (allowing suit by members of tribe to enjoin state officers from interfering with alleged right under treaty to use state highways without having to pay for licensing fees and truck permits). Moreover, when the Supreme Court turned back a § 1983 official-capacity suit by Para-

guay's Consul General asserting violations of a prisoner's rights under the Vienna Convention, it did so
because the rights he asserted were those of Paraguay, which is not a "person." Breard v. Greene
(1998). The Court simply did not discuss whether
the Convention could be a "law" within the meaning of § 1983.

Nevertheless, there is doubt whether § 1983
should be read as providing a remedy for treaty
violations. The current text of the statute refers to
deprivations of rights secured by "the Constitution
and laws." It notably does not mention treaties,
which are the third form of supreme federal law
expressly mentioned in the Supremacy Clause, in
addition to "the Constitution" and "laws." *Cree,
supra,* appears to assume that because treaties are a
form of federal "law," violations of rights under
treaties can be assimilated to the "and laws" language of § 1983. It is far more likely, however, that
the additional reference to "laws" was a reference
to federal statutes only. Other contemporaneously
enacted statutes include the trilogy mentioned in
the Supremacy Clause, including the general federal
question statute enacted in 1875 ("Constitution,
laws, and treaties"), the habeas corpus statute of
1867 ("constitution or laws or treaties"), and the
1867 revision of § 25 of the 1789 Judiciary Act
allowing for direct review of state court decisionmaking in the Supreme Court ("Constitution, treaties, or laws"). Moreover, as noted above, there is
even an argument that only civil rights statutes
were being cross-referenced by the words "and

laws," although this particular argument was rejected by the Court in *Maine v. Thiboutot, supra.* But the *Thiboutot* Court did so because it saw the "plain meaning" of the statute as providing a remedy that "broadly encompasses violations of federal statutory as well as constitutional law." The plain meaning of § 1983 should therefore exclude rights under treaties.

On a similar rationale, litigants might try to characterize fundamental norms of customary international law as a species of federal law, actionable under § 1983. Recently, the Supreme Court made clear that at least some aspects of customary international law could be treated as a species of federal common law. Sosa v. Alvarez–Machain (2004) (indicating that, under the 1789 Alien Tort Statute, redress might be had for certain violations of the law of nations as a species of federal common law). But it is not clear that § 1983 supplies a cause of action for violations of rights under federal common law. See Hoopa Valley Tribe v. Nevins (9th Cir. 1989) (noting absence of authority for "incorporating federal common law into [§ 1983's] scope"). *Sosa*, moreover, took a narrow approach to what would amount to a violation of the law of nations, lest the Alien Tort Statute supplant actions under § 1983 and "create an action in federal court for arrests by state officers who simply exceed their authority."

CHAPTER 6

MUNICIPAL LIABILITY

Overview

Cities, counties, and other local governmental entities are suable under § 1983. As a matter of statutory interpretation, they are among the class of suable "persons" to which § 1983 refers, and, in addition, they cannot claim state sovereign immunity. This is in stark contrast to the states themselves and to state agencies and other arms of state government, who are not suable "persons" (and who could also claim sovereign immunity). Nevertheless, local governments are not liable in damages for the constitutional harms inflicted by their officers on a vicarious liability or respondeat superior basis. Instead, a local government will be accountable in a damages action under § 1983 for the unconstitutional acts of one of its officials only if the plaintiff can show that the official acted pursuant to some law, custom, or policy of the governmental entity. The unauthorized, random unconstitutional acts of a local official are therefore not ordinarily attributable to the entity for which the official works for purposes of liability under § 1983, although the official herself may still be personally liable in damages (subject to immunities that the official herself might raise). On the other hand, if a local government can be liable in damages because its official acted pursuant to some custom or policy, the entity itself cannot claim any kind of good faith or other immunity, even if its official might be able to raise such a defense.

The parameters of what constitutes governmental custom or policy have been the subject of intense dispute. In a series of decisions, the Supreme Court has held that not just formal legislative enactments, but also the individual decisions of those who are final "policymakers" can subject local governments to monetary liability. In addition, it has concluded that sometimes an entity's failure to train its officials can subject it to liability for their otherwise apparently random and unauthorized unconstitutional acts, as can a failure properly to screen at the time of hire. Local governments may, of course, be subject to injunctive relief. But they will not be subject to punitive damages even for their grossly unconstitutional acts. For better or worse, the precedents in the area are some of the most convoluted in all of § 1983 litigation.

A.   Entity Accountability and Its Limits

1.   Local Governments as Suable "Persons"

In Monell v. New York City Dept. of Soc. Servs. (1978), the Court held that cities were among the "persons" who could be sued under § 1983. In so doing it reversed a portion of its earlier decision in Monroe v. Pape (1961), which had held that cities could not be sued under § 1983 at all. See Chapter

2. The reason for the shift was partly based on historical evidence—largely the same historical evidence that led to the opposite conclusion in *Monroe*. There, the Court held that the Reconstruction Congress's rejection of the "Sherman Amendment" suggested that Congress meant not to make cities accountable for the constitutional violations of their officials. The Sherman Amendment would have made cities strictly liable for the lawless violence of private parties and would have effectively imposed upon cities an affirmative duty to keep the peace. There was much opposition at the time, some of it constitutionally grounded, to the notion of imposing such "positive" duties on local governments, and the Amendment was defeated. *Monroe* inferred from the rejection of municipal liability in the one instance in which it was proposed that Congress meant to foreclose municipal liability in all instances. See Chapter 2.

The *Monell* Court, however, read the Amendment's rejection as signifying little about the possibility that a city might be made liable, not for the acts of private persons, but for the unconstitutional acts of its own officers. No constitutional barrier would be presented to municipal liability in those circumstances, nor, the Court concluded, would the Reconstruction Congress have thought so either. The Court then looked at other historical evidence which convinced it that municipal corporations should be treated as natural persons for liability purposes, and to evidence of the Reconstruction Congress's intent to make municipalities accountable under § 1983. The Court stated that its "holding ... [was], of course, limited to local government units which are not considered part of the State for Eleventh Amendment purposes."

2. Foreclosing Respondeat Superior Liability

In a second part of the opinion, the *Monell* Court concluded that Congress did not intend municipalities to be held liable "unless action pursuant to official municipal policy of some nature caused a constitutional tort." That meant that a municipality could not be held liable simply because it employed the wrongdoing official, "or, in other words, a municipality cannot be held liable on a respondeat superior theory." The Court again referred to the Sherman Amendment's rejection—this time to limit § 1983's scope. The two policies behind respondeat superior liability—(1) reduction of injuries if employers had to bear their cost, and (2) spreading the cost of accidents (to the community)—were both reasons that had been unsuccessfully put forth in defense of the Sherman Amendment.

But the Court also invoked statutory language to justify its restriction on respondeat superior liability. It focused on the part of § 1983 which speaks of the liability of "persons who ... shall subject, or cause to be subjected, any person" to a deprivation of her constitutional rights. The Court saw this language of causation as prohibiting any theory of vicarious liability of a city for the unconstitutional acts of its agents. It is arguable, of course, that a city, like any employer, inflicts injury or "causes" the injuries to be inflicted when its employee injures someone while carrying out his job. But the Court's restrictive reading of the causation language requires a greater nexus between the local governmental entity and the unconstitutional act of its officials, above and beyond simply having employed the wrongdoer:

> Instead, it is when execution of a government's policy or custom, whether made by its lawmakers or by those whose edicts or acts may fairly be said to represent official policy, inflicts the injury that the government as an entity is responsible under § 1983.

Monell, supra. The Court thus ensured that a local government would be liable under § 1983 only when its "custom" or "policy" was the "moving force" behind the unconstitutional action of one of its officers.

3. The Consequences of *Monell*

(a) In Theory

The Court's reasons for its decision are hardly airtight. The tea leaves of the rejection of the Sherman Amendment seem able to support almost any result. And the language of causation in § 1983 certainly does not compel the conclusion that employer liability should not attach unless the agent acted pursuant to custom or policy. Certainly no such limitation exists for employer liability in the private sector; a private employer can be liable for a tort committed by his employee in the course of employment even when the employee violated the employer's policies. Indeed, in *Monroe*, it was determined that an official's actions could be attributable to the government for state action purposes, and that he could act "under color of" law for § 1983's purposes, even when he did *not* act pursuant to custom or policy, so long as he was acting in the course of employment.

Thus, after *Monell*, a local officer can still be held accountable in damages under § 1983 for his unconstitutional actions in the performance of his job, whether or not he acted pursuant to any law, custom, or policy of the entity for which he works. His actions are attributable to the government and therefore they violate the Constitution. But the governmental entity will be liable only if its officer acted pursuant to custom or policy, because the official's acts are *not* always attributable to the government for § 1983 municipal liability purposes.

(b) In Practice

In practice, *Monell* brought a substantial change to the manner in which local governmental accountability for the constitutional violations of its officials was addressed. Prior to *Monell* (and after *Monroe*), if a party wanted to sue a local government, he could do so only for injunctive relief, and then, only by naming the relevant government official in her official capacity. City of Kenosha v. Bruno (1973). After *Monell*, it was possible to sue the local governmental entity in its own name for such relief, because an injunction against the enforcement of an unconstitutional ordinance or practice would typically meet *Monell*'s custom-or-policy requirement. In addition, prior to *Monell*, cities could not be sued for damages under § 1983; only their officials could be. But after *Monell*, a party could sue a city directly, in addition to or as an alternative to suing individual officers, and municipal liability could attach assuming *Monell*'s custom-or-policy requirement was satisfied.

By making cities suable persons, therefore, *Monell* was significant insofar as it gave § 1983 plaintiffs a real shot at significant monetary recovery when municipal officials (who might be able to invoke personal immunities for their good faith actions) have acted unconstitutionally pursuant to local law, custom, or policy. On the other hand, rejection of respondeat superior liability suggests that the Court may have perceived that it was unfair to make the local electorate financially accountable for its officials' actions unless those actions achieved a kind of public notoriety through legislative enactment or pervasive practice, or were undertaken by those who might be accountable to the public.

B. The Uncertain Contours of "Custom or Policy"

1. Formal Policies versus Random Acts

(a) Formal Policy

Implementing the custom-or-policy requirement has proved to be something of a chore. But some cases will be easy. Action by local officials to enforce an unconstitutional ordinance passed by a city council, for example, would clearly be action pursuant to custom or policy of the entity. Here, custom or policy is embodied in the formal lawmaking efforts of legislators. And, because of personal immunity doctrines, suit would be brought not against those who passed the ordinance, but against the city itself and/or those enforcing the ordinance.

(b) Random and Unauthorized Official Acts

At the other extreme, the random illegal search by an individual police officer or the isolated use of excessive force by the rogue cop are presumably the very sort of acts for which *Monell* meant to exclude municipal liability. They are ordinarily actions not undertaken pursuant to custom or policy (absent evidence to the contrary), and the only nexus between these events and the city is the fact of employment—a fact that *Monell* says is not enough for municipal liability to attach under § 1983. It is what lies between the example of formal lawmaking on one end of the spectrum and the example of the bad-apple police officer on the other that has caused the courts difficulty.

2. "Custom" and Informal Policy

Perhaps also easy to conceptualize, yet not so easy to establish to a factfinder, are unconstitutional acts taken pursuant to an informal, unwritten policy of an entity in the form of "custom or usage." As the Supreme Court said in Jett v. Dallas

Indep. School Dist. (1989), this sort of policy could arise "by acquiescence in a long-standing practice or custom which constitutes the 'standard operating procedure' of the local governmental entity."

The question then becomes one of degree: How often must a particular sort of behavior manifest itself before it can be considered to be "custom"? The Court's concerns in this and related areas suggest that the practice must be sufficiently long-standing and wide-spread to show that high-ranking or policymaking officials had actually or constructively acquiesced in and condoned the particular activity. Thus, merely showing that the particular behavior happened on more than a few, or even on a number of occasions, should probably be insufficient to establish a "custom." Rather, to come in under this rubric, the behavior ought to be sufficiently regularized as to be the "standard operating procedure," as referred to in *Jett*. See Lytle v. Doyle (4th Cir.2003) ("persistent and widespread" practices may amount to custom or usage having the force of law); Jeffes v. Barnes (2d Cir.2000) (concluding that "code of silence" within police department could be found to be "standard operating procedure" and retaliation for violating it "pervasive").

Of course, showings of fewer incidents of unconstitutional action may suffice for other theories of municipal liability, such as deliberate "failure to train." Below at § C. But some courts seem willing to equate a pattern of similar acts of officers with a "custom," even if those acts, although frequent,

liable under *Monell*. The county prosecutor, said a plurality, had been delegated "final policymaking authority" to make such searches, and "municipal liability may be imposed for a single decision by municipal policymakers." *Pembaur*'s significance rests with the plurality's recognition that policymaking could take place outside of lawmaking bodies and did not have to involve rules of general applicability. Rather, policy could be made by those individuals, as *Monell* itself said, "whose edicts or acts may fairly be said to represent official policy."

The less than definitive result of the *Pembaur* plurality decision on the "policymaker" question was repeated in another plurality decision reviewing a First Amendment challenge to retaliatory actions taken against a public employee for the exercise of his free speech rights. St. Louis v. Praprotnik (1988). The employee-plaintiff brought a § 1983 action against the individuals who allegedly retaliated against him, and he also sued the city for which he worked. This time, however, the Court concluded that those who retaliated against the plaintiff were not policymakers, insofar as they did not have the delegated power to make employment policy so much as to implement to it. And even if they implemented a constitutional policy unconstitutionally, the city could not be held liable under *Monell*.

Significant about *Praprotnik* was the plurality's conclusion that state law determined who was and who was not a policymaker. And under state law, perhaps only the Mayor and Aldermen of the city, or the city's Civil Service Commission had responsibilities to formulate employment policy. The fact that the power to hire, fire, and transfer employees had been delegated to subordinate officials did not convert the latter into policymakers, even when review of their decisions by the Commission was cursory at best. Finally, as the entire Court later made clear, the task of identifying policymakers is a question of law for the district court to decide—not the jury—and a variety of materials may be relevant to that determination, including evidence of de jure as well as de facto policy. *Jett, supra*.

Despite the inconclusiveness of *Pembaur* and *Praprotnik*, some things stand out. First, the "easy cases" noted above still remain: Unconstitutional actions taken pursuant to statute or long-standing custom will subject a city to liability under § 1983; actions by the rogue cop will not. Second, the acts of lawmaking bodies will subject a municipality to liability, even if it is a single act that is not itself especially legislative in nature. For example, in Owen v. City of Independence (1980), a city was held liable when the city council voted to fire the city's chief of police and, in so doing, violated his procedural due process rights to a pre-termination hearing. And in Newport v. Fact Concerts, Inc. (1981), a city was held liable when the city council voted to cancel an appearance by a musical group for reasons that violated the Constitution. Third, the single unconstitutional act of a "policymaker" can also subject a city to liability. Note, however, that sometimes an ostensibly local official, such as a sheriff, may be considered a policymaker for the (immune) state rather than the (possibly non-immune) local entity that employs him. McMillian v. Monroe County (1997).

4. *Monell* in Flux

Lower courts have taken varied readings on the "custom or policy" question, both with respect to the issue of how pronounced an informal, unwritten practice of officials must be before it rises to the level of custom or policy, and with respect to the problematic task of identifying policymakers after *Pembaur* and *Praprotnik*. On the latter issue, some courts have found cities liable for the acts of those high-ranking officials who had been formally or informally delegated "final" unreviewable decision-making authority with respect to particular matters. From this perspective, every time such an official acts on such matters she forges a small piece of what—in the aggregate—amounts to "policy." This approach seems to accord with the Supreme Court's decision in *Jett, supra*, in which the Court appeared willing to look to evidence other than "positive law" in identifying those whose edicts or acts may fairly be said to represent official policy as a matter of state law. If, in fact, a city's practice is to make a particular official's decisions unreviewable, then perhaps the official should be treated as a policymaker even if state law purports to deny him that status as a formal matter.

Other courts, however, have concluded that even when a city official is given ostensibly unreviewable authority to make final decisions, it does not necessarily amount to authority to make rules or policy. This narrower "separation-of-powers" approach sharply distinguishes lawmakers (policymakers) from law enforcers (decisionmakers), and focuses primarily on formal rather than functional characteristics of officials' roles. The downside of such an approach, however, is that it may be fairly easy for municipalities to avoid liability so long as they have boilerplate prohibitions on how laws are to be enforced, as a matter of municipal "policy."

C. "Failure to Train" as a Basis for Municipal Liability

It is sometimes possible to show that otherwise isolated unconstitutional action by an official has been taken pursuant to custom or policy when the action is the result of a city's "failure to train." The failure-to-train theory, however, is necessarily a limited one. This is so because it can almost always be argued that if only a particular officer had been better trained, he would not have acted unconstitutionally. If that was all that one had to show to put local governments on the hook for their employees' actions, then the failure-to-train approach would threaten to convert nearly all individual officer liability into municipal liability. A failure-to-train theory therefore has the potential to swallow up *Monell*'s no-respondeat-superior rule if interpreted too broadly. Consequently, so long as the Court desires to adhere to *Monell*'s principles of limited municipal liability, failure-to-train must be accommodated to *Monell*'s own strictures.

1. Inaction versus Deliberate Indifference

The Supreme Court has concluded that a failure to train employees can provide a basis for municipal liability "only where the failure to train amounts to deliberate indifference to the rights of persons with whom the [officials] come in contact." City of Canton v. Harris (1989). "Deliberate indifference," moreover, is to be judged by a largely "objective" standard under *City of Canton*, not a "subjective" one.

It will therefore not be enough for a plaintiff to allege that the city has a training program, which is its "policy," and that her injury occurred at the hands of an officer trained by that program. The program may have been perfectly adequate, and the officer's actions may have been unlawful for other reasons. Not only, then, must it be shown that the program itself is inadequate, but it must also be shown that inadequate training is itself official "policy" within the meaning of *Monell*. As stated in *City of Canton*:

It may seem contrary to common sense to assert that a municipality will actually have a policy of not taking reasonable steps to train its employees. But it may happen that in light of the duties assigned to specific officers or employees the need for more training is so obvious, and the inadequacy so likely to result in the violation of constitutional rights, that the policymakers of the city can reasonably be said to have been deliberately indifferent to the need. In that event, the failure to provide proper training may fairly be said to represent a policy for which the city is responsible, and for which the city may be held liable if it actually causes injury.

Sometimes, the need for a certain type of training will be "obvious" from the outset—as with the use of deadly force by police officers. Failure to provide training in such circumstances might well be found to constitute deliberate indifference and hence the local government's custom or policy. *City of Canton, supra.* In other contexts the need for training may not be obvious from the outset, but may become obvious over time, as when policymakers are faced with a pattern of constitutional violations of a particular kind. Estate of Novack v. County of Wood (7th Cir.2000). How stark a showing must be made is obviously a case-by-case determination. Past violations would presumably have to bear closely on the particular harm complained of, as opposed to a showing of "past generalized bad police behavior." Carter v. Morris (4th Cir.1999). But the Court had concluded before *City of Canton* that an unconstitutional policy of inadequate training could not be inferred from a single incident of unconstitutional use of deadly force. Oklahoma City v. Tuttle (1985). And presumably, simple negligence in training will not be enough to satisfy the requirements of *City of Canton* either. Springfield v. Kibbe (1987) (O'Connor, J., dissenting from dismissal of certiorari).

Note that, a finding that the law was not clearly established at the time of the alleged wrongdoing, may foreclose liability on a failure-to-train theory because deliberate indifference to an obvious risk of constitutional harm would be difficult to establish. Joyce v. Town of Tewksbury (1st Cir. 1997). In this limited respect, the officer's personal immunity from damages liability could, as a practical matter, translate to entity immunity from damages. Although, in most settings, the presence of immunity on the officer's part will have no bearing on municipal liability, here, the same considerations that would result in officer immunity would likely mean the failure of a failure-to-train argument.

2. Causation

Even if inadequate training does amount to custom or policy in the *Monell* sense, it must still be shown that the failure to train actually caused the unconstitutional action in question. That is because the unconstitutional action could be the result of something besides the lack of training even when there has been a deliberate failure to train. And for the action in question to be traced to a deliberate failure to train, it may also have to be shown that *different* training would have resulted in different action on the part of the officer.

In addition, because entity liability presupposes an underlying constitutional violation by an officer of the entity (see Los Angeles v. Heller (1986)), "a section 1983 failure-to-train case cannot be maintained against a governmental employer in a case where there is no underlying violation by the employee." Young v. City of Mt. Ranier (4th Cir.

2001); compare Fagan v. City of Vineland (3d Cir. 1994).

D. Fault in Hiring

In Bryan County v. Brown (1997), the Supreme Court rejected municipal liability for the excessive force used by a deputy sheriff whose background and prior brushes with the law had been overlooked by policymakers when he was hired. The Court concluded that where a policymaker's acts were not themselves unconstitutional (and did not command another to engage in unconstitutional acts), local government liability could attach only when those acts were taken with "deliberate indifference" to "obvious" or highly predictable specific consequences. In addition, the plaintiff had to show that there was a direct causal link between the policymaker's fault in hiring and the particular deprivation of constitutional rights. In the hiring context, this meant that a § 1983 plaintiff had to do more than show a generalized risk of harm arising from inadequate scrutiny of a prospective employee's record. Rather, the plaintiff had to show that the employee's background made the specific risk of his particular use of excessive force a plainly obvious consequence of his being hired. Although the Court did not rule out the possibility that such a showing might be made in the proper case, it purported to erect a very high barrier to municipal liability based on fault in hiring. It is possible, although by no means certain, that the *Bryan County* inquiry (regarding deliberate indifference to an obvious or highly predictable specific consequence), may be applicable to the failure-to-train cases as well.

E. Individual "Supervisory" Liability

A remaining category of § 1983 liability for individual officers is related to the concerns raised by *Monell* and *City of Canton*: the personal liability of superiors for the acts of their subordinates (even if the supervisor is not a policymaker). *Monell* itself had suggested that the "mere right to control, without control or direction having been exercised and without any failure to supervise" would not give rise to supervisory liability under § 1983. And after *City of Canton* and *Bryan County*, it is difficult to imagine that the Court would allow for such supervisory liability, absent either direct participation by the supervisor in the subordinate's wrong, or behavior on the part of the supervisor himself— through action or inaction—that was "deliberately indifferent" to constitutional rights as called for by *City of Canton*. Carter v. Morris (4th Cir.1999); Febus–Rodriguez v. Betancourt–Lebron (1st Cir. 1994). As such, the standard for supervisory liability should resemble that for municipal liability in the "omissions" or inaction context. See Randall v. Prince George's County (4th Cir.2002) (requiring "proof of multiple instances of misconduct" by subordinates before permitting supervisory liability to attach).

F. The Future of *Monell*

The no-respondeat-superior regime of *Monell* has been subjected to constant criticism, both for its convolutedness as well as for its disallowance of monetary recovery from local governments for ad

hoc constitutional violations by their officers. Three
Justices recently indicated that *Monell* made the
Court "spin ever finer distinctions" and that "we
should reexamine the soundness" of *Monell's* limitation on vicarious liability. *Bryan County, supra*
(Breyer, J., joined by Stevens and Ginsburg, JJ.,
dissenting). Of course, monetary nonrecovery is also
a consequence of rules of individual officer immunities, as discussed in the next Chapter. In this respect, the battle that raged in Monroe v. Pape
(1961) between Justices Douglas and Frankfurter
over when, if ever, monetary relief should be available for the nonsystemic, ad hoc violations of the
Constitution caused by governmental officials (see
Chapter 2), continues. These issues are also related
to the concerns expressed by the line of cases associated with Parratt v. Taylor (1981), where the Court
found that remedies under state tort law would be a
suitable monetary remedy for some governmental
deprivations. See Chapter 3. But if *Monell* and
other doctrines are convoluted, or result in no
award of monetary damages for ad hoc violations of
the Constitution, is it the limit on respondeat superior liability in *Monell* that needs to be rethought?
Or is it perhaps that part of *Monell* that made cities
financially liable in the first place?

CHAPTER 7

STATE SOVEREIGN IMMUNITY

Overview

States cannot be made defendants in actions brought under § 1983. The reasons for the limitation are twofold. First, constitutionally based doctrines of sovereign immunity associated with the Eleventh Amendment prevent federal courts from exercising jurisdiction over suits by private parties against a state without its consent. Second, states are not suable "persons" within the meaning of § 1983. As a consequence, states cannot be sued in state courts under § 1983 any more than they can be sued in federal courts. This is not to say that relief cannot be obtained that might effectively run against the state under § 1983. As discussed below, it has long been possible to obtain injunctive relief that effectively runs against the state by suing appropriate state officials to compel their future compliance with the Constitution. In addition, the sovereign immunity and statutory barriers to suing states are applicable against only the state itself, its agencies, and other arms of the state. These barriers are not applicable when the defendants are local governments, such as cities and counties, or other political entities that are not arms of the state. Nor is sovereign immunity applicable when damages are sought from state officers in their individual capacities, although officials may sometimes claim personal (as opposed to sovereign) immunity from such monetary awards. See Chapter 8.

A.   Sovereign Immunity and Individual Officer Suits

More than a hundred years ago, in Hans v. Louisiana (1890), the Supreme Court concluded that sovereign immunity principles associated with Article III and the Eleventh Amendment barred suits brought by private parties in federal court against states without their consent—even suits seeking to redress unconstitutional state action. *Hans* was a suit by Louisiana investors against their state to compel it to make good on interest payments on state-issued bonds. The state's actions in failing to pay out as promised were alleged to run afoul of the Constitution's Contracts Clause. U.S. Const. art. I, § 10. The Court held that sovereign immunity barred the suit despite the language of the Eleventh Amendment, which declares only that federal courts lack jurisdiction over suits against states brought by a citizen of "another" state and says nothing about suits brought against a state by one of its own citizens. The Court seemed to say that limitations on such suits against states antedated the Constitution and that the Eleventh Amendment was merely illustrative of an immunity principle carried forward in the Constitution itself. Much maligned of late, *Hans* remains good law.

Hans hardly meant, however, that constitutional norms would be unenforceable against states and their officials. As discussed in Chapter 1, a variety of common law mechanisms have long guaranteed enforcement of the Constitution, if perhaps in less convenient ways than a direct action against the states themselves. Also, the equally famous case of Ex parte Young (1908), made clear that state officials threatening to enforce an unconstitutional statute could be enjoined in federal court, without running afoul of the Eleventh Amendment. The underlying action in *Young* was a suit to enjoin the Minnesota Attorney General from enforcing what were alleged to be unconstitutional statutes respecting railroad rate schedules. (For reasons noted in Chapter 1, *Young* (like *Hans*) was not brought under § 1983 (although it would be today), but directly under the federal question jurisdictional statute, 28 U.S.C.A. § 1331.)

Obviously, Young was being sued because of who he was—the state official charged with enforcement of state law. But the Supreme Court concluded that to the extent that the state statutes authorizing his behavior were unconstitutional, Young was stripped of his official authority and was no longer cloaked with the mantle of the state. He was therefore merely an individual threatening to engage in tort-like behavior who could be enjoined, without regard to sovereign immunity.

The theory underlying *Young* is sometimes said to be a "fiction" insofar as the Court seemed to pretend that only an individual, not the state, was being held accountable in a federal court. Of course, there was some tension in the Court's apparent conclusion that Young's acts sufficiently implicated state action for purposes of the Fourteenth Amendment, yet were at the same time sufficiently distinct from the state so as not to implicate Eleventh Amendment concerns. Nevertheless, the equitable and legal precedents for suing individual officers for their common-law harms were sufficiently well-ingrained even before *Young* that the Court had little trouble in concluding that such suits were not ones forbidden against the state.

For example, the Supreme Court had allowed actions against individual officers for damages for their tortious harms when it was alleged that they were acting pursuant to an unconstitutional statute. The officer was able to be sued individually because the unconstitutional law gave the officer no authority to act, and left him suable as an ordinary tortfeasor who could be personally liable in damages for his common-law harms. Such damages suits were not thought to implicate the Eleventh Amendment or state sovereign immunity. E.g., Virginia Coupon Cases (1885). And the precedents in the injunctive context were based on similar reasoning. E.g., Osborn v. Bank of the United States (1824). What was new about *Young* was that it was not clear that the harm about to be suffered by the railroads (the threatened injury to property from enforcement of an unconstitutional rate schedule) was a traditional common-law injury, although the Court noted that the harm was "akin to a tort."

Young is therefore often said to have involved an action based on the Constitution itself rather than on state tort law, although the opinion itself is not entirely clear about the point.

What was also new about *Young* was that the case arose under federal law, unlike the typical common law action brought against state officials. In those older actions, state authorization was raised by the official in his defense to the plaintiff's state-law or common-law claim, and the question of the constitutionality of the state authorization arose only by way of the plaintiff's reply to that defense. In *Young*, the Court apparently considered the plaintiff's well-pleaded complaint (i.e, the bill in equity) to have itself raised the constitutional question. Otherwise, given the nondiversity of the parties in *Young*, the case could not have arisen under federal law given other developments that same year regarding the necessity for federal jurisdiction to appear on the face of the plaintiff's own pleading, as opposed to in the defendant's possible defense. Louisville & N.R.R. v. Mottley (1908). Although pleading in equity may have allowed a plaintiff to anticipate the defense in a way that pleading actions at law did not, the result made it easy for later generations to say that the claim in *Young* effectively involved an implied right of action for equitable relief, directly under the Constitution.

B. Retrospective versus Prospective Relief

Although neither *Hans* nor *Young* was styled as a § 1983 suit at the time, their message had clear import for such suits after § 1983 was resuscitated in the 1960's. When, for example, litigants brought a § 1983 action to enjoin an Illinois administrator of a welfare benefits program to compel him to calculate welfare benefits consistent with federal law and to have him disgorge wrongfully withheld welfare benefits to a class of beneficiaries, they met with only partial success. Edelman v. Jordan (1974). The effort to obtain prospective injunctive relief was upheld, largely on the basis of *Young*. But the effort to obtain monetary relief from the state for past-withheld benefits was rejected, largely on the basis of *Hans*, even though the plaintiffs had named only a state official and not the state as a defendant. Neither aspect of the decision, however, was obvious.

1. Prospective Injunctive Relief

First, with respect to injunctive relief, *Edelman* was arguably a considerable step beyond *Young*. *Young* had involved a simple negative injunction of a state official that told him to stop what he was about to do. It did not purport to tell the official how to carry out his job, other than to tell him not to. And it did not tax the imagination too greatly to indulge the fiction that in such circumstances Young was an individual wrongdoer, acting without lawful authority, and that suit against him could be rationalized as not being a suit against the state.

By contrast, the injunction in *Edelman* required the state official to undertake affirmative steps to carry out his duties under state law consistent with federal law. Although distinctions between affirmative and negative injunctions may not always carry much explanatory force, it seems clear that the affirmative injunctive relief in *Edelman* was qualitatively more intrusive on the state and its operations than the simple negative injunction in *Young*. Certainly that was true of later judgments for far more complex injunctive relief that were entered against state officials in institutional reform litigation in the wake of Brown v. Board of Ed. (1954). It was therefore more difficult to view the suit in *Edelman* as anything other than a suit against the entity itself insofar as a state official was being ordered to carry out his official functions under state law in a particular way.

Historically, moreover, such requests for affirmative relief against state officials would have been problematic from the perspective of sovereign immunity. E.g., Pennoyer v. McConnaughy (1891); Kentucky v. Dennison (1861). And, far from being stripped of his authority, Edelman was sued on the assumption that he would continue to exercise his official authority. However, from the time of decisions such as *Brown, supra*, federal court awards of affirmative and sometimes complex injunctive relief against state and local officials to bring public institutions into compliance with the Constitution had become commonplace. So, in some respects, *Edelman* merely ratified what had already come to pass. But by exempting affirmative injunctive relief directed against state officials from the Eleventh Amendment's prohibition, it turned into grand fiction what had only been a light fiction in *Young*.

2. Retrospective Damages Relief

Second, with respect to damages, the Court concluded that the *Young* fiction would apply only to requests for prospective relief (such as an injunction) but not to retrospective relief (such as an award of damages for past wrongs). Any award of damages that "must be paid from" the state treasury would violate principles of sovereign immunity even if only an official had been named as the defendant.

The reasons given by the *Edelman* Court for the prospective/retrospective dichotomy were not clear, and certainly no such distinction is suggested by the terms of the Eleventh Amendment. But the opinion rightly noted that dipping into the state's treasury to remedy its past violations of the law had traditionally been a problem for federal courts. For example, Chisholm v. Georgia (1793)—a pre-Eleventh Amendment decision whose outcome (allowing an individual to sue a state in federal court) provided the impetus for the Amendment's ratification—had been a common-law breach-of-contract action brought by a South Carolina citizen to compel the State of Georgia to pay for goods it had purchased from the plaintiff. And although *Hans* (in contrast to *Chisholm*) was a constitutionally based suit, it too was an action that sought to compel a state to make good on its financial promises. The sanctity of the state treasury from damages judgments for a state's past violations of law therefore seemed to go to the core of what it was that sovereign immunity protected, even in *Edelman*.

For these very reasons, suits against individual officers of the state that seek damages from them personally are not, and have never been thought to be, suits against the state barred by the Eleventh Amendment. And the fact that the state might voluntarily agree with its officers to indemnify them for damages liability in § 1983 cases can hardly convert an otherwise permissible § 1983 damages action against the officer into an impermissible one against the state. See Sales v. Grant (4th Cir.2000) ("a state's promise of indemnity cannot invest governmental officers with sovereign immunity"); cf. Regents v. Doe (1997) (finding Eleventh Amendment implicated even though state university was indemnified). Because a judgment against an officer in his personal capacity would not have to be paid by the state absent such an agreement, individual officer suits for damages do not present a case where relief "must be paid from" the state treasury. If such voluntary indemnification agreements could create a sovereign immunity problem for damages actions against individual officers, then the state would have the unfettered power to make its officers absolutely immune from personal damages awards under § 1983. Presumably, states lack the power to amend § 1983 in such a fashion.

C. "Ancillary" Monetary Impacts

Nevertheless, the *Edelman* Court had to acknowledge that states are sometimes obligated to expend money from their treasuries to comply with orders of permissible prospective injunctive relief. For example, implementing school desegregation remedies or reforming a prison system to bring it into compliance with the Constitution obliges a state to expend money in order to comply with the federal court's order of injunctive relief. Such expenditures, even if they came from the state treasury, were justified despite the Eleventh Amendment, said *Edelman*, because they were merely "ancillary" to the permissible order of prospective injunctive relief. Moreover, while such compliance may necessitate expenditures, it would not involve payment to identifiable individuals whom the state had allegedly wronged.

The difference between permissible ancillary relief and impermissible retrospective awards is hardly, as the Court itself acknowledged, the difference between night and day. Even injunctive decrees in the area of institutional reform litigation, which *Edelman* allows, have a "retrospective" look to them, because such decrees seek to undo the status quo and remedy the present-day effects of past illegality. Predictably, the Court has struggled with the prospective/retrospective and the ancillary-relief concepts. For example, it once found no Eleventh Amendment problem with a federal court order to inform welfare beneficiaries of means under state law to recoup wrongfully withheld past benefits. Quern v. Jordan (1979). But it did find an Eleventh

Amendment problem when a similar order was not part of an injunction issued by a federal court to redress a continuing violation of federal law. Green v. Mansour (1985). The Court has also upheld awards of attorney's fees against states under the 1976 Civil Rights Attorney's Fees Awards Act as ancillary relief when state officials have been sued successfully for injunctive relief. Missouri v. Jenkins (1989); Hutto v. Finney (1978). Of course, such an award is not ancillary in the sense of being a cost routinely paid in litigation by losing parties who have litigated in good faith; nor is the award like the inevitable expense of having to comply with an order of injunctive relief. But the Court apparently considers the "ancillary" label as necessary if fees are to be awarded against the state, given the fee statute's insufficiently clear abrogation of state sovereign immunity.

Arguably what the Court has tried to do with its prospective/retrospective distinction is to accommodate, perhaps uneasily, the competing constitutional claims of sovereign immunity and the supremacy of federal law. It found a way to give meaning to sovereign immunity by continuing to apply it to bar suits for damages that would necessarily run against the state (although effectively ignoring the problem in the injunctive relief context), while simultaneously giving meaning to the supremacy of federal law by ensuring that, at a minimum, states could be judicially compelled to cease their ongoing or threatened illegal behavior and to comply with the Constitution and laws in the future.

By reversing the usual preference for monetary over injunctive relief, however, the Court effectively gave states a free bite at violating federal law until a suit for injunctive relief was brought. Perhaps one way of looking at this part of the *Edelman* decision is that the Court implicitly concluded that a state was entitled to the heightened "notice" associated with an injunction against its officials before it could be held financially accountable to private parties for violating their rights under federal law or the Constitution, at least absent any clearer notice of abrogation of immunity than is supplied by the language of § 1983. And *Edelman* provides for vindication of the underlying federal norm, even though individually recoverable damages are unavailable against the state itself.

D. Abrogation, Waiver, and States as Suable "Persons"

Under traditional sovereign immunity analysis, states can be sued if their immunity is waived, even though sovereign immunity is in the nature of a limitation on subject matter jurisdiction. Clark v. Barnard (1883). But waivers are not easily found, and they tend to be narrowly construed. Nevertheless, the modern Supreme Court has allowed that, if Congress acts with sufficient clarity in enacting statutes under its acknowledged power to enforce, for example, the Fourteenth Amendment, it can legislatively "abrogate" the states' sovereign immunity from suit. Seminole Tribe v. Florida (1996); Fitzpatrick v. Bitzer (1976). Such abrogation, however, only remotely resembles a notion of true waiver or consent. The theory must be that there was an antecedent waiver to the extent that § 5 of the Fourteenth Amendment might be read to permit Congress to legislate directly against states. (Whether the Reconstruction Congress(es)—which never made states directly suable for their constitutional violations—would have so understood § 5 is another question.)

Given this power, one might assume that § 1983 itself has abrogated the states' sovereign immunity from suit in federal court, insofar as § 1983 is the acknowledged vehicle to enforce (among other things) the guarantees of the Fourteenth Amendment. In Quern v. Jordan (1979), however, the Supreme Court concluded that Congress had not spoken with the requisite degree of clarity needed to abrogate the states' sovereign immunity because § 1983 did not expressly declare that "states" could be sued for violations of the statute. Use of the all-purpose statutory term "persons" to define the class of those who could be sued was insufficiently clear for the Court. This was true even though the 1871 drafters may have been operating under the assumption that the term "persons" could include corporate and governmental bodies, and even though the Court itself had concluded that cities and counties were suable "persons." See Chapter 6.

A related but not identical issue was whether states might nevertheless be suable "persons" in *state* court. Until relatively recently (see Alden v. Maine (1999)) sovereign immunity was sometimes thought to be relevant only to federal court jurisdiction. It was therefore argued that the crystal-clear language required for finding a congressional abrogation of state sovereign immunity from suit in federal court might not be required in deciding whether, as an ordinary matter of statutory interpretation, states were among the suable "persons" to whom § 1983 was addressed. In other words, the statutory interpretation of "persons" under § 1983 might have required merely ordinary evidence of state suability (for suit in state court under § 1983) rather than the extraordinary evidence of state suability required to find that § 1983 had abrogated state sovereign immunity from suit in federal court.

Nevertheless, the Court dispatched the idea in Will v. Michigan Dept. of State Police (1989), when it applied its Eleventh Amendment-inspired, crystal-clear-language-of-abrogation approach to the arguably simpler question of statutory interpretation. By concluding that states were not suable "persons" within the meaning of § 1983, states became no more suable in state court under § 1983 than they could be in federal court. *Will*'s holding is therefore in line with later decisions such as *Alden, supra*, that refuse to distinguish the state's sovereign immunity based on whether suit is brought in state versus federal court.

E. Section 1983 Litigation after *Seminole Tribe* and its Progeny

The Supreme Court has concluded that Congress cannot abrogate the states' sovereign immunity from suit at the behest of an individual when it acts under its Article I Commerce Clause powers, no matter how clearly it speaks. Seminole Tribe v. Florida (1996). Thus, for example, a state could not now be directly suable against its wishes by private parties in federal court for a violation of an environmental clean-up statute if the Commerce Clause was the power pursuant to which the environmental statute was passed. Compare Pennsylvania v. Union Gas Co. (1989) (overruled by *Seminole Tribe*). Nor could a state be sued by a private party in state court in such an action. *Alden, supra.*

The Court has distinguished, however, Congress's power to abrogate state sovereign immunity when acting pursuant to its (post-Eleventh Amendment) powers conferred in the Reconstruction-era amendments, as when it lifted state immunity in employment discrimination actions brought under the 1972 amendments to Title VII of the Civil Right Act of 1964. Fitzpatrick v. Bitzer (1976). In *Fitzpatrick*, the Court concluded that Congress acted validly under § 5 of the Fourteenth Amendment in implementing the command of the Equal Protection Clause (even though Title VII, unlike the Equal Protection Clause, can be violated merely on a showing of disparate treatment). See also Tennessee v. Lane (2004) (upholding abrogation of state sovereign immunity under provisions of Title II of the Americans with Disabilities Act as they relate to court access); Nevada Dept. of Human Res. v. Hibbs (2003) (upholding abrogation of state immunity under Family and Medical Leave Act of 1993 as appropriate legislation to remedy gender discrimination in workplace).

In most respects, therefore, *Seminole Tribe* and its progeny should have little impact on § 1983 actions, in part because § 1983 was passed primarily to enforce the Reconstruction-era amendments, and more importantly, because the Court has already held that Congress did *not* abrogate state sovereign immunity when it enacted § 1983, since Congress did not speak clearly enough. *Will, supra.* But if Congress wanted to, it could presumably abrogate the states' sovereign immunity from suit for violations of the Fourteenth Amendment (including violations of those provisions of the Bill of Rights incorporated through the Due Process Clause) by exercising its powers under § 5 with the requisite degree of clarity. To the extent that § 1983 is employed to remedy actual violations of the Constitution, there would appear to be little argument that the statute provides anything other than "congruen[t] and proportional[]" relief. Compare Kimel v. Florida Bd. of Regents (2000); City of Boerne v. Flores (1997). But Congress has not taken such a step.

Nevertheless, there may be some potential for fallout from *Seminole Tribe* for a few § 1983 cases. One issue raised by *Seminole Tribe*—a suit to enforce a purely statutory, not a constitutional right— was the scope of the Ex parte Young fiction. The Court not only disallowed suit against the state under the federal statute that was at issue in *Seminole Tribe*, but the Court also disallowed a *Young-*

type action for injunctive relief against the Governor of Florida. The Court explained that the federal statute in question expressly allowed for suits against the state, and that Congress had apparently intended this to be the exclusive remedy—even to the exclusion of a suit against the wrongdoing official based on the *Young* rationale. As noted in Chapter 5, some § 1983 actions are based on violations of federal statutes that may have been enacted pursuant to Commerce Clause or spending powers, rather than under the Fourteenth Amendment. *If* those underlying federal statutes specifically purport to allow suit against only the state itself—as did the statute at issue in *Seminole Tribe*—then they could not be enforced in federal court on their own; and they arguably would not support a § 1983 action for prospective injunctive relief against the wrongdoing official for a violation of the underlying federal statute either.

It is not likely, however, that the *Seminole Tribe* decision meant to suggest more broadly that the *Young* fiction would be unavailable for injunctive relief against state officers whenever the underlying claim was based on a statute passed pursuant to Congress's pre-Reconstruction-era powers. If it did, the Court would have to revisit cases such as *Edelman*, because *Edelman* itself was a § 1983 suit to enforce welfare statutes enacted under Congress's spending power. Because § 1983 does not purport to provide for suits directly against the state (but only against individuals and local governments), there should ordinarily be no problem under *Semi-*

nole Tribe if § 1983 is used to enforce federal laws enacted pursuant to a pre-Reconstruction era power. As to such statutes, *Seminole Tribe* would not disable Congress from providing for their prospective enforcement against state officers consistent with principles of sovereign immunity.

Finally, if the Court were writing on a clean slate, fee awards against the state for some § 1983 claims enforcing federal "laws" could have presented interesting questions under *Seminole Tribe*. As noted above, under the 1976 Attorney Fees Awards Act, 42 U.S.C.A. § 1988(b) (discussed in Chapter 11), the Court has held that states are liable for the plaintiff's attorney fees when state officials have been successfully sued in their official capacities for injunctive relief. Missouri v. Jenkins (1989); Hutto v. Finney (1978). The Act, however, lacks anything like a clear statement that states will be monetarily liable for fees in such event. What is more, even if the Act had spoken clearly, it is open to question (given *Seminole Tribe*) whether Congress could compel payment of fees from the state in § 1983 actions that seek to enforce rights under federal statutes enacted only pursuant to Congress's Article I powers (e.g., suits to enforce welfare rights against state officials). But right or wrong, the Court has made clear that attorney fees against the state are justified as "ancillary" to an award of injunctive relief against its officials, and, like other "costs" of litigation (as uniquely defined by the 1976 Act), their payment by the state has been held not to implicate sovereign immunity at all. *Jenkins, supra.*

Jenkins was pre-*Seminole Tribe*; it was a Fourteenth Amendment case, not an "and laws" case; and its reasoning is hardly airtight. But if *Jenkins* is right, and assuming the underlying award of injunctive relief against a state official is not in question, then the award of fees against the state will not be in question either, no matter what the underlying basis for the § 1983 claim.

F. What Are Arms of the State?

Sovereign immunity protects only the state, state agencies, and other arms of the state. Historically, it has not protected cities, counties, and other local governmental entities. Lincoln County v. Luning (1890). Consistent with such treatment, the Court has also concluded that local governmental entities, unlike states, are suable persons under § 1983. Monell v. New York City Dept. of Soc. Servs. (1978). While the availability of sovereign immunity will often be a simple matter to determine, the status of various hybrid governmental entities—such as school boards, water and resource management districts, and entities created by interstate compact—may be harder to decipher.

In resolving whether an entity is an arm of the state, and thus entitled to immunity, courts have looked to a variety of factors. Some of these factors are formal, such as the nominal status of the entity under state law. For entities that are less obviously "local" than cities and counties, more significant are functional considerations, including the independence and separate political and financial accountability of the entity. Perhaps the most important of these functional concerns is the ability of the entity to generate its own resources from which any judgment might be paid without having to require resort to the state treasury. Emphasis on economic autonomy comports with the conclusion in *Edelman* that sovereign immunity is implicated only when payment of any judgment "must" come from the state. E.g., Jacintoport Corp. v. Greater Baton Rouge Port Comm'n (5th Cir.1985); see also Cash v. Granville Cty. Bd. of Ed. (4th Cir.2001) ("principle factor . . . is whether judgment would have to be paid from the State's treasury").

The significance of this particular factor is highlighted by the Supreme Court's decision in Hess v. Port–Auth. Trans–Hudson Corp. ["PATH"] (1994). In deciding (in a non–§ 1983 context) on the Eleventh Amendment status of PATH—an entity created by an interstate compact between New York and New Jersey—the Court concluded that it was not an arm of the state even though it was the offspring of two states. Although lines of political control over PATH reached to state officials of the compacting states, the financial independence of the bi-state entity warranted denial of Eleventh Amendment protection. Cf. Regents v. Doe (1997) (Eleventh Amendment implicated even though state university was indemnified).

Nevertheless, some lower courts have concluded that individuals who were ostensibly county or local government officials were employees of the state when they were carrying out the task of enforcing state law. For example, in Scott v. O'Grady (7th Cir.1992), a county sheriff was considered to be a state, not a county, employee when evicting persons pursuant to a state court writ of assistance. And another court held that when a city prosecutor prosecuted defendants on state criminal charges, she was, to that extent, a state employee. Pusey v. City of Youngstown (6th Cir.1993).

Then, in McMillian v. Monroe County (1997), the Supreme Court came to a similar conclusion. It held, based on the structure of Alabama's government, that sheriffs represented the state rather than the (nonimmune) county when acting in a law enforcement capacity. The Court looked to state law to answer the *Monell* question whether the sheriff was a "policymaker" for the state or the county in the area of law enforcement. Although the Court was careful not to say that all sheriffs (even in Alabama) always represented the state rather than their county, *McMillian* is in tension with the Court's sovereign immunity decisions which have looked to a variety of factors (of which local law is only one) to resolve whether a suit is, as a matter of federal law, against the state under the Eleventh Amendment.

G. Individual versus Official Capacity Suits

1. Officer Liability

The prospective/retrospective relief dichotomy set up in *Edelman* requires attention to how a suit under § 1983 is styled. If damages are sought personally against a state or local official, no Eleventh Amendment problem is usually presented, and the suit can be styled as one against the officer in his or her individual capacity. Obviously, after Monroe v. Pape (1961), most suits against officers involve actions they have taken under color of law, and, in some sense, are directed at "official" acts. But such official action does not mean that the § 1983 suit should be brought against the state officer in his "official" capacity. If personal liability for damages under § 1983 is sought for a state officer's action taken under color of law, the suit against the officer must be brought against him in his individual or personal capacity, and *not* against him in his official capacity. Hafer v. Melo (1991). Indeed, if suit is brought against an officer in his official capacity only, the Court has concluded that only the entity for which the officer works has been effectively named as the defendant, and that the officer himself has not been named. Kentucky v. Graham (1985). In short, it will not be possible to recover damages personally from an officer (state or local), if he is sued only in his official (rather than his individual or personal) capacity.

2. Entity Liability

If a party brings only an official capacity action, recovery may therefore be had only against the entity; and that, in turn, can be problematic for the reasons discussed in this and in the last Chapter. In suits against local and municipal officials sued in their official capacity only, typically no Eleventh

Amendment problem will be presented, but the custom-or-policy limitation respecting the liability of local governments will be triggered. See Chapter 6. Thus, in a suit for damages under § 1983, it may make sense to name a officer in her individual and official capacities (or to add the local government by name) if the plaintiff is unsure whether the custom-or-policy requirement can be made out and when recovery might only be possible against the officer alone.

But if suit is brought against a *state* official in her official capacity only, sovereign immunity will be implicated. If the suit is for monetary relief, it will be barred by sovereign immunity because the state has been effectively named as the defendant. Thus, in a suit for damages under § 1983, it makes no sense to name a state official in his individual and official capacities because recovery can be had (if at all) against the officer alone. If it is a suit for prospective injunctive relief, however, suing the state official in her official capacity is typically not a problem, even though doing so is ordinarily tantamount to naming the entity for which the official works. In this context the *Young/Edelman* fiction will apply, and the suit will not be dismissed on sovereign immunity grounds. Indeed, suing the official in her official capacity for injunctive relief may be obligatory if attorney's fees from the state are also sought. *Graham, supra.*

Strict compliance with the *Young* theory of individual liability might well suggest also naming the state official in her individual capacity as well as her official capacity when suing for injunctive relief. But the Supreme Court seems willing to assume that official-capacity suits are the proper mechanism for injunctive relief that effectively runs against the entity. A suit seeking to recover damages from a state officer for her past constitutional harms, as well as injunctive relief to prevent future harm, can readily be styled as a suit against the named officer in both her individual and official capacities.

H.   Pendent Claims Under State Law

1.   The *Pennhurst* Limitation

Young's individual officer fiction does not carry over into suits for injunctive relief based on *state* law, even when the state law claim would otherwise be pendent to a § 1983 claim brought against the proper official. In Pennhurst State School & Hosp. v. Halderman (1984), the Court had before it a suit for injunctive relief to reform a state mental institution. The plaintiffs' initial theories of relief had been based on federal statutory, federal constitutional, and state law grounds. Officials of the state institution were named as defendants on all claims for relief. Although the state-law claim for injunctive relief arose out of the same events that gave rise to the federal claims, the Supreme Court eventually concluded that the state-law injunctive claims were in fact suits against the state which sovereign immunity forbids.

The Court's reasoning was that such suits, because of the relief they generated, were "in effect" against the state, even though only state officials, and not the state, were named as defendants. Of course, that was equally true of the suits based on federal constitutional grounds. But the Court seemed to say that such suits were tolerated under the fiction of Ex parte Young to accommodate the enforcement of the supremacy of federal law and the Fourteenth Amendment. No such toleration of the fiction was necessary, said the Court, when the injunctive claim for relief against state officers was based on state law.

Pennhurst was seemingly at odds with earlier decisions of the Court in which injunctive relief had been entered on non-federal theories of relief against state officials. E.g., Siler v. Louisville & N.R.R. Co. (1908). And, following the reasoning of *Young*, if an officer who acted in violation of federal law was stripped of his authority, then he would arguably have been stripped of it when he acted in violation of state law, too.

Older cases such as *Siler*, however, were ones in which the relief did not involve the imposition of complex affirmative obligations on state actors that more dramatically resembled relief against the state itself. Those older cases might well have regarded affirmative relief such as that in *Pennhurst* as amounting to an impermissible suit against the state, whether the underlying legal theory was state law *or* federal law. See Pennoyer v. McConnaughy (1891). The newer forms of permissible injunctive relief to secure compliance with the Constitution had clearly stretched the fiction to a point beyond which the Court was prepared to go, at least when the supremacy of federal law was not at issue. *Pennhurst* itself, of course, makes no distinction between affirmative and negative injunctive relief. So, if injunctive relief is sought in federal court against a state official to have him comply with state law, the claim will now be barred by sovereign immunity.

2. Limitations on *Pennhurst*

Pennhurst also has its limits, however. It should not bar pendent claims based on state law for damages against state (or local) officials sued in their personal capacities. Such suits have never been thought to implicate sovereign immunity concerns. Thus, if supplemental jurisdiction otherwise exists under 28 U.S.C.A. § 1367 (see Chapter 18), pendent damages claims against individual officers based on state-law grounds should not be a problem. Similarly, suits for injunctive or monetary relief based on state law against local governmental entities that are not arms of the state ought not to be barred by *Pennhurst*. Sovereign immunity is simply not implicated in suits brought against such entities.

Although there is language in *Pennhurst* suggesting that injunctive relief against a county would not be allowed in that case, that may merely reflect the fact that the local governments were, with respect to the administration of the particular program at issue, not independent from the state as a matter of state law. When state-law-based injunctive relief against state or local governmental entities is concerned, it makes sense to defer to state-law characterizations of the role of the particular entity within the state's governmental structure in assessing its immune status in federal court. In addition, abstention doctrines may sometimes counsel hesitation when federal courts would be put in the position of telling local governments and their officials what powers they have as a matter of state law, especially when the question is unclear. Louisiana Power & Light v. City of Thibodaux (1959). In this respect, *Pennhurst* constitutionalizes (in suits against state officers) what would otherwise be a sensible albeit discretionary limit on federal court authority.

CHAPTER 8

PERSONAL IMMUNITIES

Overview

The premise of Monroe v. Pape (1961) was that state and local officials could be personally liable for their constitutional violations. Although neither *Monroe* nor § 1983 suggests that those who violate the Constitution may claim personal immunity from liability, subsequent decisions have concluded that virtually all public officials may be able to claim some form of personal immunity from damages awards for their discretionary acts. Law enforcement and most other administrative officials enjoy qualified immunity which enables them to avoid personal damages liability if they can show that they acted in objective good faith—i.e., that a reasonable officer would not have known that his actions violated the Constitution. In short, for these officials, mistaken judgments reasonably arrived at are off-limits to damages awards under § 1983. Officials who act unconstitutionally in their judicial or prosecutorial capacity typically enjoy an *absolute* immunity from damages as do legislators and many others who engage in lawmaking functions. By contrast, private parties who act in concert with state or local officials can act under color of law for purposes of § 1983, and even engage in state action for purposes of the Fourteenth Amendment, and yet may be *un*able to invoke official immunity. Finally, although various immunities may attend § 1983 damages actions, injunctive relief is typically treated differently. Generally, there is no immunity from injunctive (or declaratory) relief, except for those acting in a legislative capacity. The Constitution therefore remains at least prospectively enforceable under § 1983 against non-legislative officials.

A. Good Faith Immunity

On its face, § 1983 creates a species of tort liability that admits of no immunities. Nevertheless, some forms of immunity for discretionary acts of officials were well ingrained at common law. Based on this history, and based on the assumption that Congress in 1871 did not mean to override such common-law immunity, the Supreme Court has concluded that most officials deserve some form of immunity, at least from damages liability under § 1983 for their constitutional violations. Despite this approach, however, some of the Court's decisions on immunities seem to be more grounded in policy than in history, especially immunities for law enforcement and executive branch personnel.

After a number of false starts, the Supreme Court concluded that law enforcement officials and other members of the executive branch may invoke a qualified good faith immunity from awards of damages for constitutional harms that they inflict. Harlow v. Fitzgerald (1982). The good faith immunity test is said to be "objective": Would a reasonable official have known that his actions violated the constitutional rights of the § 1983 plaintiff? If not, the defendant officer will not be liable in damages for his constitutional violation. The Court has made clear that qualified immunity is an affirmative defense that must be pled by the officer in his Answer to the Complaint, Crawford–El v. Britton (1998), and there is no special pleading requirement that would compel the plaintiff, in her Complaint, to anticipate the defense.

Although *Harlow* itself indicated that an official's *actual* knowledge ("knew or should have known") that his acts violated the Constitution would result in a loss of immunity (even if a reasonable officer might not be expected to know), later decisions from the Court have effectively ignored this "subjective" element. So have most lower courts. And although *Harlow* was a *"Bivens* action"—a constitutional action involving a federal official (see Chapter 17)—the decision was quickly embraced as the standard for § 1983 actions. Davis v. Scherer (1984). Thus, state and local officers will be personally accountable in § 1983 actions only when their unconstitutional acts violate "clearly established constitutional rights of which a reasonable official would have known."

The decision in *Harlow* corresponds to what scholars have called a "colorable legality" model of official accountability, as opposed to a "legality" model. The latter would hold officials financially accountable any time they violated the law—a kind of strict liability; the former holds them immune from such relief if their unlawful acts were plausibly lawful. The two models existed at common law and competed with each other at various historical periods. And the two models continue to exist, insofar as a "legality" model still generally applies to claims for injunctive relief, while the "colorable legality" model applies to most law enforcement and administrative officials sued for damages. In other words, a defense of good faith or qualified immunity will not ordinarily allow an officer to avoid injunctive relief to cease his continued unconstitutional behavior. But the same defense will bar an award of damages against the officer.

1. Freedom to Act in Areas of Uncertain Legality

The purposes of qualified immunity are thought to be twofold. First, without such an immunity, there would arguably be a disincentive for officers to act in areas of uncertain constitutionality even though their actions might later be determined to be constitutionally permissible. Bold or vigorous enforcement of the law would be discouraged. In theory, even though an official's contemplated activity might be on the constitutional side of the line, the line itself is hard to discern, surrounded as it is by the proverbial gray area separating lawful from unlawful activity. Fear of stepping over that line would counsel a rational official to stay out of the gray area altogether and to forgo behavior that might actually be lawful. By allowing immunity for all discretionary actions taken in the gray area—the

area in which a reasonable official could not be
expected to know where legality ended and illegality
began—officials will be encouraged to act more
boldly, all the way up to the line of constitutionally
permissible behavior rather than short of it.

Of course, this gray area immunity also gives the
official the ability to step *over* the line of constitutionally acceptable behavior and still avoid damages, so long as the officer is acting in the area of
uncertain legality. As a consequence of such an
immunity, constitutional norms may go marginally
underenforced, because officials are liable not for all
of their unconstitutional acts, but only for their
clearly unconstitutional acts—acts of which the officer will have "fair warning." Hope v. Pelzer (2002).
The trade-off is between (1) compensation for all
unlawful activity and (2) encouraging law enforcement officials to do whatever may be constitutionally permissible by allowing them to do some things
that are constitutionally impermissible. The Court's
qualified immunity doctrine has honored the second
of these two values over the first.

2. Freedom from Trial

Second, the immunity for law enforcement officials is designed to allow them to avoid trial and
even pre-trial discovery in some cases lest they be
kept unnecessarily from the performance of their
duties. Consequently, the Court has "repeatedly . . .
stressed the importance of resolving immunity
questions at the earliest possible stage in litigation." Hunter v. Bryant (1991). Prior to its decision

in *Harlow*, the Court had experimented with tests for qualified immunity that imposed liability when an officer acted with subjective bad faith or ill will (even though his conduct might otherwise have been objectively reasonable). This enabled plaintiffs to succeed in imposing liability by proof of malice or bad faith, and it enabled a plaintiff to avoid dismissal on summary judgment under Rule 56, Fed. R. Civ. P., because of the presence of factual questions surrounding the officer's state of mind.

Harlow's focus on objective reasonableness thus limited the possibility that the immunity issue would survive summary judgment. And the fact that qualified immunity in federal court partakes in some measure of a right to avoid trial as well as liability would also permit a court to compel a plaintiff in a pleading subsequent to the initial Complaint to engage the qualified immunity issue. *Crawford-El, supra.* But the test of objective reasonableness does not always guarantee early resolution of the immunity issue

As discussed further below, the Court has indicated that the immunity inquiry is only the second step in a two-step inquiry. The first inquiry is to identify whether the plaintiff has alleged (or, at the summary judgment stage, will have sufficient evidence to satisfy a factfinder that) a violation of the Constitution. If the answer to that question is "yes" the court will then (and only then) need to resolve the second question of qualified immunity.

Saucier v. Katz (2001); Sacramento Cty. v. Lewis (1998).

Thus, if a pure question of law is presented, with no underlying factual dispute, summary judgment may be proper, either because the plaintiff has not alleged (or would not be able to show) a violation of the Constitution. For example, a female plaintiff who claims she was denied her constitutional right to enroll in a particular state high school without regard to gender may or may not state claim for relief under the Equal Protection Clause and § 1983. If a court were to conclude that such a practice did not run afoul of the Constitution, the case could be dismissed without having to reach the question of qualified immunity. Even if a court were inclined to find that the plaintiff's allegations, if true, did amount to a constitutional violation, the uncertainty that currently surrounds the constitutionality of such single-sex secondary institutions would likely make the school officials immune from a damages judgment for excluding her. A motion to dismiss a § 1983 damages action on immunity grounds would therefore be appropriate in such a case. (But, as noted above, there is no similar immunity from injunctive relief, and good faith would be irrelevant to the availability of such relief if the court were to conclude the refusal to enroll was indeed unconstitutional.)

On the other hand, unresolved factual issues may foreclose pre-trial resolution of the immunity issue, but not always. For example, in a damages action alleging an unreasonable search and seizure, there may be factual issues surrounding the facts of which the officer was aware. In Anderson v. Creighton (1987), the Court stated that when a § 1983 plaintiff alleges an unreasonable search and seizure, the (objective) inquiry into reasonableness called for by the Fourth Amendment is made in light of facts known (subjectively) to the officer. If, under even the most plaintiff-favorable reading of those facts, there would still not be a constitutional violation, the court could resolve the matter pre-trial. In such a case the plaintiff's case would be dismissed because of the plaintiff's inability to show a violation of the Constitution. Even if such a plaintiff-favorable reading of the facts would show a constitutional violation, a court might still be able to conclude as a matter of law that any violation would not have involved "clearly established constitutional rights of which an objectively reasonable official would have known." In such a case, the plaintiff's case would be dismissed on qualified immunity grounds. But if such a reading of the facts would show a constitutional violation, and the court concluded that the violation (if proved) did implicate clearly established constitutional rights, summary judgment would be denied, and the case would have to go to trial.

For example, if there is a dispute over whether an officer who shot a fleeing felon had reason to believe that the shooting victim posed an imminent threat to human life, summary judgment will not be available. Similarly, if the plaintiff and defendant have a genuine dispute about the information that the officer possessed at the time of a search, and under the plaintiff's version of the facts there would be a clear lack of probable cause, summary judgment should be denied. And, of course, if the defense at summary judgment is in the nature of "I didn't do it," summary judgment would also have to be denied if the plaintiff comes forward with evidence sufficient to rebut the denial. Johnson v. Jones (1995).

Likewise, if the constitutional claim against a public official is one that itself hinges on subjective motivation—such as a claim that the official discriminated in hiring against the plaintiff because of race—then summary judgment may also be problematic. That is because, even if the equal protection right to be free of race discrimination under the given factual circumstances may be very clear, there still remains the underlying question of the defendant's subjective motivation or racial animus. Despite the risk that such allegations, perhaps easily made, might defeat the purposes of qualified immunity if not backed up with substantial evidence at the time of summary judgment, the Court has rejected a requirement that the plaintiff come forward at the summary judgment stage with evidence from which a factfinder could find by clear and convincing evidence that the defendant was impermissibly motivated. Crawford–El v. Britton (1998). All that is needed under Rule 56 is evidence from which a rational factfinder could find impermissible motivation by a preponderance of the evidence.

Note, however, that in the context of § 1983 actions for Fourth Amendment violations, the question is not simply "Was there probable cause?" or "Was the search reasonable?" but: "Was the officer reasonable about the existence of probable cause, or the reasonableness of the search?" Thus, an officer might commit an "unreasonable" search and seizure and yet be found to have acted "reasonably" under *Harlow* and its progeny. Saucier v. Katz (2001). As long as the officer was not unreasonably unreasonable in such a setting, he will be immune from damages. In *Saucier*, the Court reaffirmed its approach in Anderson v. Creighton (1987), and stated that the question whether an officer had used excessive (i.e., unreasonable) force in effecting an arrest was a separate question from whether the officer acted unreasonably for purposes of immunity. Given that Graham v. Connor (1989) requires an inquiry into objective reasonableness as a prerequisite to finding a Fourth Amendment violation in the first instance (see Chapter 4), the practical effect of *Saucier* is a "doubling [of] the 'objective reasonableness' inquiry" in search and seizure cases. *Saucier* (Ginsburg, J., dissenting). Whether there should be a separate "objective reasonableness" requirement for all other constitutional violations that require proof of defendant's subjective deliberate indifference, such as certain Eighth Amendment claims brought by prisoners, may still be an open question post-*Saucier*. See Ford v. Ramirez–Palmer (9th Cir. 2002) (concluding, however, that *Saucier* would require the separate inquiry).

3. Assessing Reasonableness

Deciding whether the constitutional right in question was "clearly established" can be tricky business. It forces an endlessly debatable question: How clear is clear enough? "This inquiry," the Court has said, "must be undertaken in light of the specific context of the case, not as a broad general proposition[.]" *Saucier, supra.* The constitutional right in question, therefore, must have been clearly established at an "appropriate level of specificity": "Would it be clear to a reasonable officer that his conduct was unlawful in the situation he confronted?" *Id.* Often, results will turn on the level of generality at which a court articulates the underlying constitutional right. Compare, e.g., Brosseau v. Haugen (2004) (defining right to be free from use of excessive force in a highly contextualized manner and finding qualified immunity), with Groh v. Ramirez (2004) (defining warrant particularity requirement of Fourth Amendment at a relatively high level of generality and finding no qualified immunity).

Nevertheless, the fact that the precise issue has not been decided does not automatically ensure qualified immunity. Anderson v. Creighton (1987). In other words, some reasoning by analogy from other precedents may be required of the reasonable public official in ascertaining whether the law is "clearly established." See Hope v. Pelzer (2002) (rejecting lower court's requirement that there be a "materially similar" precedent; rather, the question is whether sufficiently analogous precedents provided "fair warning" "even in novel factual circumstances"). But the controlling or sufficiently analogous precedent will likely have to be from the Supreme Court or from the Circuit whose law is applicable to a particular public official, absent "a consensus of cases" of such persuasive authority that an officer could not have supposed his actions were constitutional. Wilson v. Layne (1999). See also the opinions concurring in and dissenting from the denial of rehearing en banc in Robles v. Prince George's Cty. (4th Cir.2002).

In *Wilson, supra*, a damages action under § 1983, the Court held that the Fourth Amendment was violated when police allowed the media to accompany them into a suspect's home while serving a warrant. Thus, the search was constitutionally unreasonable. But it also upheld the qualified immunity of the officers because no controlling authority was in place at the time of the ride-along to the effect that the practice was unconstitutional. Thus, the officers were reasonable in their conducting of a constitutionally unreasonable search.

The decision in *Wilson* was also one of the first which indicated that ordinarily, the court resolving an immunity issue should first answer the question whether the plaintiff has alleged the deprivation of a constitutional right. As noted above, if the answer is "no," then the case should be dismissed. If the answer is "yes," then the court should answer the second question, i.e., whether the right was "clearly established." See *Saucier, supra*; County of Sacramento v. Lewis (1998). Prior to decisions such as *Wilson*, courts sometimes punted on the question of whether a constitutional right had been implicated simply by assuming that, even if it had been, it was not clearly established at the time. Such efforts obviously had the potential to stymie the development and elaboration of constitutional doctrine, and *Wilson* seemed to put an end to it.

Nevertheless, there have recently been doubts raised about whether *Wilson's* rigid sequencing requirement makes sense. Brosseau v. Haugen (2004) (Ginsburg, J., concurring, joined by Breyer and Scalia, JJ.). It forces courts to reach out to decide perhaps difficult and complex questions of constitutional law that might be easily avoided by resorting first to the simpler question of immunity. Also, there are other ways in which constitutional rights can ordinarily be articulated other than in § 1983 damages actions, such as in § 1983 injunctive actions or by way of defense in criminal or civil enforcement actions. In addition, the sequencing requirement creates potential problems on appeal, as when an officer prevails on qualified immunity grounds but has lost on the constitutional question that was decided first. If the officer, who won, is not permitted to appeal the constitutional ruling, then *Wilson's* rule somewhat perversely encourages articulation of constitutional rights, but potentially at the expense of appellate review. Perhaps, therefore, flexibility in sequencing would make more sense unless there is a risk that the particular constitutional issue would otherwise go systematically unaddressed.

4. Interlocutory Appealability

The "freedom from the distractions of trial" rationale for qualified immunity has also resulted in the conclusion that federal court decisions rejecting claims of qualified immunity are immediately appealable, at least when the lower court has concluded that a particular set of facts violates "clearly established" law. Mitchell v. Forsyth (1985). Thus, under the so-called collateral order doctrine developed in Cohen v. Beneficial Industrial Loan Corp. (1949), immediate review is available to make sure that the right to avoid trial (which the good-faith immunity doctrine seems to embody) can be enforced. Compare below at Chapter 13, § B, 2.

In fact, multiple appeals may be allowed on the immunity issue. For example, a defendant might move to dismiss a claim based on qualified immunity and lose; the order would be immediately appealable. But even if he should lose on that appeal (because, for example, further discovery is needed on certain underlying factual questions), he will still be able to re-raise the immunity issue on summary judgment in the trial court. And if that motion is denied, the immunity issue would be immediately appealable a second time. Behrens v. Pelletier (1996).

Unlike individuals, however, a municipality's "immunity" from damages under § 1983—i.e., whether a particular official's actions were taken pursuant to custom or policy—is not an issue that is immediately appealable. Swint v. Chambers County Commission (1995). The Supreme Court has characterized the municipality's immunity as an immunity from the imposition of liability, not an immunity from trial itself. Moreover, even if there are individual officers who can obtain an interlocutory appeal under *Mitchell*, a city can get no "pendent [interlocutory] appellate jurisdiction" over the denial of its own motion for summary judgment based on lack of custom or policy.

5. Beneficiaries of Qualified Immunity

Consistent with the above, qualified immunity should be available to all officials who are charged with the enforcement of laws, including members of the executive branch of state and local governments. In the past, it has been extended to school board officials, Wood v. Strickland (1975); police officers, Pierson v. Ray (1967); members of a prison disciplinary committee, Cleavinger v. Saxner (1985); and a state governor, Scheuer v. Rhodes (1974). Unlike state governors, however, the Nation's Chief Executive—the President—has an absolute immunity from damages for unconstitutional acts taken as President, as discussed in Chapter 17.

B. Absolute Immunity of Judicial Actors

In contrast to law enforcement and executive branch officials, persons acting in a judicial capacity are accorded an absolute immunity from § 1983 suits for damages for all of their judicial acts—no matter how erroneous or objectively unreasonable— at least if they are acting within their jurisdiction. Pierson v. Ray (1967). Indeed, liability will not even attach for acts, including malicious and corrupt ones, that happen to be "in excess of jurisdiction" unless they are undertaken in a "clear absence of all jurisdiction." Thus, in Stump v. Sparkman (1978), an Indiana judge of general jurisdiction was held absolutely immune when sued under § 1983 for having entered an ex parte order, without notice or hearing, to allow sterilization of a minor on the petition of her parents. Although state law neither gave the parents the right to consent to their child's sterilization nor expressly provided for any judicial approval of sterilization procedures for uncommitted persons, damages under § 1983 were unavailable against the judge despite the judge's clear violation of due process. Absolute immunity (unlike qualified immunity) therefore protects judicial actors from violations of even clearly established law.

The main functional reasons given for the immunity are that judges are too easy a target for the countless numbers of disgruntled losing parties in lawsuits, that other avenues ordinarily exist for the correction of judicial error, and that judges must be free to act without apprehension of personal consequences to themselves. Indeed, the dissent's argument in *Stump* that the judge's action was not "judicial" was premised on the arguable absence of certain of these factors in the order allowing sterilization, including the absence of meaningful appellate correction of error.

The Supreme Court has also sought to draw historical support for its rule. At common law such absolute immunity inhered in judicial acts of judges of courts of general jurisdiction even when taken in excess of their jurisdiction, so long as the acts were colorably within the judge's jurisdiction. Under the modern Court's view, it may be fair to say that so long as a judge acts reasonably with respect to her jurisdiction she may actually act beyond it, and do so with impunity insofar as monetary relief under § 1983 is concerned.

Nevertheless, not all decisions of judges are subject to absolute immunity. First of all, injunctive relief may be entered against a judge in limited circumstances, and no immunity will attach at all in such settings. In addition, the Court has stated that judicial immunity can be defeated, even in § 1983 damages actions, when (1) the judge's act is "not taken in a judicial capacity"; or (2) "though judicial in nature" the act is "taken in complete absence of jurisdiction." Mireles v. Waco (1991).

Thus, when a judge fired a probation officer for sexually discriminatory reasons, the Court held that the function was an administrative, not a judicial act, and therefore subject only to qualified immunity. Forrester v. White (1988). And in Zarcone v. Perry (2d Cir.1978), the Second Circuit apparently found that a traffic court judge's mock sentencing of a courthouse coffee vendor for making bad coffee was not protected by absolute immunity, either because it was in excess of all jurisdiction, or because it was not a judicial act. At the same time, however, the Supreme Court has held that a judge's order to his bailiff to go out into the hallway and "with excessive force" to apprehend a tardy attorney, was subject to absolute immunity because the

act of compelling counsel's appearance (even if not
the command to use excessive force) was the kind of
function ordinarily performed by a court and therefore was a judicial act. And the order itself, while
"in excess of" the judge's authority, was not made
in the "absence of all jurisdiction." *Mireles, supra*;
cf. U.S. v. Lanier (1997) (leaving open the question
whether state judge—who made sexual assaults, in
chambers, on female parties to litigation in his
court—acted "under color of . . . law" under criminal counterpart of § 1983, 18 U.S.C.A. § 242, for
willful deprivation of constitutional rights).

Lastly, it is important to remember that the
absolute judicial immunity which the Court has
recognized is merely a default rule. If Congress
wishes, it may abrogate this and perhaps other
personal immunities of state or local officials from
damages in § 1983 suits. This possibility roughly
corresponds with the Court's debatable methodolo-
gy in its immunity cases which assumes that, in
enacting § 1983, Congress did not by its silence
mean to override existing common-law immunities.
Thus, if Congress speaks, such override can occur.
For example, the Court once concluded that judges
could be personally liable for attorney's fees whenever injunctive relief is properly entered against
them, because it read the 1976 Attorney's Fee
Awards Act as lifting judicial immunity from fee
awards in such cases. Pulliam v. Allen (1984). Nevertheless, Congress later legislated to prevent fee
awards against judges, thus reversing *Pulliam*, and
thereby restoring judges' absolute immunity from

monetary liability. See Federal Courts Improvement Act of 1996, Pub. L. No. 104–317.

C. Absolute Immunity of Legislative Actors

Legislators and those who act in a lawmaking capacity are immune from damages and injunctive relief under § 1983 for their legislative acts. Tenney v. Brandhove (1951). Equitable or legal challenges to unconstitutional legislation or other legislative acts must therefore ordinarily be made by suing the proper officials charged with enforcement of the offending statute, not by suing those who enacted it. Thus, in Kilbourn v. Thompson (1881), a non–§ 1983 action to redress an illegal act ordered by the Speaker of the U.S. House of Representatives, suit was properly brought against the Sergeant-at-Arms who implemented the order. Similarly, in Powell v. McCormack (1969), there was no immunity for the low-level House employees who excluded a House member on orders of the Speaker.

The Supreme Court has found justification for its legislative immunity rule from the Speech and Debate Clause, U.S. Const. art. I, § 6, cl. 1, which expressly immunizes federal legislative officials, and also from English common-law privileges of legislators from arrest or civil process for what they say and how they vote in legislative proceedings. In addition, the Court has noted that other remedies exist against legislators who enact unconstitutional laws, including resort to the ballot box. Also, alternative avenues of relief against other officials are available to redress the enforcement of an unconstitutional legislative enactment. Ex parte Young (1908). Thus, so long as the legislator is acting "within the sphere of legitimate legislative activity," even his most egregiously unconstitutional acts are immunized under this "free speech" rationale.

The Court has expanded its legislative immunity holding to regional officials who acted in a lawmaking capacity for a bi-state entity created by interstate compact, despite the fact that these officials were not directly accountable to the electorate. Lake Country Estates, Inc. v. Tahoe Regional Planning Agcy. (1979). And it has also concluded that local legislators, like their state counterparts, are entitled to absolute immunity for their legislative actions. Bogan v. Scott–Harris (1998). Before *Bogan*, the Court had strongly hinted at that possibility when it refused to hold council members for the City of Yonkers in contempt for violating a federal court order (to which the council had previously assented, on behalf of the City) to enact needed legislation as part of a consent decree to remedy housing discrimination. Spallone v. United States (1990). So the extension of immunity to local legislators hardly comes as a surprise. What was somewhat surprising, however, was that the *Bogan* Court applied legislative immunity to a city mayor who had proposed legislation to the city council—a proposal that was alleged to be an act of retaliation against the plaintiff's free speech rights. But presumably, the city itself would not share its official's immunity and would be liable for enforcement of its unconstitutional legislation as a custom or policy. See below at § F.

Finally, care must be taken to distinguish between absolutely protected legislative activity and other functions. For example, judges of the Virginia high court were said to be engaging in a legislative function insofar as they were responsible under state law for promulgating state bar rules. Supreme Court of Virginia v. Consumers Union of U.S., Inc. (1980). Thus, in a case like *Consumers Union*, someone other than an official acting in a legislative capacity would have to be named as a defendant if the § 1983 plaintiff wanted to enjoin the enforcement of an allegedly unconstitutional state bar rule. Analogously, in the context of litigation against federal officials, statements by legislative officials made outside of the legislative confines have been held unprotected, even if they would have been protected if made within them. Hutchinson v. Proxmire (1979).

D. Prosecutorial and Related Quasi-judicial Immunities

Although prosecutors are executive branch officials who do not act in a traditional judicial capacity, the Supreme Court has nevertheless held that they are entitled to invoke a quasi-judicial absolute immunity from § 1983 damages for their decisions to bring a case and for their actions in presenting it in court. Imbler v. Pachtman (1976). In *Imbler*, the plaintiff—a former criminal defendant—brought a § 1983 action against a prosecutor for allegedly procuring and using knowingly false testimony against him. The Court concluded that the action should be dismissed. It did so by finding that, at common law, a prosecutor was absolutely immune from suit for his bringing of a prosecution even though it was brought with malice and without probable cause. The Court also concluded that the reasons for judicial immunity were implicated in a prosecutor's actions in bringing and presenting his case: Prosecutors were involved in the "judicial phase of the criminal process," which needed to be free of intimidation and harassment. Like judges, prosecutors were likely targets of lawsuits by losing defendants. And there were abundant judicial checks on unlawful prosecutorial behavior.

Of course, when it comes to injunctive relief, prosecutors have no immunity. Indeed, those charged with enforcing a law which is challenged as unconstitutional, such as a state's attorney general, are the proper subjects of suits for prospective injunctive relief against enforcement of the law. Ex parte Young (1908); Steffel v. Thompson (1974).

Nevertheless, the Court has also held that when prosecutors act in an investigatory capacity, they may assert only a qualified immunity from monetary relief, like that reserved for law enforcement personnel. In Burns v. Reed (1991), the Court held that absolute immunity did not attach to a prosecutor's erroneous advice to the police that there was probable cause to arrest a suspect, nor to his decision that the arrestee could be questioned under hypnosis. Yet the same prosecutor's decision in the same case knowingly to use misleading testimony to procure a search warrant was held to be absolutely protected. The Supreme Court's reasoning that the "out of court" activities of the prosecutor did not implicate judicial functions as immediately as the decision to prosecute (or the presentation of a case in court) was bolstered by its conclusion that, historically, absolute immunity did not accompany such administrative or investigative functions of the prosecutor.

In a similar vein, the Court concluded that absolute immunity did not attach to a prosecutor's filing of his own falsely sworn application for an arrest warrant from a court. Kalina v. Fletcher (1997). The conduct, said the Court, was not part of the advocacy functions of the prosecutor and instead put the prosecutor in the position of a complaining witness. As such, the prosecutor was only entitled to qualified immunity for the act of filing the false application (even though, as noted below, witnesses at trial usually can claim absolute immunity).

Not all persons involved in the judicial process are treated similarly, however. In contrast to prosecutors and judges, public defenders are ordinarily not suable under § 1983 because they do not act "under color of" law in representing their clients. See Chapter 2. But when they *do* act under color of law by acting in concert with other public officials, they do not get absolute immunity for their acts, largely because attorney immunity for intentional harm to one's client was never so protected at common law. Tower v. Glover (1984). And court reporters are not absolutely immune for failure to produce a transcript, in part because their duties do not require the exercise of judicial (or any other kind of) discretion. Antoine v. Byers & Anderson, Inc. (1993). The Court has also concluded, based on historical immunity and functional grounds, that witnesses at criminal trials, including police officers, have an absolute quasi-judicial immunity from damages in a later-filed § 1983 case, even when they give knowingly perjured testimony. Briscoe v. LaHue (1983). Lower courts are apparently divided over whether the absolute immunity of witnesses is applicable in other contexts, and immunity from damages liability under § 1983 has therefore been denied to grand jury witnesses in some circuits, Anthony v. Baker (10th Cir.1985), while it has been granted in others, Kincaid v. Eberle (7th Cir.1983). *Kalina*, noted above, may suggest that complaining witnesses do not have absolute immunity for their pre-trial acts.

E.   Hybrid Officials

For officials who wear more than one hat and who act in multiple capacities at different times— whether law enforcement, lawmaking, or judging— it may be necessary to inquire into the kind of function they were performing at the relevant time in order to assess their immunity. For example, in Butz v. Economou (1978), a non–§ 1983 case, an executive branch official was held to have acted in a judicial capacity when he acted as a full-time Hearing Examiner for a federal agency. In a similar vein, the Court also concluded that a judge on a state supreme court which played the leading role in the governance of the state bar might act in a legislative capacity when promulgating bar rules, but act in a law enforcement capacity when enforcing those rules in disciplinary proceedings, and in a judicial capacity when interpreting or judging their application to particular facts. *Consumers Union, supra.*

Nevertheless, the Court seems less willing to engage in this sort of strict separation-of-powers analysis the more local the official and the more indivisible his functions. In Wood v. Strickland (1975), for example, the Court found that school board officials could not claim absolute judicial immunity under § 1983 when they were sued for the discipline that they had meted out to a student following a formal hearing at which they presided and took evidence. Likewise, in Cleavinger v. Saxner (1985), the Court denied absolute immunity to members of a prison's Inmate Discipline Committee who had punished a prisoner for violating prison rules. Although the administrators "perform[ed] an adjudicatory function" they lacked the traditional attributes of judges, including independence, professionalism, procedural safeguards, and insulation from non-judicial review by other prison officials. More than anything else, these decisions seem to say that, although executive branch personnel may be required to follow procedural due process by providing notice and hearing rights, they are not thereby necessarily converted into judicial actors.

F.   Private Actors and Immunity

As discussed in Chapter 2, private parties ordinarily do not engage in state action and therefore are typically not among those who can be sued under § 1983, quite apart from questions of immunity. But sometimes private persons do engage in state action and act under color of law when they act in concert with state or local officials. In Dennis v. Sparks (1980), for example, a state court judge issued an injunction against an individual in connection with a mineral rights dispute. The party who was the subject of the injunction then brought a § 1983 claim against the judge and the party who originally obtained the injunction against him, claiming that they corruptly conspired to enter the injunction and to deprive him of his property without due process of law. Even though one of the defendants in the § 1983 action was a private party, the Supreme Court concluded that he had acted under color of law because he "was a willful participant engaged in joint action with" a state official in effecting the deprivation of rights.

Furthermore, although the judge in *Dennis* had absolute immunity from damages, the private party could not share the immunity. The Court found that historically, no "derivative" immunity for private parties existed at common law. It also concluded that the judge's own immunity would not be compromised by denying it to the private party with whom he conspired even though the judge might be required to testify in the § 1983 action.

The Supreme Court has similarly denied qualified immunity to a private party who acted in concert with public officials by invoking an unconstitutional state replevin statute against a § 1983 plaintiff. Thus, the private party, who had no derivative immunity, was held liable for the constitutional harm suffered by the plaintiff, while the officers (whose help he enlisted) were shielded from a damage award because of their reasonable reliance on the constitutionality of the replevin statute. Wyatt v. Cole (1992). The Court found that in such contexts, the rationale for qualified immunity for officers was "not transferable to private parties." Nevertheless, the Court left open the possibility that such private § 1983 defendants might be able to assert either "probable cause" or their subjective "good faith" as a defense to monetary liability.

In addition, when (unlike in *Wyatt*) private parties perform work that would otherwise be performed by governmental personnel—as when private physicians work under contract to provide prison medical care—it is perhaps less clear whether official immunity will be unavailable. In this context, it is at least arguable that qualified immunity is needed to ensure that such individuals act "decisively," and to ensure that private parties will not be dissuaded from public service. Williams v. O'Leary (7th Cir.1995). Despite these concerns, however, the Court has concluded that private guards in a privately run prison lack qualified immunity, even though they perform the same jobs as public prison guards who need breathing room to act in areas of constitutional uncertainty. Richardson v. McKnight (1997). The Court opined that market forces would suffice to keep private guards from being overly aggressive lest they be saddled with damages, or overly timid lest competitor firms provide safer or more efficient facilities. And it focused on the historical absence of such immunity while noting the possibility, as in *Wyatt*, that a probable cause or subjective good faith defense might still be raised. Interestingly, in *Richardson*, the Court assumed but did not decide that the prison guards were acting under color of state law.

The no-derivative-immunity principle has also prevented a police officer from claiming absolute (instead of qualified) immunity when sued for conducting an unconstitutional search based on an unconstitutionally authorized warrant issued by a judicial magistrate. Although the magistrate would be entitled to absolute judicial immunity from damages in a § 1983 action for any unconstitutional errors he made, the police officer who relied on the warrant might not be. The officer could prevail only if he could show that a "reasonably well-trained" officer would not have known that the search authorized by the warrant, given the underlying affidavit in support of it, was unconstitutional. Malley v. Briggs (1986). Ironically, therefore, the magistrate—as a judicial actor who should know better—will be absolutely immune, while the cop on the beat will not be.

G. Local Governments and Official Immunities

Finally, recall that in § 1983 actions, cities and counties do not have any "personal" immunity at all, nor any derivative immunity that would flow from the immunity of their wrongdoing officers. Chapter 6. Nevertheless, cities are not liable in respondeat superior, but are liable only when their officials have acted pursuant to some law, custom, or policy. So, if law, custom, or policy can be established, cities are strictly liable for the constitutional harms inflicted by their officials who implement it, even when the officials would be protected by some kind of personal (good faith or absolute) immunity.

For example, if a police officer from a city or county enforces an unconstitutional local ordinance, he may be protected by qualified immunity in a § 1983 damages action if he did not violate any clearly established constitutional norms; but the governmental entity for which he works will still be liable. On the other hand, if the police official is a state trooper acting similarly, the official himself may be immune, and the entity will be able to assert sovereign immunity from any award of damages, even if the trooper was acting pursuant to law, custom, or policy. Thus, compensation for behavior that is unconstitutional (but not clearly unconstitutional), even when taken pursuant to governmental custom or policy, may turn on the fortuity of who the wrongdoing official's employer happens to be. If it is the state, there may be no recovery at all; if it is not, there could be recovery—at least against the local government entity.

CHAPTER 9

DAMAGES AND § 1983

Overview

Section 1983 speaks of actions "at law" or suits "in equity" to redress the deprivation of constitutional rights. Accordingly, it is possible to recover the traditional range of compensatory damages from an official for the harm that he inflicts because of his constitutional violations, subject to any personal immunities of the officer. And such damages will be available against a local government when its officer has carried out official policy. States themselves, however, are immune from such awards, largely because of Eleventh Amendment concerns. In order to recover more than nominal damages from a § 1983 defendant, however, the victim of unconstitutional injury must put on proof of actual injury. In this regard, the Supreme Court has also stated that there should be no recovery beyond proved injury to reflect the "inherent" value of lost constitutional rights. Finally, punitive damages are available against individual officers, but not local governments, and only when there has been "reckless or callous indifference" to constitutional rights, or when the defendant was motivated by "evil intent."

A. Compensatory Damages

1. Standards and Proof

The Court has stated that the "basic purpose" of the § 1983 action for damages "is to compensate persons for injuries that are caused by the deprivation of constitutional rights." Carey v. Piphus (1978). Damages awards also serve to vindicate the underlying constitutional rights, and to deter future illegality (while personal immunity doctrines, by contrast, help to prevent overdeterrence). Injunctive relief, along with fee-shifting, can of course secure rights-vindication and deterrence in many cases, but injunctive relief is available only when behavior is ongoing and systematic.

Carey involved a high school student's claim that he was denied procedural due process when he was summarily kicked out of school for 20 days for allegedly smoking marijuana on school grounds. He complained that he had not been given a pre-suspension hearing or any other opportunity to contest the charges. The district court agreed that his due process rights had been denied and reinstated the student after only eight days. But the district court and the court of appeals disagreed over whether damages could be awarded for the due process denial, especially since the student had put on no evidence by which a factfinder could measure his injuries.

The Supreme Court in Carey reiterated its admonition in Monroe v. Pape (1961) that § 1983 creates a "species of tort liability," and the Court added that "the elements and prerequisites for recovery of damages ... should parallel those for recovery of damages under the law of torts." The Court stressed the compensatory purposes of § 1983, and held that the plaintiff was obligated to put on proof that he was actually injured by his deprivation of procedural due process before he could recover more than nominal damages (in *Carey*, $1.00). Of course, common-law tort rules might not provide perfect analogies for all constitutional injuries. But that simply meant that trial courts would have to engage in "the more difficult [task] of adapting common-law rules of damages to provide fair compensation for injuries caused by the deprivation of a constitutional right."

Carey concluded that if the § 1983 plaintiff in the case before it would have been suspended even if he *had* received a pre-suspension hearing, then no damages could be awarded for injury caused by the suspensions (i.e., the missed eight days). That did not mean that the plaintiff could not recover damages for the dignitary harms and possible emotional distress associated with his not having a hearing prior to suspension. But as to those injuries, the plaintiff had put on no evidence at all, even though such emotional distress "is a personal injury familiar to the law, customarily proved by showing the nature and consequences of the wrong and its effect on the plaintiff." Absent such proof, the plaintiff was entitled only to an award of nominal damages for the loss of his constitutional rights, "not to exceed one dollar."

Educated by *Carey*, § 1983 plaintiffs have been able to put on proof of and recover for virtually all of the sorts of injuries that one might see in more ordinary common-law litigation, including recovery for mental anguish and emotional distress, feelings of unjust treatment, reputational harm, economic loss, fear, anxiety, humiliation and personal indignity, as well as for physical injury and out-of-pocket expenses. Similarly, parties that succeed in their § 1983 dormant Commerce Clause or pre-emption claims should be able to recover erroneous assessments, lost profits, and other business-related losses that they have suffered. E.g., Pioneer Military Lending, Inc. v. Manning (8th Cir.1993). Expert testimony as to damages is as appropriate in a § 1983 suit as it would be in any other suit. And dignitary harms, as well as mental and emotional distress, can also be established by the victim's testimony, without the need for expert or corroborating testimony. Fisher v. Dillard University (E.D.La.1980). Interestingly, the issue of damages and their recovery has been consistently treated as a question of federal common law, although, under 42 U.S.C.A. § 1988(a)—a choice-of-law provision for filling in § 1983's silences—other gaps in § 1983 are presumptively filled by looking to state law. See Chapter 12.

2. Damages and the "Inherent" Value of Constitutional Rights

If § 1983 plaintiffs must put on proof of "actual injury" in addition to showing that their constitutional rights have been violated, then it would seem difficult to compensate (other than nominally) for the supposed "inherent" value of lost constitutional rights. That suggestion was borne out in Memphis Community School Dist. v. Stachura (1986). A school teacher who had been dismissed in violation of his free speech rights sought reinstatement and compensatory damages, including damages for mental anguish and lost wages. He also sought and obtained an instruction from the trial court allowing the jury to assess damages based on the inherent value of the rights in question because, as the trial court instructed the jury, "damages for this type of injury are more difficult to measure than damages for a physical injury or damages to one's property." The trial court instructed the jurors that "[t]he precise value you place upon any constitutional right which you find was denied to Plaintiff is within your discretion," and told them that they might want to consider "the importance of the right in our system of government."

The Supreme Court in *Stachura* concluded that *Carey* barred such an instruction and held that the abstract value of a constitutional right could not form the basis for a § 1983 damages award. The fact that *Carey* was a procedural due process case and that *Stachura* involved a deprivation of a "substantive" constitutional right did not matter. The Court purported to distinguish some prior precedents in the area of voting rights denials in which it had upheld "presumed damages" without any particular proof of injury. The Court stated that presumed damages were a rough substitute for (and not a supplement to) a fully compensatory award when there has been "certain" injury that might be difficult to establish. No rough substitute was needed in *Stachura* given the ready availability of proof of plaintiff's injuries. And the effort to award damages based on the abstract importance of a right was not related to compensation for injury, as were presumed damages. Presumed damages, therefore, may only be available in the unusual case in which the constitutional harm is so intangible as to defy proof of quantification.

Taken together with *Carey*, *Stachura* strongly suggests that even though the Constitution may protect interests that go beyond those that the common law might have protected, injuries arising from a constitutional deprivation will ordinarily have to be reducible to common-law components in order to be compensated. Perhaps the conclusion is inevitable, if juries are to make rational awards of damages. But even if there remains a role for "presumed" damages in some uncertain handful of cases, the Court's common-law model itself leaves the possibility that some uniquely constitutional dimensions of official illegality may go uncompensated, at least when the common-law analogies run out. Of course, personal immunities of officers also mean that the system is prepared to tolerate non-compensation in favor of other values. And it is doubtful whether the Constitution itself requires a damages remedy for all of the interests that it protects.

3. The Role of State Law

The Supreme Court's damages rulings indicate that uniform federal common-law rules ordinarily apply in § 1983 litigation, not state law. The Court has not lately invoked 42 U.S.C.A. § 1988(a), which often requires federal courts to resort to state law when § 1983 is silent on particular questions, to resolve questions of damages. See Chapter 12. To be sure, the Court looks to common-law principles, generated sometimes by state courts in developing its damages rules. But the Court has not felt obliged to look to the law of any particular state in developing its damages rules. Lower courts have also, if less consistently, ignored state law in § 1983 actions particularly when it would have worked a restriction on recovery, even when the theory of recovery is in the nature of a wrongful death action which may otherwise be shaped by state law. E.g., Berry v. City of Muskogee (10th Cir.1990); Bell v. City of Milwaukee (7th Cir.1984). And some courts have similarly ignored state law in such cases even when it would have enhanced recovery. Gilmere v. City of Atlanta (11th Cir.1989).

Nevertheless, there is at least some (if doubtful) precedent for thinking that, when the constitutional violation results in death, § 1988 applies and that it permits the adoption of state-law damages rules, at least when they are rights-reinforcing. E.g., Brazier v. Cherry (5th Cir.1961); cf. Sullivan v. Little Hunting Park, Inc. (1969). But these decisions antedated the Supreme Court's rather more consistent use of federal common law to resolve damages and immu-

nities issues under § 1983. In any event, if there is
a constitutional violation and death results, recovery should be available as a matter of federal law by
the decedent's survivors for the various injuries
suffered by the decedent because of the defendant's
unconstitutional acts, without having to engraft a
state law "wrongful death" cause of action onto
§ 1983. And if, for some reason, the decedent's
§ 1983 claim would not survive him, or if state
"survival" statutes severely limited the damages
recoverable for loss of life, those limits might be
ignored as "inconsistent" with the compensatory
and deterrent policies of § 1983. State law, however, will likely be relevant in determining who it is
that may bring the surviving constitutional claim
that would have belonged to the decedent. Robertson v. Wegmann (1978).

A true "wrongful death" claim, moreover, is
properly the claim for the injury suffered by those
who survive the decedent; it is not the § 1983 claim
that belonged to the decedent that survives him.
Although the lower courts are divided, plaintiffs
probably should not be able to bring claims under
§ 1983 for their own injuries that arise from the
unconstitutional taking of the life of another, even
if state law would allow for it by statute in analogous circumstances. Compare, e.g., Valdivieso Ortiz
v. Burgos (1st Cir.1986) (denying recovery) with
Grandstaff v. City of Borger (5th Cir.1985) (allowing it). Although the decedent's relatives may suffer
derivative "injury," it is doubtful whether their
own constitutional rights have been denied just

because the decedent's have been. And it would be questionable in many cases whether any loss they suffered was, as to them, more than negligently inflicted. Robertson v. Hecksel (11th Cir. 2005); Russ v. Watts (7th Cir.2005). If there are state-law claims that belong to the survivors—such as state wrongful death claims—they can be brought pendent to a proper § 1983 action on behalf of the decedent.

B. Punitive Damages

1. Against Individual Officers

Punitive damages have historically been available under ordinary tort law to deter and punish egregious behavior. Punitive damages are available under § 1983 to achieve similar goals. When a defendant's unconstitutional conduct is shown to be motivated by evil intent, or when it involves reckless or callous indifference to the federally protected rights of others, a jury may award punitive damages against the official. Smith v. Wade (1983). In *Smith*, a Missouri prison inmate sued prison officials under § 1983 after he had been beaten, harassed, and sexually assaulted by his cellmates. He claimed a denial of his Eighth Amendment right to be free of cruel and unusual punishment because of the defendant prison guards' awareness of the likelihood of an assault. The jury awarded punitive damages in addition to compensatory damages—an award that the Supreme Court upheld.

The *Smith* Court dispatched the idea that punitive damages could be awarded only when the defendant was motivated by subjective ill will or malice. Relying on the history of punitive damages at common law when § 1983 was enacted and on developments thereafter, the Court concluded that a showing of subjective ill will or malice was a sufficient but not a necessary condition to a punitive damages award. A violation of an objective standard of "callous or reckless indifference" would also suffice for punitive damages. Of course, that standard was not far removed from the standard for a compensatory award because, given personal immunity doctrines, compensatory liability would attach only if the officer had violated "clearly established" constitutional rights. See Chapter 8. And today, a prison official's deliberate indifference to known risks is the prerequisite for a failure-to-protect claim as in *Smith*. Farmer v. Brennan (1994) (discussed in Chapter 4). Thus, punitive damage liability could easily follow on a showing of substantive liability for compensatory damages in such a case. Even when the standard for punitive damages is met, however, such damages are not a matter of right; they are still discretionary with the jury.

Jury awards of punitive damages are themselves subject to procedural as well as substantive due process limitations, as the Court has held on review of state court punitive damage awards in non-§ 1983 litigation. Pacific Mutual Life Ins. Co. v. Haslip (1991); State Farm v. Campbell (2003). But in the federal court system, because of the standard set up in *Smith*, and because the factfinder is ordinarily instructed about the nature and purpose of punitive damages, and also because there is post-verdict review of such awards, procedural due process should ordinarily not be a problem. Nevertheless, some measure of substantive review respecting the reasonableness of any punitive damages award may now also be appropriate in individual cases, for example, when there is only a nominal award of compensatory damages and punitive damages are high. The more general subject of jury trial rights in § 1983 litigation is taken up in Chapter 18.

2. Against Local Governments

Municipalities are not subject to punitive damages awards, even when their officials act pursuant to official policy, and even when that policy shows "callous or reckless indifference" to constitutional rights. Newport v. Fact Concerts, Inc. (1981). In *Fact Concerts*, a city council voted to revoke a concert promoter's license after the promoter signed up a particular band ("Blood, Sweat & Tears") which the city council thought would attract a "rowdy and undesirable audience." In its successful First Amendment and Due Process Clause challenge to the city's actions, the promoter obtained a substantial punitive damage award against the city, but the Supreme Court vacated the award. In addition to pointing to the lack of historical evidence that cities were liable for such damages at common law, the Court noted that the only parties punished by an award of punitive damages against the city would be the "blameless" taxpayers who would have to pick up the tab. Punitive damages and retribution, said the Court, were more properly addressed to individual governmental wrongdoers.

After *Fact Concerts*, however, the "blameless" taxpayers still will have to pick up the tab for the compensatory damages awarded against the city for its unconstitutional official policies, and they will have to do so even when a city's violation is in good faith—i.e., objectively reasonable—rather than grossly unconstitutional. Owen v. City of Independence (1980). With the result in *Fact Concerts* it is useful to compare the decision in Spallone v. United States (1990), discussed below in Chapter 10, in which the Court upheld a colossal contempt sanction against a city (and thus, its "blameless" taxpayers) for the obstinate refusal of city council members to comply with a federal court order, while freeing the council members themselves of any personal obligation to pay contempt sanctions.

CHAPTER 10

INJUNCTIONS AND DECLARATORY RELIEF

Overview

In addition to damages, § 1983 plaintiffs may also seek injunctive and declaratory relief which can run effectively against either state or local governments. In the case of states, however, relief must be sought against the appropriate state officer, not the entity itself. To obtain injunctive relief, moreover, a plaintiff must meet certain requirements familiar to equity, as well as requirements of justiciability, including standing to sue. As discussed below, such equitable standing may be difficult to establish in challenges to informal law enforcement practices as opposed to other regulatory action by government. More complex injunctive relief, such as that involved in structural reform litigation, also raises federalism concerns regarding intervention by federal courts in the everyday functioning of state and local governments. Partly because of such concerns, prison reform litigation under § 1983 is now governed by an especially stringent set of congressional standards. In addition, federalism issues are raised in the post-judgment context of enforcement of constitutional remedies against recalcitrant defendants, and also when defendants seek relief from ongoing judicial oversight and other injunctive decrees.

A. Prerequisites for Equitable Relief

Injunctive remedies are a familiar component of equity jurisdiction and are available in § 1983 actions in the proper case. Even though equitable remedies are traditionally said to be more extraordinary than legal remedies such as damages, this familiar hierarchy is sometimes turned upside down in the context of constitutional and civil rights litigation. For example, "negative" injunctions to halt or prevent a state or local official from enforcing an unconstitutional law are quite commonplace, and have been a fixture of the federal courts at least since Ex parte Young (1908), if not before. See Osborn v. Bank of the United States (1824). And even more complex, "affirmative" or "structural" injunctive relief, such as that involved in school desegregation and other institutional reform litigation, has become a staple of the federal courts in the last fifty years. Brown v. Board of Ed. (1954). Many of these injunctive decrees have been entered with only lip service to traditional equitable requirements and in disregard of the common law's preference for legal over equitable relief.

1. Adequacy of Legal Remedies

Equitable relief is traditionally unavailable when legal remedies are adequate to redress the injury. But this prerequisite often receives less than prominent attention when denial of prospective injunctive relief will result in the loss of constitutional rights. For example, reinstatement of a public employee who is found to have been discharged because of his race is probably the norm, to be denied only in exceptional circumstances. This is true despite the common law's familiar resistance to awards of specific performance and its reluctance to enter such awards when personal services are involved. Arguably, front pay and other damage assessments against the wrongdoing defendants might be sufficient to redress the injury in such a case. But injunctive relief (in the form of reinstatement) seems almost to be a presumptive or preferred remedy in such cases, although the point often goes unmentioned. Perhaps in some cases damages remedies are more obviously inadequate, as when an individual seeks an award of tenure against a state university that denied tenure on an discriminatory basis, or when an individual seeks to enroll in a public institution on a non-discriminatory basis. But even in these sorts of cases, the propriety of injunctive as opposed to monetary relief often goes unmentioned.

Structural injunctions in institutional reform litigation, almost by definition, rarely present circumstances in which monetary awards or reparations for past victims of systemic illegality would be preferable to bringing a defendant into future compliance with the Constitution. Indeed, the preference for injunctive over monetary relief in these contexts (in a reversal of the common law's hierarchy) is also reflected in the Court's sovereign immunity decisions. There, awards of injunctive relief against states (through state officials) to secure compliance with the Constitution are more easily tolerated than awards of damages against the state, even when there have been acknowledged past violations. See Chapter 7. In such cases, mandating future compliance may be the minimally acceptable remedy to keep the Constitution from becoming a dead letter.

2. Irreparable Harm

Another traditional requirement of equity—that the party seeking equity show irreparable harm— also often goes unmentioned in cases in which the § 1983 plaintiff can show that constitutional rights will be lost absent prospective injunctive relief. That is, demonstrating the impending loss of constitutional rights, rather than some (possibly additional) showing of irreparable harm to economic or other interests, is itself frequently enough to satisfy this requirement, especially when non-economic behavior is at issue. For example, the irreparable harm faced by protesters who are barred by an unconstitutional ordinance from parading is probably the irretrievable loss of free speech rights. In this respect, the "inherent" value of such rights is vindicated by way of an injunction, without actual proof of economic loss. Compare Memphis Community Sch. Dist. v. Stachura (1986), discussed above in Chapter 9.

Nonetheless, courts sometimes still engage in more traditional analysis and focus on irreversible financial loss associated with the loss of constitutional rights before granting relief. For example, in Hughes v. Cristofane (D.Md.1980), the court focused on the financial ruin faced by the owner of a topless bar who claimed a city ordinance violated his rights to free expression under the First Amendment. Traditionally, equity focused on irreparable harm to property, not liberty, and this may explain why some courts still focus on such concerns. Section 1983, of course, now protects against deprivations involving either property or liberty, Lynch v. Household Finance Corp. (1972), although that was not always true. Hague v. C.I.O. (1939) (Opinion of Stone, J.) (suggesting that § 1983 protects "liberty" not "property").

3. Likelihood of Prevailing on the Merits

If parties wish to be protected in their exercise of constitutional rights against threatened enforcement of unconstitutional laws, preliminary injunctive relief is critical. Such relief lets a party engage in the very activity she believes to be protected, without fear of prosecution pending trial on the merits. An important additional requirement for "preliminary" injunctive relief—that is, injunctive relief pending the outcome of trial—is a showing that the plaintiff is likely to prevail on the merits. Parties must also be able to show a genuine threat of enforcement of the challenged statute against them before they can seek injunctive relief. However, because of principles of equitable restraint, these same parties must ordinarily not be subject to any state court enforcement proceedings at the time they bring their federal action nor until they obtain an order of preliminary injunctive relief. See Chapter 15.

4. Balance of Harms

If the party seeking injunctive relief can meet these criteria, most courts will then consider the relative harms to the parties and the public arising from the grant or denial of the injunction. This is the classic "balancing of the equities" that courts have long performed as a precondition to injunctive relief, and it is said to be left to the discretion of the trial judge. It includes a consideration of possible irreparable harm to the plaintiff if the injunction is not granted, and (at least implicitly) the irreparable harm to the defendant if it is, i.e., harm that cannot be undone by the defendant's later prevailing on the merits. But again, in constitutional litigation, the balance is often weighted in the direction of granting injunctive relief, especially when the showing as to likelihood of success by the plaintiff is strong.

B. Structural Injunctions: Federalism, Justiciability, and Remedial Discretion

The fact that many traditional equitable maxims may go slighted in § 1983 litigation does not suggest that equitable considerations may not bar injunctive relief in a particular case. It merely suggests that the presumptive availability of injunctive relief in a successful challenge to unconstitutional action is likely to be defeated only when there are particularly good reasons for doing so. Many of those reasons, discussed below, are associated with problems of "justiciability"—the appropriateness of judicial consideration of particular claims in Article III courts—and with problems of judicial "federalism"—the proper role of the federal judiciary in our system of government.

Of course, it should be remembered that § 1983 itself—and the injunctive remedies that it sanctions—was designed as an intrusion into the functioning of state and local governments insofar as it supplied a mechanism to remedy violations of the Constitution. But federal court intervention can put federal judicial officials in positions of control, both financial and otherwise, over local institutions; and such intervention substitutes the decisions of life-tenured judges for those of more politically accountable officials. The Supreme Court's concern about such possibilities has therefore prompted it to put curbs on the freedom of federal courts to fashion equitable remedies to redress unconstitutional patterns or practices of official illegality.

1. Unconstitutional Law Enforcement Practices

In Rizzo v. Goode (1976), the Supreme Court signaled that justiciability and federalism concerns would serve as a limit on the scope of complex equitable relief entered by federal courts to redress constitutional violations. In *Rizzo*, a class of plaintiffs seeking to reform the city's police department sued the Philadelphia police commissioner, its mayor, and others. The plaintiffs alleged that they had been subject to a pattern of unconstitutional mistreatment at the hands of police officers and that the defendants were liable under § 1983 because of their authorization and encouragement of such behavior and their failure to prevent recurrence of such behavior. Plaintiffs put on evidence of some 40 instances of alleged police brutality, although constitutional violations were found in fewer than half of those instances. When those acts had been complained of to city officials, however, the officers were seldom disciplined. The district court found that, although these incidents were not pursuant to any policy of the city, they were neither "rare" nor "isolated." The district court therefore ordered the defendants to draft a detailed and comprehensive program for dealing with civilian complaints, and to put into force a directive governing the manner for handling complaints by the police department. The Supreme Court, however, overturned the award of injunctive relief.

(a) Justiciability Concerns

First, the *Rizzo* Court doubted whether Article III's case-or-controversy requirement had been satisfied. In O'Shea v. Littleton (1974), the Court had held that "[p]ast exposure to illegal conduct does not in itself show a present case or controversy regarding injunctive relief." Although past wrongs might have been evidence bearing on whether there was a "real and immediate threat of repeated injury" to the plaintiffs it was only guesswork whether such injury would recur. *O'Shea* was a class action claiming that African–Americans and others had been victims of a continuing pattern and practice of discrimination in the enforcement and administration of the Cairo, Illinois criminal justice system. Plaintiffs alleged that local law enforcement and judicial officials discriminated against the plaintiffs, that they had engaged in punitive bond-setting in violation of the Eighth Amendment, that higher sentences were imposed on African–Americans, and that officials compelled class members who could not pay modest fines to endure jury trials and risk prison sentences. Plaintiffs sought wide-ranging injunctive relief to stop these practices and to monitor the administration of the city's justice system in the future to prevent recurrences.

Based on the pleadings, the *O'Shea* Court concluded that the claims had to be dismissed. Even if some in the plaintiff class had suffered such harms in the past, there was no "present case or controversy regarding injunctive relief" unless a class member could also show some "continuing, adverse effects" from the past illegal conduct. Alternatively, the plaintiffs might show a genuine threat of future injury, but to do so, they would have to establish that they would violate the law again, be arrested again, and be subject to the same illegal behavior again. No such allegations had been made.

These particular observations were reiterated with a vengeance in a later Supreme Court decision, Los Angeles v. Lyons (1983). A § 1983 suit to enjoin the future use of an allegedly unconstitutional choke-hold by the Los Angeles Police Department was brought by an individual who had been a victim of the choke-hold in the past. Although the plaintiff had standing to bring a § 1983 damages action, the Court concluded that he could not sue for injunctive relief. The choke-hold had resulted in the deaths of 16 people, most of whom were African–American males like the plaintiff. Nevertheless, the Court held that the plaintiff had not shown (and presumably could not show) with sufficient certainty that he would have another encounter with the police. Even if he could make such a showing, he could not establish that the choke-hold would then be applied *to him*. Only if he alleged that "all" police "always" used the choke-hold in citizen encounters or that the city "ordered or authorized" them to act in such a manner could he sue for injunctive relief.

Of course, if an individual complains of an illegal police practice (as in *Lyons*) that is unrelated to the enforcement of an unconstitutional statute, it is almost always a matter of some speculation whether the complaining party will again engage in illegal activity and be arrested, much less subjected to the same illegal practice by the police incident to arrest. For example, suits brought by individual victims of past racial profiling seeking to enjoin its future use will need to surmount the high barrier erected by cases such as *Lyons*. But the more routinized the practice the easier that task will be.

Thus, it is usually much easier to make a prospective challenge to the enforcement of an unconstitutional law or policy when the government and the regulated party are in an ongoing relationship, such that the threat of enforcement against the party is virtually assured. To illustrate: an ongoing business that is subject to a particular regulation will readily satisfy the Court's equitable standing concerns in a constitutional challenge to that regulation. However, police abuse litigation, because it usually deals with informal patterns and practices of behavior by the police, and because the particular individuals who encounter the police do so only irregularly, is especially resistant to complex injunctive relief at the behest of individuals. Sometimes, therefore, only a lawsuit brought by the United States alleging a pattern and practice of unconstitutional police behavior under 42 U.S.C.A. § 14141 will be able to overcome the justiciability concerns associated with equitable remedies against police abuse. E.g., United States v. Los Angeles (9th Cir.2002); United States v. City of Columbus (S.D.Ohio 2000). Insisting that government be the enforcer in such settings is perhaps what justiciability doctrines are designed to do anyway.

(b) "Our Federalism"

In *Rizzo* and *O'Shea* the Court also invoked the language of Younger v. Harris (1971), to the effect that equity, comity, and federalism play an important, sub-constitutional role in limiting the injunctive powers of the federal courts. In *Younger* (discussed in Chapter 15), the Court concluded that federal courts should not ordinarily enjoin ongoing state criminal proceedings even when they are based on unconstitutional statutes. It concluded that based on principles of "Our Federalism," federal courts ought to dismiss a party's § 1983 action seeking injunctive relief against enforcement of an unconstitutional statute that formed the basis of an ongoing state criminal proceeding against that same party. So long as the constitutional challenge could be raised by way of defense in the state proceeding, *Younger* calls for dismissal of the federal proceeding.

O'Shea, however, did not involve the enforcement of unconstitutional statutes in state courts. Instead, injunctive relief was sought that would control or prevent the occurrence of specific illegal events that might take place in the course of future criminal proceedings brought under apparently valid laws. But the Court believed that the relief requested would necessarily involve federal court interruptions and day-to-day supervision of ongoing state criminal proceedings that *Younger* meant to foreclose. And in *Rizzo*, unlike even in *O'Shea*, the order of injunctive relief would not have interfered with any criminal proceedings at all. Only law enforcement practices and other executive branch illegalities were at issue. Although recognizing this fact, and noting that principles of federalism were "perhaps entitled to their greatest weight in efforts to enjoin criminal prosecutions," the *Rizzo* Court invoked *Younger* and admonished that injunctive relief would impose a sharp and impermissible limitation on the police department's "latitude in the 'dispatch of its own internal affairs.'"

Rizzo and *O'Shea* were decided before many of the modern-day municipal liability decisions such as Monell v. New York Dept. of Soc. Servs. (1978) and City of Canton v. Harris (1989). See Chapter 6. Today, if the plaintiffs' proof is sufficient (which it arguably was not in *Rizzo*), a city can be made monetarily liable for injuries arising from its deliberate failures to train its police in the face of unconstitutional police behavior. But the language of "Our Federalism" from a case like *Rizzo* or *O'Shea* might impose an additional limitation on the scope of injunctive relief directed at remedying the same sort of policies. In addition, injunctive relief against judges under § 1983 (which was sought in *O'Shea*) can now be obtained only when "a declaratory decree was violated or declaratory relief was unavailable." 42 U.S.C.A. § 1983, as amended by the Federal Courts Improvement Act of 1996, Pub. L. No. 104–317.

2. The Limits of Remedial Discretion

Related concerns have surfaced in other contexts of institutional reform litigation, including school desegregation, housing discrimination, prison reform, and mental health care litigation. Simple, negative injunctive relief telling officials to halt their unconstitutional behavior is often not enough in such cases. The status quo itself may be the product of illegality, and affirmative injunctions to transform the status quo are often appropriate. It is a familiar notion of equity to restore victims of illegality to the position they would have occupied but for the illegality. But in nearly all cases of complex injunctive relief, the Court has admonished federal judges not only to restore victims of unconstitutional conduct to the position they would have occupied absent such conduct in devising their remedies, but also (1) to take into account the public's interest in running its own local institutions; and (2) to fashion remedies so that they do not exceed the scope of the constitutional violation.

Of course, there is no single remedy or set of remedies to put a public institution back into compliance with the Constitution and to eliminate the present effects of past constitutional violations. And equity has been traditionally known for its flexibility in shaping remedies. Thus, considerable discretion rests with district courts to fashion remedies for constitutional violations, within the pair of parameters noted above.

In the school desegregation context, for example, the Court has upheld far-reaching equitable relief to remedy past de jure segregation, including such affirmative relief as bussing, race-conscious student reassignment, and novel educational programs, including curriculum redesign and various remedial programs. Swann v. Charlotte–Mecklenburg Board of Education (1971); Milliken v. Bradley (1977) (*Milliken II*). At the same time, it has usually honored local autonomy respecting the structure of state and local governments and refused interdistrict pupil-reassignment remedies when district lines themselves were not drawn or maintained for racially discriminatory purposes. Milliken v. Bradley (1974) (*Milliken I*). Thus, the Court once threw out a remedy designed to redress segregation in a predominantly African–American inner-city school district that would have required bussing of students to and from outlying, predominantly white, but independent, suburban school districts. Even though the interdistrict remedy may have been the only realistic one to achieve meaningful desegregation, the Court in *Milliken I* was reluctant to have federal judges restructure local governmental entities and their financing, at least when their structure and financing were not themselves unconstitutional. Interdistrict remedies that would include "innocent" districts have therefore been routinely rejected.

In Missouri v. Jenkins (1995), the Supreme Court again concluded that the limits of remedial discretion had been overstepped in a school desegregation context. It rejected a district court's "elaborate" remedy consisting of district-wide capital improvements, course enrichment, and extracurricular enhancement designed to promote "desegregative attractiveness" and to make a predominantly black school district more attractive to white students who had fled to outlying suburban districts. By seeking to turn the entire urban district into a "magnet district" to stop interdistrict white flight when an interdistrict remedy would have been unavailable under *Milliken I*, the trial court had abused its discretion.

C. Declaratory Judgments

Under 28 U.S.C.A. § 2201, a party "in a case of actual controversy within [a district court's] jurisdiction" may obtain a declaration of the rights of the parties. The availability of declaratory relief in § 1983 cases is no less than it is in other areas. In fact, in a great deal of constitutional litigation, noncoercive declaratory relief as to the constitutionality of a piece of legislation or a governmental practice is as much sought as any other, coercive remedy such as damages or an injunction. Requests for declaratory relief often accompany requests for injunctive relief, although declaratory relief need not satisfy the traditional equitable prerequisites of irreparable harm, for example, or the lack of adequate legal remedies. Steffel v. Thompson (1974). Declaratory relief in federal courts is, however, made discretionary by statute.

Requests for declaratory relief are less necessary in damages actions, because in deciding whether a § 1983 plaintiff should be compensated for a rights violation, a court will necessarily have to make a determination of whether rights have been violated. Of course, declaratory relief is not usually available in federal court in challenges to unconstitutional rates or taxes in light of judicial glosses on the tax and rate injunction statutes, 28 U.S.C.A. §§ 1341–1342. And it is no more available in the face of an ongoing state court enforcement proceeding than an injunction would be under the equitable restraint doctrine of Younger v. Harris (1971). Samuels v. Mackell (1971). See Chapter 15.

There is no requirement, however, that a party seek coercive relief—damages or an injunction—as a co-requisite to seeking declaratory relief. Sometimes a declaratory judgment is sought on its own. This might make sense if a party wishes to challenge the enforcement of a practice or statute and there is fear that traditional equitable prerequisites will not be met for some reason (even though justiciability prerequisites can be satisfied). Assuming that there is no ongoing state enforcement proceeding against the § 1983 plaintiff, he may obtain a declaratory judgment respecting a statute challenged on constitutional grounds if he can show a "genuine threat" of its enforcement against him sufficient to satisfy traditional justiciability and case-or-controversy concerns. *Steffel, supra*; cf. *Lyons, supra*.

An award of declaratory relief, moreover, can provide the basis for an award of attorney's fees in the proper case. See Chapter 11. Although, unlike an injunction, a declaratory judgment cannot itself be enforced by contempt, it can serve as the basis for a later award of injunctive relief, 28 U.S.C.A. § 2202, and can be enforced by an injunction to protect or effectuate the federal court's order of declaratory relief. 28 U.S.C.A. § 2283. *Samuels, supra*. Although a declaratory judgment's preclusive effects are less than certain, it ought to have sticking power in later state court litigation brought by the state against the same § 1983 plaintiff. Preclusion in favor of third parties is particularly troublesome, however, especially when it is remembered that non-mutual preclusion rules are relaxed against the government, even when it has previously litigated and lost on an issue. Cf. United States v. Mendoza (1984).

It is open to question, however, whether a state or local official, concerned that the statute which he may be about to enforce is unconstitutional, can obtain—as a plaintiff—a declaratory judgment of the statute's constitutionality in a § 1983 declaratory judgment action. First of all, there may be justiciability problems—including ripeness, case-or-controversy, and standing concerns—associated with the state's bringing suit against an individual who has not yet but who may wish to violate a state statute. If the statute is currently being enforced against that individual in state court, perhaps those concerns are removed. And perhaps a genuine threat of enforcement respecting a particular individual may be shown even short of commencement of such an enforcement proceeding in state court.

Other problems may attend such a declaratory judgment, however. It is questionable whether the state or its officials suing in their official capacity are "persons" who may sue under § 1983. Cf. Breard v. Greene (1998) (stating that Paraguay was not a "person" under § 1983, nor were its officers suing in their official capacity). As a matter of declaratory judgment law, it is less than clear whether a would-be defendant to a federal cause of action may always turn the tables and bring a declaratory action against the would-be plaintiff, at least when the declaratory plaintiff has no cause of action of his own under the relevant federal statute.

Franchise Tax Bd. v. Construction Laborers Vacation Trust (1983). Finally, there is the sense, expressed by the Court in *Franchise Tax Board*, that a state forum provides a satisfactory venue for the state and its officials to enforce and obtain interpretations of its own enactments. ("There are good reasons why the federal courts should not entertain suits by the States to declare the validity of their regulations, despite possibly conflicting federal law."). Although the decision in *Franchise Tax Board* did not involve an interpretation of § 1983, the sentiment it expressed was a general one, and it suggests that declaratory relief arguably should not be as readily available to state and local officials enforcing state and local statutes as it is to those against whom those statutes are enforced.

D. Coercive Enforcement of Remedies

1. Damages Judgments

Under Rules 69 and 70 of the Federal Rules of Civil Procedure, federal court damages judgments are enforceable in the same manner that they would be under state law. In the case of individual officer liability, a federal court § 1983 damages judgment can be enforced in the same manner as it could be against an individual judgment debtor, including the garnishment of wages or the attachment of the judgment debtor's property if payment of the judgment is resisted. But a damages judgment cannot be enforced against the government for which the officer works if relief has been sought against the official in his personal capacity only.

Things can become more problematic when enforcement of monetary relief is sought against a state or local governmental entity. Enforcement against a state is possible in some cases, for example, where the state is liable for attorney's fees incident to obtaining injunctive relief entered against a state official sued in his official capacity. And enforcement of monetary awards against a municipality is possible since cities have become suable persons under § 1983. If the officer has acted pursuant to custom or policy and either (1) the city has been made a defendant, or (2) the officer (whether or not he has been sued in his individual capacity) has been sued in his official capacity and the city has had notice and an opportunity to respond, it can be held liable in damages under § 1983.

In such cases, state-law limitations on the enforcement of judgments against state and local entities have been ignored when the supremacy of federal law would be impaired. For example, in Gary W. v. State of La. (5th Cir.1980), state officials dragged their feet in complying with the payment of attorney's fees in an institutional reform case brought against state officials under § 1983. The state argued that under its law, payment of money from the state in connection with any judgment against it was discretionary, and that the § 1983 plaintiffs' attorneys were obliged to line up and wait along with other judgment creditors of the state's until the state passed the necessary appropriations bill. The district court and the Fifth Circuit disa-

In concluding that the trial court had exceeded its discretion, the Supreme Court stated that respect for the integrity and functioning of local governments required that a tax increase—an "extraordinary" remedial measure—could be undertaken only if "no permissible alternative" would have accomplished the task. Nevertheless, the Court upheld a modification of the taxation order that had been made by the appellate court. The appellate court had concluded that the trial court could simply order the school district to levy adequate property taxes, at a level that the school district (not the federal court) chose to set. If the tax ordered by the school district exceeded the maximum allowed by the state constitution, then the federal court could simply enjoin enforcement of the state tax ceiling. The latter order arguably gave the school district greater autonomy in how it would come up with the necessary funds than did the trial court's order which had set the rate and imposed the tax itself.

The dissent in *Jenkins* objected that the order, even as modified, amounted to "judicial taxation." But the Supreme Court had previously suggested that a federal court might order local officials to raise adequate taxes (without setting the amount of tax itself) to pay for the costs of school desegregation. Griffin v. County School Board of Prince Edward County (1964). And there had been a long tradition (primarily in nineteenth-century municipal bond default cases) of federal courts' compelling local officials to exercise power they had under state law to levy taxes to satisfy federal court judgments against local entities. Wolff v. New Orleans (1881); Amy v. The Supervisors (1871).

Where the decision in *Jenkins* probably broke new ground, however, was in allowing a federal court to order state officials to raise taxes in a manner contrary to state law. In the past, state officials had been ordered to carry out powers that were theirs to exercise under pre-existing state law, but subject to any bona fide state-law limits on their powers. Only when, for example, the state-law limitation on state taxation itself had been unconstitutional or had been imposed to thwart the enforcement of a federal judgment, were limitations on state power ignored. Graham v. Folsom (1906); Meriwether v. Garrett (1880). The state tax ceiling in *Jenkins* was neither unconstitutional in itself, nor enacted to thwart enforcement of a federal court order. The inability to enjoin the operation of the state tax ceiling, however, might have made effective enforcement of the injunction in *Jenkins* impossible. On the other hand, being able to order state officials to do things that are not within their specific power to do under state law—when the limitation on their power is not itself unconstitutional—presents troubling federalism concerns of its own, not unlike those at issue in *Milliken I*, in which the Court honored nondiscriminatory state law in disallowing an interdistrict remedy.

3. Contempt

Problems of enforcement can become even more dramatic when public officials resist valid federal court orders. In Spallone v. United States (1990), the City of Yonkers and various council members resisted a federal court order to remedy housing discrimination. A federal court had found that the city had engaged in past intentional discrimination, and as part of the court's remedy, it had ordered the city to establish public housing in a predominantly white section of the city from which African–Americans had been historically excluded. After the city had initially failed to comply, the parties entered into a consent decree under which the city, through the city council, agreed that it would pass the necessary enabling legislation to carry out the federal court's decree. The council, however, balked again, declaring a moratorium on public housing, even though it had already approved the consent decree. The district judge then indicated that he was prepared to hold the council members and the city in contempt if the requisite legislation was not passed.

When the council took the position that it would not pass the requisite legislation, the court held the city and the council members in civil contempt. The city was fined $100 for the first day of noncompliance, with the fine to double, daily. (By the twenty-fifth day, the fine would exceed $1 billion, and it would continue to double, daily.) The individual council members were each to be fined $500 per day until they complied. The Court of Appeals affirmed, although it capped the city's daily fine at $1 million per day.

The Supreme Court upheld the contempt fines against the city, but not against the council members individually. Acknowledging the trial court's broad equitable powers to remedy past discrimination, the Court cautioned that in devising any equitable remedy a federal trial court was obliged to "take into account the interests of state and local authorities in managing their own affairs, consistent with the Constitution." In addition, the "extraordinary" nature of the contempt power required the district court to use the "least possible power adequate to the end proposed." The council members, unlike the city, were not individual parties to the lawsuit. Moreover, it was not clear that sanctions against the city alone would have failed to do the trick. Personal fines against the legislators would cause them to act out of personal financial motivation, said the Court, and thereby skew the normal legislative process. In addition, the fines would "come close to" undermining notions of absolute legislative immunity. The result was that the cost of the council members' individual noncompliance was spread among the general electorate.

Spallone is an unusual case. The council members had, after all, not merely resisted a decree; they had resisted a decree that they had already agreed to (on the city's behalf). And it is at least curious that the Supreme Court apparently assumed that the political process would work in such a way that it was not unfair to hold the populace vicariously liable for the grandstanding of their elected representatives. While collective financial responsibility is the ordinary result when a legislative body passes unconstitutional statutes, the act of standing in contempt of an order that the same legislator has already agreed to, seems to make the transgression somewhat less legislative in nature. The decision contrasts with the Court's concern for the "blameless" taxpayers of a city, who do not have to pay punitive damages for the wanton disregard of the law by its officials (see above at Chapter 9). In addition, the Court has shown little reluctance in the past to hold other sorts of officials, particularly law enforcement officials, in contempt for their violations of federal court orders. Ex parte Young (1908).

E. Relief from Continuing Injunctive Relief

1. Achieving Compliance

The effort to get out from under a consent decree or judicial order of complex injunctive relief need not always entail contempt. In recent years state and local officials have increasingly sought to eliminate continuing federal judicial oversight of their public institutions by establishing that they have achieved compliance with the Constitution—e.g., that a formerly dual school system is now "unitary" or that offending prison conditions have been alleviated. While the goal of restoring local control at that point would seem to be a compelling one, it is sometimes difficult, where complex injunctive relief is concerned, to ascertain when compliance has been achieved. Wrongdoing institutions are typically under an order to eliminate the so-called continuing effects of past unconstitutional action, and it is not always clear when the last vestiges of such past illegality have been rooted out.

For example, in Freeman v. Pitts (1992), a school board sought to bring an end to federal court supervision under a 1969 consent decree to dismantle its dual school system. Determining that "unitary status" had been achieved with respect to pupil assignment and transportation, the district court eliminated its affirmative orders with respect to those matters. But it kept in force its orders respecting other areas such as faculty hiring and expenditures on physical facilities, where compliance had not been achieved. The Court of Appeals reversed, concluding that a school system was not unitary, and thus not eligible for relief from federal court oversight, until all vestiges of discrimination had been alleviated. The Supreme Court upheld as within the district court's discretion the decision to withdraw incrementally its oversight of certain areas, while retaining jurisdiction over the entire school system until the remaining vestiges had been eliminated. The Court did so despite the obvious concern that a remaining "vestige of discrimination in one factor [could] act as an incubator for resegregation in others." Id. (Souter, J., concurring). See also Board of Ed. of Oklahoma City v. Dowell (1991) (setting forth standards for dissolving desegregation decrees); Pasadena City Bd. of Ed. v. Spangler (1976).

2. Relief from Hard Bargains

Sometimes state or local officials seek to get out from under a court-supervised consent decree, not because they have achieved compliance, but because compliance has become too onerous or perhaps because subsequent developments have shown that the bargain they entered into was simply a bad one. Relief from judgment is ordinarily governed by the flexible standards of Rule 60(b), Fed. R. Civ. P., which the Supreme Court has held applicable to modification of consent decrees, and which requires a showing of a "significant change in facts or law that warrants revision." *Rufo v. Inmates of Suffolk Cty. Jail* (1992); see also *Frew v. Hawkins* (2004).

In *Rufo*, for example, the state had agreed in a consent decree to end the double-bunking of prisoners, but it later turned out that it might not have been constitutionally obligated to do so in all cases. Of course, the mere fact of intervening legal change is not in itself enough to warrant modification of a decree. And *Rufo* was careful to admonish lower courts not to rewrite consent decrees to make them conform only to "the constitutional floor." Indeed, while no single element of a consent decree may be constitutionally required, each of the elements of the decree may be necessary in the aggregate to eliminate unconstitutionality in the institution under scrutiny. And it may be appropriate to hold a state or local government to an element of a decree that was at the heart of the agreement. Nevertheless, in these contexts, the Court is clearly sympathetic to the concerns of the local decisionmakers who must implement the decrees, and in *Rufo* the Court concluded that the trial court should have been more willing to consider modification of the decree at issue. "The upsurge in constitutional reform litigation since [*Brown*], has made the ability of a district court to modify a decree in response to changed circumstances all the more important." *Rufo* therefore specifically rejected the applicability in the public law context of United States v. Swift & Co. (1932), which had required a showing of "grievous wrong" evoked by new and unforeseen conditions before a consent decree could be modified.

The decision in *Rufo* makes sense. The ability of a particular administration of a state or local government to enter into consent decrees that tie the hands of successor governments in perpetuity creates an especial need in institutional reform litigation for the kind of safety valve suggested by Rule 60(b). *Frew v. Hawkins, supra*. Of course, the solemn promises of state officials made during the course of litigation must have some binding effect between the parties to the litigation that produced the decree. But the flexibility of Rule 60(b) should be able to accommodate those concerns as well.

3.　Prison Litigation Reform Act

Congressional action has gone farther than *Rufo*, however. Federal law now allows state or local officials to move for immediate termination of any previously entered prospective relief in prison reform litigation that was "approved or granted in the absence of a finding by the court that the relief is narrowly drawn, extends no further than necessary to correct the violation of the federal right, and is the least intrusive means necessary to correct the violation of the federal right." 18 U.S.C.A. § 3626(b)(2), as amended by Prison Litigation Reform Act of 1995 (PLRA), Pub. L. No. 104–134. The statute provides for a mandatory automatic stay of any previously entered injunctive relief beginning 30 days after filing of the motion (subject to an additional 60 days extension on good cause shown), and the stay continues to operate until such time as the district court rules on the propriety of continued injunctive relief. Id. at § 3626(e)(2). Thus, the prior injunctive relief is temporarily undone upon the passage of the statutorily prescribed time, and remains so until such time as the district judge is able to render a decision as to whether it should be permanently undone, or modified, or left in place, consistent with the PLRA. In fact, a similar set of standards now applies to the initial entry of injunctive relief in prison reform litigation, whether the case is litigated or is resolved by a consent decree.

Although the new statute allows for the district judge to undo existing judicial judgments that have become final, Congress is probably not without power to order reconsideration of outstanding decrees along new lines that it has established, primarily because federal courts retain continuing jurisdiction over most such orders for injunctive relief. Compare Plaut v. Spendthrift Farm, Inc. (1995) (striking down, on Article III and separation of powers grounds, a federal statute that retroactively re-opened federal court damage judgments). And, by definition, these remedial limitations in the PLRA cannot go so far as to disallow constitutionally "necessary" relief.

The automatic stay provisions were potentially more troubling. In Miller v. French (2000), the Court concluded that the stay provisions were mandatory, and that they trumped any equitable powers in the federal courts to delay operation of a stay of relief beyond the statutory requirements. In addition, the Court upheld the stay provisions against a separation of powers challenge and specifically distinguished the decision in *Plaut, supra*. There, the Court had struck down a congressional statute that allowed for the reopening of judgments in cases seeking damages that had become final, and over which the courts were exercising no continuing jurisdiction. The Court purported to leave open what it considered to be the separate due process question of whether the time constraints might ever prove too short for meaningful consideration of the earlier decree in light of the new congressional criteria, before the stay would go into effect.

CHAPTER 11

ATTORNEY'S FEES

Overview

It is unlikely that the rights associated with § 1983 would be enforced without lawyers who were willing to bring suit. But under the "American Rule" each party ordinarily has to pay for his own attorney—an economic reality that could be problematic for many § 1983 plaintiffs. Congress modified the American Rule in the Civil Rights Attorney's Fees Awards Act of 1976 (now codified as the paragraph (b) of 42 U.S.C.A. § 1988), by substituting what the Court has read as a largely one-way version of a loser-pays rule for a host of civil rights actions, including suits under § 1983. The statute thus provides a financial incentive to bring lawsuits which might not otherwise attract attorneys, either because only injunctive (rather than monetary) relief is sought, or because the likelihood of substantial damages is uncertain. This latter uncertainty is driven both by the difficulty of establishing particular constitutional violations and satisfactorily proving injury, and by various doctrines of official and sovereign immunity that kick in even when a constitutional violation can be established and injury proved.

Under the Fees Act as construed by the Court, reasonable attorney's fees are ordinarily available to prevailing plaintiffs in § 1983 litigation; they are ordinarily unavailable to prevailing defendants unless the plaintiff's suit has been brought in bad faith. The courts have developed this largely one-way reading of the statute, despite its neutral (i.e., two-way) fee-shifting language.

A presumptively reasonable fee is said to be reached by calculating the hours reasonably expended and the prevailing rates in the community for similar services. "Success" under the statute, however, means something more than the lawsuit's serving as a catalyst to get the defendant voluntarily to modify his unlawful behavior; yet it might mean something as little as an award of nominal damages or any other relief entered by the court. Nevertheless, the degree of success is highly relevant to the ultimate determination of what is a reasonable award. Finally, despite the barrier of sovereign immunity, the Supreme Court has held that states themselves are obligated to pay attorney's fees under § 1988 when their officials have been successfully sued in their official capacities for injunctive relief.

A. The Rationale Behind Statutory Fee Shifting

The Supreme Court made clear in Alyeska Pipeline Service Co. v. Wilderness Society (1975) that fee shifting is generally unavailable in litigation in federal courts in the absence of specific statutory authorization. The Court relied on what it called the "American Rule," which was little more than the common-law tradition that each party pay for his own counsel costs, win or lose.

Alyeska was not a foregone conclusion, however. In the past, the Court had upheld fee shifting out of a "common fund" generated for shareholders in a securities class action, and it had also upheld fee shifting when a union member successfully sued his union to vindicate statutorily protected free speech rights which it had denied him, thereby arguably benefiting all members of the union. Mills v. Electric Auto–Lite (1970); Hall v. Cole (1973). Moreover, in the past, the Court had apparently considered it to be part of a federal court's equitable powers to reimburse litigation costs, including counsel costs. Sprague v. Ticonic National Bank (1939). And even at common law, fees could be shifted when a party had litigated in subjective bad faith.

As a result of *Alyeska* and its default rule making fees ordinarily unavailable from the losing party, a cloud was thrown over public law litigation. Without the incentive of fees in the event of success, there was a risk that rights might go unenforced under § 1983. Costs of litigation are often high and most lawyers are unwilling to work for psychic gratification alone. In addition, many would-be § 1983 plaintiffs are impecunious. Although contingent fee arrangements might be available in particular cases that resembled traditional tort cases (as with a police beating), many of the rights that § 1983 serves to vindicate would not possess such allure in the legal marketplace. And many times no monetary relief is sought, but only injunctive or declaratory relief, which generates no fund at all from which counsel might be paid.

Congress responded to the *Alyeska* Court's decision with the 1976 Attorney's Fees Award Act, which provides in relevant part, as now modified:

42 U.S.C.A. § 1988(b). Attorney's fees

In any action or proceeding to enforce a provision of [various civil rights statutes, including § 1983], the court, in its discretion, may allow the prevailing party, other than the United States, a reasonable attorney's fee as part of the costs, except that in any action brought against a judicial officer for an act or omission taken in such officer's judicial capacity such officer shall not be held liable for any costs, including attorney's fees, unless such action was clearly in excess of such officer's jurisdiction.

The Act was packaged with a detailed (some might say "cooked") legislative history which is a staple of judicial decisions on fee issues arising under the statute. See S. Rep. No. 94–1011 (1976); H.R. Rep. No. 94–1558 (1976). The legislative history, despite the apparently contrary wording of the statute, strongly suggests that the fee-shifting provisions of the statute were to be in one direction only: in favor of the prevailing § 1983 plaintiff—i.e., the party who successfully vindicated federal rights. In the legislative history, Congress referred to pre-*Alyeska* decisions stating that "If successful plaintiffs were routinely forced to bear their own attorney's fees, few aggrieved parties would be in a position to advance the public interest by invoking the injunctive powers of the federal courts." Newman v. Piggie Park Enterprises, Inc. (1968). And, despite the emphasis on such injunctive issues, Congress also made clear that the statute intends for fee shiftwrg to apply in damages cases as well.

The legislative history acknowledges that such prevailing plaintiffs act as "private attorneys general" in vindicating important public law norms that benefit not just the individual litigant, but society at large. It further declares that prevailing civil rights counsel should be compensated "as is traditional with attorneys compensated by a fee-paying client 'for all time reasonably expended on a matter.'" It also indicates that governmental entities, including states, will be liable for fees when injunctive relief is obtained against their officials, even though the statute's language is completely silent about state liability for fees. Finally, the legislative history makes clear that a defendant's litigating in good faith is not an excuse for avoiding fees.

B. Judicial Elaboration of the Fees Act

1. Prevailing Parties

To be a prevailing party, a § 1983 plaintiff must obtain from the court some actual relief on the merits of his claim that alters the legal relationship between the parties. This can include an order requiring the defendant to pay an amount of money (including nominal damages) or an order for injunctive relief. Declaratory relief can also be enough, provided the declaratory judgment alters the parties' ongoing legal relationship and benefits the plaintiff by affecting the defendant's behavior toward him. Farrar v. Hobby (1992). Even if a case does not go to trial, but ends in a consent decree entered by the court altering the defendant's challenged behavior, a plaintiff may be considered to have prevailed. Maher v. Gagne (1980). But a party whose suit merely serves as the "catalyst" in causing the defendant voluntarily to change its behavior, without any award or order of relief from the court, will not be considered to have prevailed. Buckhannon Bd. and Care Home, Inc. v. West Virginia Dept. of Health and Human Resources (2001).

It is not necessary that a plaintiff prevail on all issues to be considered "prevailing" (although lack of overall success may be reflected in the reduced size of any fee award). Instead it is enough that the plaintiff succeeds on "any significant issue" that achieves some of the benefit the party sought in bringing suit. It is unclear, however, whether a § 1983 plaintiff who prevails only on his supplemental state-law claim(s) will be considered prevailing for the purposes of § 1988. He arguably should be so considered, however, if the reason for deciding on state-law grounds was to avoid having to reach the federal issues in the case. And a party who loses a damages action under § 1983 because the defendant is immune cannot recover fees simply because the court determines the officer's actions were unconstitutional.

Not all plaintiffs who prevail in one of the ways just noted will be able to recover fees, however. The Court has held that plaintiffs who do not hire an attorney to represent them but who proceed *pro se* will not be entitled to recover reasonable attorney's fees even if they succeed and even if the pro se plaintiff was a lawyer representing herself in her own § 1983 action. Kay v. Ehrler (1991).

2. Assessing a Fee's Reasonableness

(a) The Lodestar

The Court has stated that the place to start in assessing the reasonableness of a fee award for a successful plaintiff "is the number of hours reasonably expended on the litigation multiplied by a reasonable hourly rate." Hensley v. Eckerhart (1983). Such assessments are typically made at the conclusion of the litigation at a hearing before the district court in which the contesting parties put on documentary or live testimony (or both) to establish what a reasonable fee should be. Although neither the statute nor the legislative history defines what a reasonable fee is, courts have made use of a multi-factor analysis to which Congress also made reference in the House and Senate Reports to the Fees Act. Those factors are: (1) the time and labor required; (2) the novelty and difficulty of the questions; (3) the skill requisite to perform the legal service properly; (4) the preclusion of other employment by the attorney due to acceptance of the case;

(5) the customary fee for similar work; (6) whether the fee is fixed or contingent; (7) time limitations imposed by the client or the circumstances; (8) the amount in dispute and the results obtained; (9) the experience, reputation, and ability of the attorneys; (10) the "undesirability" of the case; (11) the nature and length of the professional relationship with the client; and (12) awards in similar cases.

This "lodestar" figure, representing reasonable hours expended and reasonable rates, is said to be a presumptively reasonable fee. But the lodestar itself might be adjusted upward or downward depending on particular circumstances, such as the "results obtained." Nevertheless, the Court has made it difficult to obtain an upward adjustment of the lodestar based on "exceptional results"; on the other hand, the Court has cautioned that a fee award should not be reduced simply because the plaintiff, who has obtained excellent results, failed to prevail on every contention raised in a lawsuit. Even losses on some claims will not be discounted as hours unreasonably spent, when those claims arose out of a "common core of facts" or were otherwise closely related to prevailing claims. Although lower court decisions respecting the calculation of a reasonable fee are treated deferentially, the Supreme Court and the federal appeals courts have shown an unusual fascination with reviewing fee awards.

(b) Proportionality in Fee Awards and Damages Judgments

In City of Riverside v. Rivera (1986), Mexican–American plaintiffs in a police-abuse case recovered a little over $33,000 in total damages when they succeeded in proving to a jury 37 incidents of civil rights violations by a municipality and five of its police officers (out of an original 23 defendants). The fee award, however, was nearly a quarter of a million dollars. The Supreme Court narrowly upheld the fee award. A plurality concluded that the vindication of constitutional rights "cannot be valued solely in monetary terms," and that it would be improper to limit fees, based on a tort analogy, to some fixed percentage or proportion of the total recovery. That particular conclusion was later strengthened in Blanchard v. Bergeron (1989), when the Court concluded that a contingent fee arrangement entered into between counsel and client could not serve as a cap on an award under the fee statute.

The dissenters in *City of Riverside* argued that no rational party would expend tens of thousands of dollars to recover on claims worth only a small part of that amount, and that similar "billing judgment" considerations should enter into the assessment of a reasonable fee award. But the plurality observed that civil rights cases often result in "nominal or relatively small damages awards" and that successful judgments deter future illegality, "particularly . . . in the area of individual police misconduct." Requiring the fee recovery not to exceed some proportion of damages would deter vindication of constitutional rights, they said, and Congress itself had legislated on the assumption that private fee arrangements were inadequate to ensure vigorous enforcement of civil and constitutional rights.

The Court would eventually conclude, however, that an award of only nominal damages might make a plaintiff a prevailing party within the meaning of the Fees Act, but that if the nominal award was because of a failure of proof, then "the only reasonable fee is usually no fee at all." Farrar v. Hobby (1992). Language in *Farrar* suggests that "consideration of the amount of damages awarded as compared to the amount sought" may now be a more significant factor than it arguably was in *City of Riverside*. Purely technical or de minimis relief may entitle a party to "prevailing" status, but it bears heavily on the propriety of a fully "compensatory" fee award. And in such cases, courts need not work through the "twelve steps" before making an award of low fees or no fees at all. *Farrar, supra*.

Nevertheless, the decision in *City of Riverside* was grounded on the district court's own detailed findings respecting the size of the jury award of compensatory damages. The district judge had specifically found there to be a "reluctance of jurors to make large [compensatory] awards against police officers," that the issues were complex, and that the fee award would serve to vindicate the public interest in redressing illegal police action that had been "motivated by a general hostility to the Chicano community in the area where the incident occurred." A majority of the Supreme Court therefore assumed that the factual findings of the district judge would have to be upheld unless they were "clearly erroneous" under Rule 52, Fed. R. Civ. P.

3. The Risk of not Prevailing

For many years, successful § 1983 litigants were able to convince courts to adjust the lodestar figure upward (sometimes significantly) to account for the risk of not prevailing. Non-contingent counsel— lawyers who are paid their fees by their clients—are able to keep those fees, win or lose. Civil rights counsel who lose will recover nothing unless they have been paid along the way. A lawyer who will get paid only in the event her client is successful would presumably not bill that client at the same (i.e., lower) rate that she would charge if she were being paid without regard to results.

In the contingent fee context, the risk of non-recovery, as well as the lost time-value of money, is accounted for by a contract through which the lawyer may take a substantial percentage of the plaintiff's ultimate recovery. In such cases the fee received is often well in excess of what a client would have paid the lawyer on an hourly basis had he been able to do so. Indeed, if one were to break down the ultimately obtained contingent fee into an effective hourly rate, that rate might seem quite inflated over "reasonable hourly rates." But the difference between the effective hourly rate represented by the contingent fee contract and the ordinary, non-contingent hourly rate which would have been charged a fee-paying client reflects compensation to the attorney both for the free loan of ser-

To some extent, these concerns may be overblown. In the private market for legal services, it may be that some of an attorney's losing contingent cases are "paid for" by the winners, and that fact may be reflected in the size of the typical fee arrangement that represents an aspect of risk over and above the risk in any particular case. But eliminating an enhancement for that additional systemic risk is no reason to refuse to incorporate any incentive at all to take account of the risk of not prevailing in a particular case. To be sure, in *Hensley, supra*, the Court held that a prevailing party could not recover for time spent on losing issues that were wholly unrelated to the claims that were victorious. But outright elimination of a risk enhancement with respect to claims on which the plaintiff did prevail probably runs counter to Congress's wishes. If civil rights claims are supposed to compete equally with other claims in the marketplace—i.e., both contingent as well as fee-paying (risk-free) claims—then *City of Burlington* promises that they will not. And if an enhancement for the risk of not prevailing amounts to a kind of subsidy to plaintiff's counsel for the cases she will eventually lose, it is not clear that such a subsidy is inconsistent with Congress's goal that such civil rights claims compete equally in the marketplace. Compare 42 U.S.C.A. § 1997e(d) (greatly restricting fees in prisoner litigation by requiring "proportiona[lity]," between fees and recovery, that up to 25% of the prisoner's monetary award be used to pay his lawyer's fees, and that rates otherwise be capped).

Of course, if the risk of not prevailing in any given § 1983 case is not to be a factor in fee awards, then presumably it should not be a factor when the risk of non-recovery is slight and the case is a "sure winner." But some courts have refused to award fees in such contexts, on the assumption that the private contingent fee market could absorb such cases, and that a statutory fee is unnecessary. See Zarcone v. Perry (2d Cir.1978). Such a result, however, seems counter to *City of Burlington*, and the decision in Blanchard v. Bergeron (1989), that a contingent fee arrangement should not serve to limit statutory fees under § 1988. Similarly, the fact that a particular plaintiff can well afford § 1983 counsel should not be a reason for refusing a reasonable fee award insofar as fees are meant to have a deterrent function as well as a compensatory one. Besides, denial of fees in a "sure winner" of a case, or in a case with a fee-paying plaintiff, would be a windfall to the wrongdoing defendant.

4. Defendant Fees in § 1983 Litigation

Successful civil rights plaintiffs customarily recover fees absent extraordinary circumstances. The unsuccessful defendant's good faith in litigating and losing on the merits is said to be no defense to a fee award. Hutto v. Finney (1978). By contrast, despite the neutral, two-way fee-shifting language of § 1988, those who successfully defend § 1983 actions generally recover fees under § 1988 only when the plaintiff has brought or maintained the lawsuit on objectively unreasonable grounds.

In Christiansburg Garment Co. v. EEOC (1978), an employment discrimination case brought under Title VII of the 1964 Civil Rights Act, the Court stated that prevailing defendants could recover fees from a losing plaintiff when the underlying claim was "frivolous, unreasonable or without foundation, even though not brought in subjective bad faith." The Court concluded that Congress understood the 1976 Fees Act to have borrowed Title VII's "objective" bad faith standard for awarding fees to prevailing defendants, and the Court has since applied it in § 1983 litigation without much discussion. Hughes v. Rowe (1980). Nevertheless, "subjective" bad faith has always provided a basis for fee shifting at common law and quite apart from statutory provisions such as the Fees Act. Chambers v. NASCO, Inc. (1991). And neither *Alyeska* nor the 1976 Act purported to eliminate the possibility of fee-shifting on such grounds. So, if a losing § 1983 claim is brought in bad faith—whether objectively or subjectively—counsel fees may be awarded against a plaintiff and in favor of a defendant, under one rationale or another.

Even when these standards for defendant fees are met, however, a number of courts have further concluded that the goal of a defendant fee award is not to compensate the defendant by rewarding him a fully compensatory lodestar figure. Instead, the award is viewed as punitive, and should therefore reflect a sum that will penalize the plaintiff and deter him and those similarly situated from such litigation in the future. Thus, in Faraci v. Hickey–

Freeman Co., Inc. (2d Cir.1979), an appeals court reduced a fully compensatory fee when the plaintiff, who had brought the suit in objective bad faith, had limited resources. But in Munson v. Friske (7th Cir.1985), another appeals court upheld a fully compensatory award when there had been a showing of improper subjective motivation in bringing suit. Although plaintiff's inability to pay a defendant fee award is probably not a reason not to enter such an award, it may be relevant to the ultimate size of the fee award. Wolfe v. Perry (6th Cir.2005).

C.　Who Pays the Fee Award?

1.　Damages Actions

It is easy enough to state the principle that a losing defendant pays a fee award to a successful § 1983 plaintiff. But given the complexities surrounding suits against officers in their individual and official capacities, and the problems with suing governmental entities, application of the principle can be problematic. If an officer is successfully sued for damages in his individual capacity only (i.e., personally) for his violation of the Constitution, fees may obviously be awarded against the officer himself; the entity that employed him will not be liable for such fees in an individual-capacity-only damages action. Kentucky v. Graham (1985). If, however, the officer is found to be immune (even if he may have violated the Constitution) he will not be liable for any fees because the plaintiff will not have prevailed against him. In such suits, the officer's liability for fees will track his liability for damages. Of course, when it is appropriate to sue a local government for damages inflicted by one of its officers— i.e., when he has acted pursuant to official policy— and damages are recovered against the entity, the entity will also be on the hook for fees. In such a case, assuming the officer is not himself immune from damages, the city and the officer will both be liable for fees. If the officer is immune, of course, he will be off the hook altogether; but if the plaintiff has otherwise prevailed on the merits against the city, the city will be liable for both the damages judgment and the attorney's fees.

2. Injunctive and Declaratory Relief

Things become trickier when suit is for declaratory or injunctive relief. In such suits, the plaintiff could often simply name the local government entity as a defendant (but not the state, or a state agency, given its sovereign immunity and the fact that it is not a suable person under § 1983; see Chapter 7). Or, the plaintiff might name as a defendant the responsible official. The naming of the official in his official capacity effectively joins the governmental entity who employs him, assuming the entity gets notice of the suit and has the opportunity to respond. Hafer v. Melo (1991). If injunctive or declaratory relief is granted in such a case, the entity will be liable for the fees under § 1988. Indeed, if an official is successfully sued only in his official capacity, *only* the governmental entity can be liable for fees. Brandon v. Holt (1985). And in a proper case of declaratory or injunctive relief against a state officer in his official capacity, the state and its treasury could be liable for the fees, insofar as the Court has decided (not unproblematically) that sovereign immunity imposes no barrier to such awards. Missouri v. Jenkins (1989); Hutto v. Finney (1978). Even if those cases were correctly decided, one might still question whether such fees can be awarded against the state itself when § 1983 is being used to vindicate rights under federal statutes that Congress has enacted under its Article I powers. Seminole Tribe v. Florida (1996). Finally, when a judge is the proper subject of injunctive or declaratory relief, however, fees cannot be assessed against the judge personally—at least not when the judge has been sued for acts taken in his "judicial capacity" that were not "clearly in excess" of his jurisdiction. Compare Pulliam v. Allen (1984) (holding the contrary under an earlier version of § 1988).

3.　Bad Faith and Other Misbehavior

Finally, when litigation has been pursued in bad faith, the plaintiff herself will ordinarily be held liable for the defendant's fees under § 1988, subject to the limitations noted above. But there are occasions on which counsel for either side in § 1983 litigation can be held personally liable for fees because of various kinds of misbehavior, pursuant to statutory provisions, rules or fee-shifting theories common to all federal court litigation. For example, under Rule 11, Fed. R. Civ. P., monetary sanctions may be assessed against an attorney, his firm, or, in some instances, the party, for certain improper representation of claims, defenses, or other contentions and allegations. Sanctions may also be assessed against attorneys or parties under other Rules for failures to comply with and respond to discovery. And under 28 U.S.C.A. § 1927, federal courts have express power to punish lawyers who "multipl[y] the proceedings ... unreasonably and vexatiously" by making lawyers pay for costs associated with their conduct, including payment of opposing counsel's fees. In addition, the Supreme Court has held that federal courts have the inherent power to protect the integrity of their own proceedings and, in narrow circumstances, to impose monetary sanctions—including attorney's fees—on parties or their attorneys for behavior that is vexatious, wanton, or oppressive. *NASCO, supra*; Roadway Express, Inc. v. Piper (1980).

D. Litigation Costs Other than Counsel Fees

The ordinary expenses of litigation typically involve not only counsel expenses, but other related costs as well, including out-of-pocket expenses of counsel, expert witness fees, and paralegal and law clerk expenses. These are all items for which an attorney would bill a fee-paying client. And if the private-attorney-general theory is to be taken seriously, failure to compensate for these litigation costs could significantly skew the incentives that § 1988 was supposed to provide. Therefore, in Missouri v. Jenkins (1989), the Court allowed separately billed paralegal and law clerk time to be charged to the losing party under § 1988 as part of a reasonable attorney's fee.

But later, in West Virginia University Hosp., Inc. v. Casey (1991), the Court held that expert witness fees (in the six-figure range) incurred by the successful plaintiffs in a suit under § 1983, although "essential" to the litigation, were not recoverable under the Fees Act as then written. The Court's reasoning was that two other statutes already covered the area: 28 U.S.C.A. §§ 1920 and 1821(b). These two statutes generally provide for taxing (to the losing party) various "costs" in federal court litigation, including expert witness fees, but limited recovery for experts to (then) $30 per day. The distinction between treatment of paralegal costs (which §§ 1920 and 1821(b) do not mention) and expert witnesses had been lost on lower courts, who had concluded that "the time spent by the expert is a substitute for lawyer time, just as paralegal time is" and that failure to allow for reimbursement would mean that the lawyer would do the work himself. *Casey* remains the law in § 1983 actions, although Congress, in the Civil Rights Act of 1991, statutorily provided for the inclusion of reasonable expert witness fees in the discretion of the district judge as part of an award of attorney's fees under § 1988(c), but only in actions brought under certain other civil rights provisions—not in actions brought under § 1983.

E. Attorney's Fees and Settlement

The prospect of having to pay an award of fees—especially an award that may easily outstrip any award of damages—creates an incentive for defendants to think hard about settlement. But that probably does not mean that injuries that are undeserving of compensation will routinely be compensated by defendants simply to avoid a fee award. Under current Rule 68, Fed. R. Civ. P., the defendant may make an offer of judgment and, if the plaintiff's ultimate recovery does not exceed that offer, the plaintiff will have to pay "costs" incurred after the making of the offer. The Court has interpreted the language in Rule 68 to mean that a successful plaintiff may not recover attorney's fees incurred by her counsel after rejection of a more-favorable-than-judgment offer from the defendant. Marek v. Chesny (1985).

Marek is a troublesome decision, however. It told a prevailing § 1983 plaintiff that she could not recover for all counsel time her attorney may have reasonably spent in prosecuting the case successfully. Rule 68, of course, does not require that the rejection of the offer be unreasonable or in bad faith, or that the counsel hours thereafter expended be unreasonable, before its no-recovery sanction attaches. Thus, as interpreted by the Court, the Rule seems to act as a partial repeal of a congressional statutory provision that would otherwise require compensation for all time reasonably spent. And that is arguably in tension with the Rules Enabling Act. 28 U.S.C.A. § 2072(b) ("such rules shall not abridge, enlarge, or modify any substantive right.... ").

The Court's response was to say that counsel had not been successful (within the meaning of the Fees

Act) to the extent that the final recovery was less than the rejected Rule 68 offer. But it is an extremely narrow definition of "success" to exclude a plaintiff who has won, but who did not to win as well as she might have won. In addition, the term "costs" in other cost-shifting provisions (such as 28 U.S.C.A. § 1920), had been specifically construed as *not* including counsel fees. Indeed, that was the basis of the decision in *Alyeska* itself. Moreover, Rule 68 was obviously designed against the common-law backdrop of the "American Rule" to encourage settlement by means of a modest sanction of requiring the prevailing party to pay post-offer court costs (excluding counsel fees), and seemed to mesh uncomfortably with public-law litigation under a fee-shifting statute.

Marek also reveals the difficulty of assessing when a Rule 68 offer is better than the results finally obtained, especially when something more than damages is at issue. Is a modest injunction with sizable damages better than a far-reaching injunction and minimal damages? Must an offer include or take account of attorney's fees incurred up to then?

Some of these issues were played out in Evans v. Jeff D. (1986). Plaintiffs had brought a class action on behalf of emotionally and mentally impaired children to redress deficiencies in public services. On the eve of trial, the defendants offered the plaintiff class virtually all of the injunctive relief that it had requested, but the offer was conditioned on plaintiffs' counsel's waiver of all fees. Although counsel accepted the settlement which was then entered by the court, counsel later argued on appeal (successfully) that the fee-waiver provision should be struck down. The Supreme Court disagreed. It concluded that the Fees Act did not proscribe simultaneous negotiation of fees and settlement, despite the risks for conflict of interest. In fact, the Court suggested that there was no ethical dilemma presented at all and that counsel had been obligated to take a settlement that gave the plaintiffs all of the injunctive relief they had asked for.

Ordinarily, counsel whose lawsuit results in a court order—even a consent or settlement decree that modifies the defendant's behavior—will recover fees for time reasonably expended. Compare *Buckhannon, supra* (rejecting possibility of a fee award where the lawsuit serves as catalyst in securing the defendant's voluntary change in behavior, absent judicial sanction) with Maher v. Gagne (1980) (upholding an award when a settlement judgment was entered by court). Nevertheless, the decision in *Jeff D.* to allow conditioning of settlement on waiver of a fee award perhaps serves as a disincentive to counsel in the future to undertake injunctive relief or structural reform litigation because they might have to forgo fees to which they would otherwise be entitled. As the dissenters noted, the "judicial policy" of fostering settlement of litigation in such a manner was inconsistent with "*congressional* policy" that sought "to create incentives for lawyers to devote time to civil rights cases by making it economically feasible for them to do so." *Jeff D., supra.*

CHAPTER 12

CHOICE OF LAW AND § 1983

Overview

Section 1983 is a sparsely worded statute. It makes no provision for a host of substantive, procedural, and remedial matters. For example, it does not define the category of suable "persons," it lacks a statute of limitations, and it makes no provision for immunities of officers or the standard for awarding compensatory or punitive damages. The courts have obviously had to supply meaning to these statutory gaps. The Supreme Court itself sometimes appears to engage in statutory interpretation, as when it decided on different occasions that the scope of suable persons included cities but excluded states. Other times, the Court seems to have developed federal common law, as when it decided that various officials would be able to assert personal immunities. On still other occasions, however, the Court has made recourse to state law under the direction of 42 U.S.C.A. § 1988(a), which the Court has read as a gap-filling device for actions under § 1983. Section 1988(a) provides in relevant part:

42 U.S.C.A. § 1988(a). Applicability of statutory and common law

[Jurisdiction in various civil rights statutes, including civil suits under § 1983] shall be exercised in conformity with the laws of the United States, so far as such laws are suitable to carry the same into effect; but in all cases where they are not adapted to the object, or are deficient in the provisions necessary to furnish suitable remedies and punish offenses against law, the common law, as modified and changed by the constitution and statutes of the State wherein the court having jurisdiction of such civil or criminal cause is held, so far as the same is not inconsistent with the Constitution and laws of the United States, shall be extended to and govern the said courts in the trial and disposition of the cause, and, if it is of a criminal nature, in the infliction of punishment of the party found guilty.

Under this provision, the Supreme Court has held that § 1983 is "deficient" because of its silence respecting a statute of limitations and the survival of § 1983 actions, and that recourse must be made to state law to supply rules for these matters. Lower courts have read § 1988 to require resort to state law to supply rules for indemnity and contribution and other matters. Resort to state law under § 1988 is said to be improper only when state law is "inconsistent" with the purposes of § 1983. Nevertheless, it is difficult to predict safely when the Court will invoke § 1988 and look to state law to fill in the gaps in § 1983, and when it will choose to interpret § 1983's silences and/or develop federal common law to fill them in.

A. Choice of Law in Federal Litigation

The choice-of-law problem in federal courts is not unique to § 1983 litigation. Any time a federal claim for relief is litigated in a federal court, choice-of-law problems arise because federal statutes are rarely gap-less. For example, federal statutes may lack provisions for limitations periods, or for indemnity and contribution among violators, and they may include terms (such as the term "children" in the federal copyright statute, or "partnership" in the federal tax code) that lack precise definition. The Rules of Decision Act, 28 U.S.C.A. § 1652, states that when federal law does not otherwise require or provide, state laws shall supply the "rules of decision" in cases where they apply. This provision might be thought (and once was thought) to supply a gap-filling mechanism for some matters such as statutes of limitations for federal laws that lacked them. Campbell v. Haverhill (1895) (patent statutes); O'Sullivan v. Felix (1914) (§ 1983). But the modern Supreme Court has generally assumed that when the federal statute on which a party sues is silent in some material respect, the courts must engage in a process of statutory interpretation to resolve ambiguities, including filling in otherwise irresolvable silences with judge-made federal common law.

Sometimes, this interpretive/federal common law process results in the creation of uniform (judge-made) rules; other times, the Court borrows state law, resulting in non-uniform (but still federal, judge-made) rules. When state law is selected in this latter manner, it is said to be applicable as a matter of federal law. It is therefore a question of "choice" to borrow state law, not a matter of compulsion. The choice between a uniform federal rule and borrowing of state law is made depending on a number of factors. Weighing in favor of a uniform rule may be the strength of the federal interests, the need for interstate uniformity, and the ease of fashioning a uniform judge-made rule. Counterweights may include the parties' expectations that local law would apply, the local governmental interests in the adoption of non-uniform (i.e., state) rules, and the ease of borrowing a ready-made set of state rules.

For example, when the federal government is a lender to a local farmer, and a question arises respecting the priority of the government's lien, should a state's commercial law regarding lien priority apply, or should a special uniform rule be created? While a uniform federal rule creates interstate uniformity on behalf of the federal government, it may create disuniformity within a state between federal governmental loans and analogous non-governmental loans and upset reasonable expectations of borrowers and lenders. On the other hand, while the choosing of state law will create *intra*state uniformity, it may create *inter*state disuniformity for the federal government (the rule for it may be different in different states) and potentially erode federal interests. United States v. Kimbell Foods, Inc. (1979). The perennial difficulty is to decide which set of disuniformities is to be preferred in particular contexts.

B. Choice of Law in § 1983 Actions: Section 1988

In § 1983 litigation, this choice-of-law process is complicated by the presence of § 1988, set forth above. In Robertson v. Wegmann (1978), the Court was faced with the problem of the "survival" of a federal court § 1983 action when the plaintiff died after his suit was filed. The original plaintiff, Clay Shaw, had sued (in federal court) the district attorney of New Orleans, Jim Garrison and others who acted in concert with him, for damages and injunctive relief arising out of a malicious prosecution of Shaw in connection with the assassination of President John F. Kennedy. Shaw had been acquitted of murder charges in a first state court criminal trial, but was then prosecuted a second time, for supposed perjury in the first trial. The second trial was enjoined when the federal district court (and later the Fifth Circuit) found that Garrison's second prosecution was a bad faith criminal proceeding brought for purposes of personal gain and with no reasonable expectation of success. Shaw died, however, leaving no relatives. The executor of Shaw's estate then sought to maintain the § 1983 damages action upon Shaw's death.

1. Deficiencies in Federal Law

There is no provision in § 1983 for the survival of an action in favor of another upon the death of the § 1983 plaintiff. This silence or "deficiency" might mean that whenever a victim of unconstitutional action dies, there should never be survival of the action in anyone. Alternatively, federal courts might feel the need to develop a uniform standard for § 1983, lest constitutional rights go systematically unremedied. On the other hand, most states have some version of a survival statute that will allow other persons, sometimes the executor of a decedent's estate, to prosecute civil actions that belonged to the decedent. Louisiana law was not terribly unusual in that respect. It allowed survival of tort claims ("personal actions") in favor of a spouse, children, parents, or siblings; otherwise, the claim abated.

The Supreme Court concluded that § 1988 controlled the question of survival of § 1983 actions (although no one seems to have argued that it did not). Section 1988, concluded the court, broke down the choice of law question into three subsidiary inquiries: (1) Was there a deficiency in § 1983?; (2) Did state law speak to the deficiency?; (3) Was state law inconsistent with the policies underlying § 1983? With respect to the first question, the Court concluded that § 1983 was "deficient" within the meaning of § 1988, for the simple reason that neither § 1983 nor any other federal statute expressly provided for the survival of § 1983 actions.

2. Requiring Resort to State Law

As its second step, the Court read § 1988 as requiring that reference be made to state law— here, state statutory law that modified what might have been any pre-existing "common-law" rule. But the selection of state law was not a matter of choice as in the usual federal-common-law process. Rather, it was a matter of compulsion under the directive of § 1988. Of course, directing the federal court to select state statutory law does not answer the additional question of *which* law of the state a court should adopt, if there is more than one obvious candidate. But in the case of the survival of actions in Louisiana, there was only one.

In addition, because there was a controlling state statute, the Court in *Robertson* managed to avoid answering the question of whether § 1988's requirement that a federal court first look to "the common law" when federal law is deficient meant that it must look to relevant state common law, in the absence of a controlling state statute. Section 1988 was enacted prior to Erie R.R. Co. v. Tompkins (1938), which debunked the notion of a "general" common law, divorced from some specific state's common law. A possible interpretation, therefore, would be that the reference in § 1988 was to the then still-in-vogue general common law, and not to any particular state's common law. The *Robertson* Court was able to avoid the question, however, because, no matter how the phrase "common law" might be interpreted in § 1988, the common law in this case had been "modified and changed by . . .

statute[].'' And § 1988 rather unambiguously declares that such state statutory modifications of the common law (however defined) would control.

3. "Inconsistencies" with § 1983 or Federal Law

(a) Abatement and "Inconsistency"

The *Robertson* Court concluded in the third part of its analysis under § 1988 that it could ignore state law only if state statute law was "inconsistent" with the policies underlying § 1983. It found, unlike the lower courts, that nothing in the policies of § 1983 would be compromised by the application of the state's statutory law of abatement. Neither the possibility that § 1983 actions would be governed by 50 different survival laws depending on where they were maintained, nor the provisions of Louisiana's law in particular, would interfere with § 1983's general goals of compensation for constitutional harm.

Louisiana's laws were not that different from the laws in other states, and were actually more generous than the old nineteenth-century common-law rule of automatic abatement of all personal injury claims. And Shaw's lack of relatives was shared, said the Court, only by "few persons." Because most such claims would ordinarily survive, state officials would still be deterred from clearly illegal actions by the prospect of a § 1983 suit. As the Court observed, "[a] state statute cannot be considered 'inconsistent' with federal law merely because the statute causes the plaintiff to lose the litigation." The Court might also have noted that the underlying constitutional norm did not go unvindicated in Shaw's case, because there had been injunctive relief against the bad faith prosecution, as allowed for by Younger v. Harris (1971). See Chapter 14. Moreover, given various personal immunities, it is often the case that many individual constitutional violations go uncompensated even when the plaintiff (or his cause of action) survives.

In contrast, in the context of implied constitutional actions against federal officials (which exist apart from § 1983 or any statute at all—see Chapter 17), the Court has concluded that a uniform federal common law rule of survival, rather than state law, is appropriate. Of course, in that context, the Court is not hamstrung by the limitations of § 1988. And perhaps there is a stronger argument for a uniform rule for claim-survival when the constitutional violation is by a federal official, rather than a state or local official. But it is at least odd that the federal courts might have less freedom to develop federal common law in § 1983 actions against official wrongdoing than in other constitutional tort cases because of the perceived command of § 1988.

(b) Examples of Inconsistency

In the last part of its analysis, the *Robertson* Court suggested limits on its reasoning. Section 1988 mandates resort to state law only if it is not "inconsistent" with federal law or the Constitution. It therefore stated that a different case would be presented if there were no survival of any tort claims at all under state law, or if there were only minimal survival provisions. Such a possibility, suggested the Court, might place too great a burden on the vindication of rights under § 1983. In addition, it stated that if the death of the § 1983 plaintiff was itself caused by the deprivation of federal rights, state abatement rules might have to be ignored. Otherwise, state or local officials would have the perverse incentive (inconsistent, presumably, with § 1983) to finish off the victims of their unconstitutional action. Some lower courts have sensibly ignored state law in such circumstances. Jaco v. Bloechle (6th Cir.1984). And in still other contexts, courts have largely rejected state-law caps on damages and other state-law limitations that would not allow for a fully compensatory remedy under § 1983. See Chapter 9.

4. The Uncertainty of § 1988's Applicability

As noted above, the Court does not always resort to § 1988 to fill in § 1983's silences. Sometimes it engages in ordinary statutory interpretation to give meaning to phrases such as "under color of" law, or suable "persons," or what it means to "cause" a deprivation. Still other times, the Court appears to have developed uniform judge-made rules with respect to such matters as the availability of compensatory or punitive damages, the personal immunities of officers, and the enforceability of so-called release-dismissal agreements as to which § 1983 is silent. Town of Newton v. Rumery (1987).

Sometimes gaps in § 1983 stay unfilled, as a matter of federal common law, even when state law would supply a workable rule of decision. For example, § 1983 has no provision for indemnity and contribution among defendants and is therefore arguably "deficient" (within the meaning of *Robertson*) with respect to such matters. Although some lower federal courts have looked to state tort law to fill this gap, others have refused to adopt state law *or* to develop an affirmative federal rule of indemnity and contribution. In so doing, of course, these federal courts are creating a federal common law rule of no indemnity and contribution in § 1983 actions. Cf. Texas Indus. v. Radcliff Materials (1981)(reaching similar result in antitrust litigation).

Perhaps the Court means to have § 1988 apply only to the more "procedural" silences in section § 1983 (for which federal law supplies no ready gap-filler, and concerning which states typically have already addressed by statute), and to use uniform federal law to govern the more arguably "substantive" aspects of § 1983. One difficulty with this explanation is that § 1988 itself refers to "remedies" as subject to § 1988's command to apply state law, and yet the Court does not seem to feel bound by § 1988 when it comes to questions of remedies (such as the standard for compensatory or punitive damages). Perhaps § 1983 is not "deficient" here, because federal common law can be (and has sometimes been) developed to fill in these gaps. But if that is true, then arguably federal law would never be "deficient," within the meaning of § 1988, because such federal common lawmaking can always be resorted to in the first instance to fill in § 1983's silences, including a silence like that for the survival of claims.

In short, it is difficult to know when courts will require resort to § 1988, and with it the presumptive applicability of state law, or when it will conclude, for one reason or another, that federal law is not deficient. Perhaps the inexact procedural/substantive distinction noted above accurately describes what the courts are actually doing in most cases, with an awareness that remedies are no longer—as they may have been in the nineteenth century—a simple matter of procedure to be filled in by reference to state law. But at least some areas are predictably governed by state law, such as survival of § 1983 claims, and statutes of limitations, as discussed in the following section.

C. Statutes of Limitations

1. State Court Analogies

The Supreme Court has also concluded that § 1983, like many federal statutes, is "deficient" as to a statute of limitations, and has therefore required resort to state law under § 1988. Board of Regents v. Tomanio (1980). Interestingly, the Court did so only after its decision in *Robertson*. Previously, the Court had resorted to state law for a statute of limitations for § 1983 as matter of federal common law, not § 1988. Johnson v. Railway Express

Agency, Inc. (1975). The three-step process outlined in *Robertson* has, in turn, been held to require federal courts hearing a § 1983 action arising in a particular state to adopt the statute of limitations for the most analogous action based on state law. "By adopting the statute governing an analogous cause of action under state law, federal law incorporates the state's judgment on the proper balance between the policies of repose and the substantive policies of enforcement embodied in the [analogous] state cause of action." Wilson v. Garcia (1985).

Nevertheless, because particular § 1983 actions might be analogized to more than one state-law cause of action, with great loss of predictability even within a state, the Court has also concluded that § 1983's purposes are best furthered by the federal courts' selection of a single ("the one most appropriate") state statute in each state for *all* § 1983 actions. For example, a § 1983 plaintiff's claim that he was unlawfully arrested and beaten might appear to be covered by possibly distinct state statutes of limitations governing false arrest, assault and battery, a specific statute governing claims against police officials for their torts, or even by a general statute for personal injuries. Such were the choices in *Wilson, supra.* Yet another § 1983 case might involve a claim of race discrimination in student admissions by a public university which might be analogized to breach of contract, intentional infliction of emotional distress, or other tortious harms.

Obviously, many of the state limitations periods arguably relevant to the police beating case would be manifestly inappropriate for the discrimination case. But the Supreme Court's admonition that there be a single state statute for *all* § 1983 claims arising in a particular state has all but forced lower courts to choose a statute that is the least common denominator, i.e., the state limitations statute for the recovery of damages for personal injuries. The Court also perceived that the personal injury analogy was consistent with § 1983's underlying purposes because a general personal injury statute would tend to cover the "broad range of potential tort analogies, from injuries to property to infringements of individual liberty." Thus, if brought as § 1983 claims, the police abuse case and the discrimination case (described above) would both be governed by the state's general personal injury limitations period.

But what happens when a state also has more than one generally applicable tort or personal injury statute? In Owens v. Okure (1989), there was a state statute for intentional torts and a (longer) residual statute governing personal injury actions. The Court, driven by *Wilson*'s search for the most general of the statutes of limitations, opted for the latter, and directed federal courts in the future to do the same. Thus, federal courts entertaining § 1983 actions must borrow "the general or residual statute for personal injury actions" when there are multiple statutes of limitations for personal injury, even ahead of one as general as an intentional tort provision. As a result, the police beating and the discrimination hypothetical described above would still be governed by the same statute of limitations.

2. Tolling and Accrual

Tolling (i.e., interruption) of the statute of limitations in § 1983 actions is governed by state law. *Tomanio, supra.* If the applicable state statute would be interrupted for some reason, then it will be interrupted in the § 1983 context as well. Indeed, the Court has suggested that other, specific tolling provisions may be applicable to the general personal injury statute of limitations that federal courts must look to. In Hardin v. Straub (1989), for example, the Court upheld the applicability of a particular state tolling rule in § 1983 cases, despite the fact that the state tolling provision was for prisoner-suits only.

Nevertheless, the question of when a state statute of limitations commences to run on a § 1983 action in the first instance ("accrual") is governed by federal law, not state law. Chardon v. Fernandez (1981). In *Chardon*, the Court concluded in an employment discrimination case filed under § 1983 that the relevant limitations period did not start at the time of discharge (as it might have under some states' laws), but at the moment when the plaintiff first learned that he was going to be terminated. The only justification for this particular twist must be the insight that the question of when a constitutional claim arises has a primarily federal rather than state dimension to it. In any event, it is an easy mistake to assume that state law regarding the commencement of a state statute of limitations will govern in federal § 1983 actions. State law may supply the statute of limitations, but federal law says when it begins to run.

3. Inconsistency

As noted above, § 1988 does not require the application of state law when state law would be "inconsistent" with federal law. That proviso applies as well to state statutes of limitations. For example, a state statute that provided a shorter period specifically for § 1983 claims would presumably be ignored as inconsistent with federal law, insofar as it discriminated against § 1983 actions. Cf. Felder v. Casey (1988) (discussed in Chapter 13). And in any event, it is unlikely that such a § 1983–specific statute would qualify as the most general personal injury statute of limitations available. In turn, most general personal injury statutes are not likely to be inconsistent with the purposes of § 1983 insofar as they might often be the most generous of the potentially applicable state provisions. In one pre-*Wilson* case (i.e., a case decided before the Supreme Court opted for a single state-limitations period), the Court refused to apply a state's six-month limitations period for filing discrimination claims before a state agency as the relevant statute for a § 1983 claim alleging race discrimination against a public employer. Burnett v. Grattan (1984). The Court concluded that the short fuse in the agency statutes was "manifestly inconsistent" with the goals of § 1983. After *Wilson*, however, it is unlikely that the specialized six-month provision would even have been the right statute to look to in the first place.

D.   Federal Statutes of Limitation?

In 1990, Congress enacted a four-year catch-all statute of limitations applicable to "civil action[s] arising under an act of Congress enacted after" December 1, 1990, if the underlying act lacked its own limitations period. 28 U.S.C.A. § 1658. In most § 1983 litigation, this catch-all statute would appear to be inapplicable. But § 1983 provides a remedy for violations of federal statutes by persons acting under color of law (see Chapter 5). It is therefore at least arguable that, if the underlying statute being enforced in a § 1983 action was itself enacted after December 1, 1990, and lacks its own limitations period, then the congressional catch-all supplies the relevant limitation period. Recently, Court made this very suggestion. City of Rancho Palos Verdes v. Abrams (2005). In *Rancho Palos Verdes*, the plaintiff sought to enforce a violation of the 1996 Telecommunications Act against a municipality through § 1983. Noting that the Court had previously held that the four year limitations period applied to "all claims 'made possible by a post–1990 [congressional] enactment,'" the *Rancho Palos Verdes* Court stated in a footnote that "§ 1658 would seem to apply" the the plaintiff's § 1983 claim enforcing the Telecommunications Act.

E.   Attorney's Fees

Finally, note that with respect to awards of attorney's fees in § 1983 actions, federal law is not deficient. In the Civil Rights Attorney's Fees Awards Act of 1976, Congress expressly allowed for a version of "loser-pays" fee shifting in suits brought under a host of civil rights statutes, including § 1983. Absent that statute, the so-called American Rule (which requires each side to pay its own attorney's fees) would have controlled in § 1983 actions in federal court. The attorney's fee statute was, interestingly, added as a new paragraph of 42 U.S.C.A. § 1988, and is discussed in Chapter 11.

CHAPTER 13

SECTION 1983 IN THE STATE COURTS

Overview

Section 1983 actions are not within the exclusive jurisdiction of the federal courts. Therefore, state courts may hear them as well. Moreover, state courts may be obligated to hear § 1983 actions if they hear analogous claims under state law. And when a § 1983 case is brought in state court, federal substantive law will control as a matter of the Supremacy Clause, even if state law is to the contrary. Thus, for example, whether a municipality is a suable "person" under § 1983 is a question of federal law and not a question of state law. Similarly, most of the remedies associated with § 1983, including compensatory and punitive damages (as well as related immunities), and the availability of attorney's fees, should also be available in the state courts, state law to the contrary notwithstanding. Nevertheless, state courts are ordinarily free to apply their own reasonable procedural rules to § 1983 cases, provided that the procedures do not discriminate against § 1983 claims by treating them worse than analogous actions under state law, and provided that the state procedures do not unduly

burden the vindication of rights accorded by
§ 1983.

A. State Court Powers and Duties

Although § 1983 was designed as a first line of
federal protection against unconstitutional state action, litigants may bring their § 1983 claims in
state court if they choose. In Martinez v. California
(1980), the Supreme Court held that federal courts
do not have exclusive jurisdiction over § 1983
claims, and that state courts have concurrent jurisdiction to hear them as well, at least when the
state's jurisdictional rules would be up to the task.

The conclusion makes sense. Neither § 1983 nor
its jurisdictional provision, 28 U.S.C.A. § 1343(3),
contains the express language of exclusive federal
jurisdiction which would ordinarily be required for
a finding that Congress had withdrawn power from
the state courts to hear particular lawsuits. Nor is
there any reason why § 1983 actions should be
held impliedly exclusive, especially when concurrent jurisdiction helps the victims of unconstitutional action by allowing them to choose the more
convenient forum. Like any federal cause of action
however, a § 1983 suit filed in state court can be
removed by the defendant to federal court. In many
cases, therefore, the § 1983 action will be litigated
in state court only when both parties have refused
to exercise their option to go to federal court. Compare Nevada v. Hicks (2001) (concluding that Tribal courts cannot entertain Native American's
§ 1983 suit against state game warden for alleged

constitutional violation in serving search warrant on tribal property).

But beyond the question of state court capacity to hear such claims is the question of state court obligation to hear them. As with claims under other federal statutes, the Supreme Court has held that state courts are under an obligation to hear § 1983 claims when they would hear analogous actions under state law. Howlett v. Rose (1990). In *Howlett*, the State of Florida refused to entertain a § 1983 action against a local school board and three of its officials arguing that it lacked jurisdiction over such claims because of state sovereign immunity. The state court's argument of purported lack of jurisdiction was rejected, primarily because the Supreme Court found that state courts would entertain similar state-law claims against school boards for the torts of their officers. Florida's refusal to hear analogous § 1983 actions therefore impermissibly discriminated against the bringing of § 1983 claims.

To the extent that Florida might have been contending that local entities were not suable in state court in a § 1983 action because of state sovereign immunity law, it was also mistaken. The Court stated that the question of suability under § 1983 was not a question of state law at all, but one of federal substantive law. The Court had elsewhere concluded, as a matter of statutory interpretation, that local entities were among the "persons" suable under § 1983. See Chapter 6. And it had also concluded that municipal liability could be imposed for the unconstitutional harm inflicted by city employees when they acted pursuant to some law, custom, or policy of the city. Florida law respecting when a local entity could be held liable under § 1983 was therefore simply irrelevant under the Supremacy Clause. U.S. Const. art. VI, cl. 1. (Recall, however, that states are not suable "persons" under § 1983, thus making them no more suable in a state court than a federal court, even if they happened to consent to suit.)

Howlett highlights how federal law controls in § 1983 actions brought in state court as a matter of straightforward application of the Supremacy Clause. First, the Supremacy Clause controls state jurisdictional choices absent a valid, nondiscriminatory jurisdictional excuse. Second, the Supremacy Clause controls questions surrounding the interpretation of § 1983, such as who is a suable "person." Third, the Supremacy Clause controls substantive questions surrounding the interpretation of the underlying constitutional (or statutory) right that a litigant is seeking to enforce through the vehicle of § 1983, such as whether the free speech rights of the plaintiff were violated.

In addition, certain of the substantive gaps in § 1983 have been filled in by what can best be called judge-made federal common law, such as the applicability and scope of individual officer immunities. See Chapter 8. Those substantive principles should also be controlled by federal, rather than state law, when § 1983 claims are litigated in the state courts. At other times, however, gaps in § 1983 have been filled in by reference to state law under the perceived command of 42 U.S.C.A. § 1988(a), such as statutes of limitations and the survival of § 1983 actions upon the death of the plaintiff. Chapter 12. When suit is brought in state court, state law will still fill in these relevant gaps, although it must be applied consistently with federal law. See below at p. 271.

B. Procedures and Remedies in State Courts

A recurring question respecting § 1983 litigation brought in state court is the extent to which litigants must adhere to state procedures and related requirements. This particular question, in turn, comprises a subset of a more general question encountered in Federal Courts law: When a litigant chooses to file her federal claim in state court, to what extent must she take state courts as she finds them? Dice v. Akron, C. & Y.R. Co. (1952). If particular procedures and remedies would be available in federal court, should they be equally available in state court? The tension is between the supremacy and uniform enforcement of federal law on the one hand, and, on the other hand, the respect that is owed to state judicial institutions as autonomous structures for resolving disputes which the parties have chosen to bring before them.

Over time, in response to the more general question, the Court has been inclined to allow state procedural rules to operate unless they discriminate against the enforcement of federal rights or unless alternative federal procedures were expressly or implicitly made "part and parcel" of the underlying federal right, and application of state law would somehow unduly burden the vindication of that federal right. Arguably, somewhat less deference to state procedures seems to have developed in the particular context of state court litigation of § 1983 cases.

1. Undue Procedural Burdens

For example, the State of Wisconsin required anyone suing a police officer or municipality for damages in state court to give notice of the claim to them 120 days before filing suit (or show that the defendants had actual knowledge of the claims). Like similar provisions in other states, the statute was designed to allow for pre-suit settlement and to reduce lawsuits against such defendants. In Felder v. Casey (1988), the Court held that the state statute could not be applied to a § 1983 action filed in state court. The Court stated that the state statute imposed a kind of exhaustion requirement on the § 1983 plaintiff in violation of precedents declaring that exhaustion of state remedies was not a prerequisite to a § 1983 action. See Chapter 2.

Of course, those decisions dealt with the question whether exhaustion of state remedies was a prerequisite to access to *federal* court, not state court. Perhaps it would therefore have made sense to say that state pre-filing requirements could not hold up one's access to a federal forum if that is where the plaintiff wanted to file her § 1983 suit, but that reasonable state procedures would have to be followed when the question was access to the state judicial system which the plaintiff had voluntarily chosen to enter. That is, the plaintiff should take the bitter with the sweet. Nevertheless, the *Felder* Court suggested that one of the rights that § 1983 protected was immediate access to a judicial forum, whether it was state or federal, free from any administrative exhaustion requirement. If that indeed is part and parcel of what § 1983 protects, then Wisconsin's notice-of-claim requirement clearly imposed an undue burden on the exercise of that right.

2. Discriminatory Procedures

Even more controversially, the Court in *Felder* concluded that Wisconsin's exhaustion requirement discriminated against claims under § 1983 by singling out suits against government and its officials for the notice-of-claim provision, whose purpose was to curb such litigation. To be sure, § 1983 suits were treated worse than most tort suits against most defendants in Wisconsin. Yet the state statute prohibited the immediate filing of, not just § 1983 claims, but any action based on state law that was brought against public defendants. So, at one relevant level of generality, there was no discrimination between § 1983 suits and other state-law suits against public officials and local governments. Consequently, the charge that Wisconsin "discriminated" against § 1983 actions is doubtful.

Issues similar to *Felder* have arisen in the context of interlocutory appeals in the state courts. Some courts have allowed for interlocutory appeals of pre-trial rejections of official immunity defenses (consistent with federal practice), while others have not. The Court, however, unanimously held that states are not obligated to provide an immediate appeal for such issues, at least when state practice generally disallows them. Johnson v. Fankell (1997). According to *Fankell*, the official's substantive rights can be fully vindicated on appeal, post-trial, although the Court had pretty clearly concluded the opposite for federal court § 1983 litigation. Behrens v. Pelletier (1996); cf. Mitchell v. Forsyth (1985) (action against federal official). In fact, the Court had stated explicitly that qualified immunity partook not only of a defense to liability, but a right "not to stand trial." *Behrens, supra. Fankell* is also in some tension with the liberal view articulated in *Felder, supra*, as to which state procedures qualify as being "inconsistent" with matters that are "part and parcel" of the substance of the § 1983 claim or defense. But *Fankell* notwithstanding, if a state's court system generally provides for some interlocutory appeals of right, then such a state may still be obliged to provide interlocutory appeals to § 1983 defendants to review the pre-trial denial of an immunity defense. The procedural nondiscrimination rationale of *Felder* would argue for nothing less.

3. Attorney's Fees and Other Remedies

The Court has unproblematically concluded that attorney's fees are available in state court under the 1976 Civil Rights Attorney's Fees Awards Act, 42 U.S.C. § 1988(b), even when the state courts would not otherwise recognize fee shifting. Maine v. Thiboutot (1980). Conversely, were a state to implement its own version of a two-way loser-pays rule for state court litigation (applicable alike to plaintiffs and defendants), it is questionable whether the rule, if in conflict with the Court's current reading of § 1988(b), could properly be applied to § 1983 litigation. The irony here, of course, is that § 1988(b) itself reads like a two-way fee-shifting rule, but it has been construed otherwise. In addition, as suggested above, the Court has also concluded that monetary damages can be available against a municipality under § 1983 even though state immunity doctrines would suggest otherwise. *Howlett, supra.*

Indeed, it is probably the case that nearly all monetary and injunctive remedies that would be available in a federal court should be available in a state court § 1983 action, and generally under the same standards as would be applicable in a federal court. Admittedly, under ordinary conflict of laws rules, questions of remedy are often pigeon-holed as "procedural," and considerable freedom is given to a forum state to ignore another state's remedial rules even when enforcing that other state's cause of action. But questions of remedy are not so easily conceptualized as procedural versus substantive when they stretch across state-federal jurisdictional lines.

To choose one example, state statutes of limitations are applicable in federal diversity actions based on state law, even though one state court might legitimately apply its own statute of limitations to a claim based on another state's law. To choose another example, federal statutory double-damages provisions have been held applicable in state courts hearing federal claims (at least when the state courts entertained analogous actions already), even though the state court might otherwise legitimately refuse to apply another state's statutory-penalties or punitive damages rules. The first example is the result of the command of Erie R.R. Co. v. Tompkins (1938); the second example is said to be a result of "converse *Erie.*"

Nevertheless, state courts that have dealt with the problem have been all over the map. For a while, some states surprisingly concluded that punitive damages in state court § 1983 actions were not governed by federal standards. E.g., Boulder Valley Sch. Dist. R–2 v. Price (Colo.1991) (burden of proof), *overruled in* Community Hosp. v. Fail (Colo. 1998); Ricard v. State (La.1980), *overruled in* Booze v. City of Alexandria (La.1994). The U.S. Supreme Court has yet to speak, but it is hard to imagine that the availability of punitive damages and the relevant burdens of proof would not be considered "part and parcel" of the underlying substantive rights associated with § 1983.

4. Pleading

A last set of "converse *Erie*" examples has to do with pleading. The federal courts have concluded that there is no general "heightened pleading" requirement in the federal courts for § 1983 claims.

Leatherman v. Tarrant County Narcotics Intelligence and Coordination Unit (1993); see also Chapter 18. And over a half century ago, over a forceful dissent by Justice Frankfurter, the Supreme Court concluded that a state court could not apply its own strict pleading rules to a case brought in state court under the Federal Employers' Liability Act. Brown v. Western Ry. (1949). Arguably, therefore, a state might not be able to apply its own strict pleading requirements to § 1983 cases brought in its own courts, at least if the Supreme Court were prepared to conclude, as it questionably did in *Brown*, that such requirements unduly burden the vindication of federal rights.

C. Section 1988, Gap–Filling, and State Courts

As noted above, when § 1983 litigation takes place in the federal courts, some of the gaps in federal law are filled in by reference to state law under the command of § 1988. It is possible to read § 1988 as a command to federal courts only and not to state courts when it comes to gap filling. But when § 1983 cases are litigated in state courts it may well be that sometimes the state law that state courts must apply is the state law that the federal courts would have applied under § 1988. For example, the Court has concluded under § 1988 that § 1983 actions in federal court are to be governed by the state's general statute of limitations for personal injury suits. Chapter 12. Were a state court to hear a § 1983 claim for a discriminatory firing of a government employee, the state court arguably must choose the applicable state statute of limitations consistent with that admonition. In other words, it may not conclude that another (for example, a more specific) limitations period is more appropriate as a matter of state law for such claims.

D. Displacement of § 1983 by State Remedies

Finally, note that not all § 1983 litigation is brought in state court voluntarily. Sometimes, litigants are told to repair to state court because the federal courthouse door is blocked. Constitutional challenges to state taxes and ratemaking are perhaps the two most conspicuous examples where Congress has placed jurisdictional limits on the federal courts. 28 U.S.C.A. §§ 1341–1342; Chapter 15. In fact, it was on direct review of a decision from state court in which the Supreme Court concluded that a dormant Commerce Clause action for damages claiming that state tax collection efforts discriminated against interstate commerce could be brought as a § 1983 suit. Dennis v. Higgins (1991).

The obvious benefit to bringing such a suit as a § 1983 action was the availability of attorney's fees in the event of a successful challenge. But *Dennis* opened a hornets' nest of potential problems. If a § 1983 remedy was available to recover taxes wrongfully assessed by the state, perhaps recovery was possible directly against the state treasury. Yet in Will v. Michigan Dept. of State Police (1989), the Court had concluded that under § 1983 as written, states could not be made defendants—not even in state court. Perhaps the relevant tax collecting official was the proper party defendant in the § 1983 action. But if the latter was true, then the collector might be able to assert qualified immunity for his good faith reliance on the constitutionality of the taxing statute. If so, then actual recovery of unconstitutionally assessed taxes might not be possible, despite the clear message of *Dennis*.

The Court managed to finesse most of these problems when, just a few years after *Dennis*, it unanimously concluded that § 1983 actions were not ordinarily available in state courts to challenge unconstitutionally assessed state taxes so long as the state had its own meaningful post-deprivation refund procedure. National Private Truck Council, Inc. v. Oklahoma Tax Comm'n (1995). Thus, where a state supplied its own refund procedure under state law for the recoupment of unconstitutionally assessed taxes, a § 1983 remedy would not be available, even in state court. The principle, said the Supreme Court, was one of comity, driven by the same respect for state procedures that prompted Congress to enact the Tax Injunction Act in the first place. *Truck Council* means that no § 1983 case would today have been possible in a case such as *Dennis* if a state court refund procedure were in place—the very case that allowed dormant Commerce Clause challenges to be brought under § 1983. Based on *Truck Council*—a tax case—it is likely that the Court would conclude that a similar limitation attaches to efforts to bring a § 1983 action in state court addressing unconstitutional rates.

CHAPTER 14

PRECLUSION AND § 1983

Overview

Given the varied contexts in which § 1983 litigation can arise, a § 1983 lawsuit may often be precluded as to some issues or claims because of prior adjudication. For example, problems of issue preclusion may arise if the § 1983 plaintiff was previously a defendant in a state court criminal proceeding in which issues that are now the subject of her § 1983 challenge were decided against her. Similarly, a § 1983 plaintiff may face problems associated with claim preclusion if she previously brought suit in state court on state law grounds as to some aspect of the official action which she later challenges on federal grounds. Initial pursuit of state administrative remedies may sometimes compromise a later-filed § 1983 action as well.

The source of the difficulty in most of these contexts is the Full Faith and Credit Act, 28 U.S.C.A. § 1738, which commands federal courts (and state courts) to give the "same" preclusive effect to prior state court judgments that the judgment-rendering state court would give them. Thus, the availability of a federal forum for the de novo consideration of federal claims and issues under

274

§ 1983 is not always available. Nevertheless, most collateral challenges to state court convictions brought under federal habeas corpus are not subject to the usual rules of preclusion. (The complex relationship between § 1983 and habeas corpus is discussed in Chapter 16.) But preclusion-like difficulties face those who bring § 1983 actions that will necessarily call into question their earlier convictions in state court.

A. Issue Preclusion

1. State Court Proceedings

Consider the factual background in a case such as Monroe v. Pape (1961): A § 1983 plaintiff whose home has been ransacked by the police sues the individual officers for their violations of his Fourth Amendment right to be free from unreasonable searches and seizures. *Monroe* itself suggested that state court remedies need not be inadequate or first tried out as a precondition to federal relief. But suppose that, prior to the trial of his § 1983 action, Mr. Monroe had been prosecuted in state court for possession of drugs that were found in his house during the search. And suppose further that, as the defendant in the state court action, Monroe timely raised the Fourth Amendment question in an effort to suppress the fruits of the search and that he litigated and lost on the question. The drugs were admitted in evidence, and Monroe was convicted. Perhaps Monroe believes that the state courts were mistaken in their assessment of whether the search violated the Fourth Amendment. He could then pursue the issue on direct review in the state court system, and if no relief was forthcoming, he could seek discretionary appellate review in the U.S. Supreme Court. But how should the federal court respond in Monroe's § 1983 damages action if it believes the state courts were wrong in their assessment of the Fourth Amendment issue?

The Supreme Court, in a case presenting almost identical facts as this hypothetical example, concluded that a federal court would have to deny a § 1983 plaintiff the opportunity to relitigate the issue of the legality of the search if a state court would also deny him the opportunity. Allen v. McCurry (1980). Under the full faith and credit statute, 28 U.S.C.A. § 1738, federal courts are required to give a state court judgment whatever preclusive effect a state court would give it. Many states following modern rules of preclusion would give a litigant who has had a full and fair opportunity to litigate a particular issue, which actually was litigated, and which was necessary to the earlier decision, no more than one round at litigating the issue. This could be true even though the party seeking to invoke preclusion in the later civil action is not precisely the same party against whom the § 1983 plaintiff was litigating in the criminal proceeding.

State preclusion rules may make allowances for changes in incentives in the litigation of a particular issue, or differences in procedural opportunities that are presented in different rounds of litigation. But the basic message from *Allen* is the same. If a state court, based on its own preclusion law, would preclude a litigant from re-raising an issue on which she had previously litigated and lost in state court, a federal court must do the same. Indeed, as discussed in § D, below, there may be additional principles that will prevent those who have been convicted from bringing damages actions over issues that were integral to a prior conviction. Heck v. Humphrey (1994). Thus, other barriers may keep some § 1983 litigants from proceeding, even if, for some reason, state preclusion law would not.

Accordingly, if Mr. Monroe would be unable to re-raise the search and seizure issue (on which he previously litigated and lost in his criminal proceeding) in a subsequently litigated tort action in state court, then he would be unable to do so in a federal court § 1983 damages action. Even if Monroe got to the federal court first, it would not help him, because in such cases the federal court would ordinarily abstain in favor of the pending state court proceeding based on principles of comity and federalism associated with the decision in Younger v. Harris (1971). See Chapter 15. It is typically the first-in-time decision, not the first-filed suit, that determines preclusive consequences. One might sensibly argue that Congress in enacting § 1983 meant to override ordinary preclusion rules because state courts and state-law enforcement proceedings were often the source of the very problems that § 1983 was meant to redress. But the argument was specifically rejected in *Allen*, largely on the basis of canons of statutory interpretation that frowned on repeals of prior legislation (such as § 1738) by implication rather than by express language.

Permutations on the problem would not change this basic message. If Mr. Monroe had had his conviction reversed in the state courts (for example, on non-Fourth Amendment grounds), but had still litigated and lost on the Fourth Amendment issue, he might still be precluded on the Fourth Amendment issue in his § 1983 action, at least if state law would still consider the issue to be precluded. If, by contrast, he had won on the issue in the state court criminal proceeding, things become more complicated. Collateral estoppel certainly allows a party who litigated and won on a particular issue to preclude the same party who litigated and lost on it from relitigating it in a later lawsuit. But due process ordinarily prevents imposing adverse consequences of collateral estoppel or issue preclusion against someone who was not a party to an earlier proceeding. If Monroe's § 1983 damages action proceeds on a theory of personal liability of the police officers, precluding them from litigating the lawfulness of the search would be troublesome. They were not, in any strict sense, parties to the state proceeding against Monroe that was prosecuted in the name of the state, or its people. It is therefore doubtful whether any state would or could allow for preclusive treatment of such issues against the individual officers in a subsequent § 1983 civil action.

2. State Administrative Proceedings

Preclusive fallout may arise from administrative proceedings that a plaintiff has invoked to remedy an alleged wrong, at least when those proceedings are judicial in nature. In University of Tennessee v. Elliott (1986), Elliott, a state university employee, voluntarily pursued administrative remedies within the university, arguing that his discharge was racially discriminatory. The administrative proceeding concluded that Elliott had not been discriminated against. Elliott's § 1983 suit (which had been filed before he pursued his administrative remedies) remained on hold while he pursued his state remedies. After his administrative claim of race discrimination was rejected, the federal district court dismissed Elliott's § 1983 Equal Protection claim on issue-preclusion grounds. The Supreme Court agreed. Although it did not believe that the preclusive effects of the administrative decision were necessarily governed by § 1738, the Court concluded that if factual findings made in a state administrative proceeding (which, the Court found, was judicial in nature) would be given preclusive effect in a later state court civil action, they should be given preclusive effect in a later-adjudicated § 1983 action as well.

The problem for litigants posed by *Elliott* is the difficult one of ascertaining when a state administrative proceeding is sufficiently "judicial" in nature that it might be given preclusive effect. When there is doubt, the decision counsels § 1983 litigants to by-pass a state's remedial administrative mechanisms that might provide a quick and inexpensive means of resolving a particular dispute, and instead counsels them to go immediately to federal court. Thus, not only is plaintiff-initiated exhaustion of state administrative remedies not required in most settings, *Elliott* indicates it is positively to be avoided in some circumstances.

Such an incentive is particularly problematic in a case such as *Elliott* in which the would-be § 1983 plaintiff also wished to pursue an employment discrimination claim under Title VII of the 1964 Civil Rights Act. In contrast to § 1983, Title VII actually *requires* exhaustion of available state administrative remedies (but gives them no preclusive effect in the later filed Title VII suit, so long as they remain unreviewed by state courts). In short, if a person in Elliott's position wants to preserve a preclusion-free federal forum for his § 1983 claim, he needs to think seriously about whether he should pursue state administrative remedies, even though the latter may be a prerequisite to possible state-law claims and perhaps, as in *Elliott* itself, to other federal claims. Of course, if the "judicial in nature" administrative procedures are coercive (i.e., not plaintiff-initiated), the would-be § 1983 plaintiff may have no choice in the matter. Because of abstention doctrines associated with coercive state administrative proceedings, the § 1983 plaintiff could conceivably be stuck with the answer given by the state system into which he has been haled. See Chapter 15.

Elliott should be distinguished, however, from the administrative proceedings that a party is obliged to invoke as a precondition to obtaining some benefit from the state, such as a license or a permit. In that setting, the administrative action may itself be the initial source of the constitutional harm that is being complained of (as distinguished from *Elliott*, where the administrative proceedings were designed to remedy a prior injury). And if so, preclusion should not prevent a de novo attack on the administrative decision under § 1983.

For example, a party who has sought a building permit from a state agency may wish to claim that the denial was a result of racial discrimination or some other violation of federal law. When that is the case, the party should be able to have immediate access to a federal court in a § 1983 proceeding against the proper defendants, free of any notion of "preclusion." This result should follow even if the administrative proceeding adhered to the quasi-judicial requirements demanded by procedural due process, and even if the state courts provide a state court forum for "appeal" of the agency's decision.

This result is strongly suggested by the non-§ 1983 decision in City of Chicago v. International College of Surgeons (1997). There the Court upheld federal jurisdiction on removal of federal-law and state-law challenges to an agency's denial of a building demolition permit. The removed proceeding had originally been filed in state court by the party denied the permit, under state statutory review procedures. Even though state law required that

the reviewing court give the agency deference on
one of the state-law based challenges, the Supreme
Court indicated that the federal court could apply
similar deference if needed. Preclusion went unmentioned, and the Court was right to ignore it. It
makes sense to view judicial review of this sort of
agency action as an original proceeding in the federal courts to which preclusion does not attach. Indeed, it is at least arguable that, in light of *College
of Surgeons*, *Elliott* got it wrong and the federal
court should have been able to review the state's
administrative action in *Elliott* to the same extent
that a reviewing state court would have been able
to.

B.   Claim Preclusion

A litigant may believe that she has suffered injuries at the hands of state officials for which both
state law and federal law provide claims for relief.
One might suppose, therefore, that the state claim
could be pursued in state court and the § 1983
claim in federal court, either concurrently or con-
secutively. This common-sense approach is a recipe
for disaster, however. In Migra v. Warren City Sch.
Dist. Bd. of Ed. (1984), a dismissed public school-
teacher brought suit against various defendants in
state court for breach of contract arising out of
events that resulted in her termination. She litigated and won on her state-law claim in state court
and recovered damages for the breach. She then
sought to recover for other damages (including for
pain and suffering) in federal court in a § 1983

action arguing that her dismissal also violated the Equal Protection Clause of the Fourteenth Amendment. The Supreme Court concluded, however, that her federal claim would have to be dismissed if the preclusion rules of the state judicial system in which she had previously litigated her state-law claim would have considered her filing of two separate actions to be claim splitting.

Many states have modern "transactional" tests for claim splitting: If two claims for relief involving the same parties arise out of a common core of underlying events, a litigant may be obliged to bring them together in a single action. Failure to bring related claims in a single lawsuit may result in a later claim's being barred by res judicata or claim preclusion. Not all states have such modern approaches to the claim-splitting problem, but a federal court is obliged to do as a state court would do. So, if a state court would call it claim splitting not to bring related claims together, the federal court must do the same.

In this respect, it does not matter that the plaintiff might have litigated and won on certain issues involved in the prior state-law claim that overlap with the issues in the later-litigated § 1983 claim. The question in such cases is one of claim preclusion, not issue preclusion, and claim preclusion (unlike issue preclusion) can apply even as to unlitigated matters. Of course, in a jurisdiction that does not recognize modern, transactional claim-preclusion rules, it might be possible for the § 1983 plaintiff to preclude the defendant from relitigation of those *issues* on which the § 1983 defendant may have previously litigated and lost in the prior state court action. But in jurisdictions with transactional rules respecting claim splitting, it is self-defeating to file federal claims in federal court and state claims in state court, and not to file all related claims together in one court.

C. *Rooker-Feldman* and Related Doctrines

As discussed above, rules of preclusion can prohibit federal court reconsideration of matters already disposed of by state courts. Another set of principles that do not go under the label "preclusion" also bar federal court interference with state court decisionmaking in analogous ways. For example, a complex set of abstention principles dictate non-interference into ongoing state court enforcement proceedings. See Chapter 15. In addition, there is a set of jurisdictional principles that limits lower federal court interference with state court proceedings that have been concluded or brought to final judgment in the state courts. Those principles make up the so-called *Rooker-Feldman* doctrine. See Exxon Mobil Corp. v. Saudi Basic Indus. (2005).

In District of Columbia Court of Appeals v. Feldman (1983), individuals who were graduates of law schools not accredited by the ABA sought admission to the D.C. bar and a waiver of its accredited-law-school-degree requirement. They were denied waivers by the highest court for the District of Columbia. Instead of seeking review of the decision in the U.S. Supreme Court under 28 U.S.C.A. § 1257, the applicants brought suit in a federal district court raising a constitutional challenge to the denial of their waiver requests arguing that the denial was arbitrary and capricious.

The U.S. Supreme Court concluded that the federal district court lacked jurisdiction over the challenge, which was "inextricably intertwined" with the D.C. high court's earlier decision. The reason given was that the D.C. high court proceedings refusing to admit an applicant to the practice of law were "judicial in nature," and direct review of any constitutional questions was therefore available in the U.S. Supreme Court under § 1257. The applicability of § 1257 meant that federal jurisdiction to review the action of the D.C. courts lay with the U.S. Supreme Court and not in the lower federal courts. Thus, federal district courts are said to lack subject matter jurisdiction to review the final decisions of state courts, or claims that are "inextricably intertwined" with them. (Habeas corpus is obviously the one major exception to this basic principle. See Chapter 16.)

Nevertheless, the *Feldman* Court simultaneously suggested that a lower federal court would have subject matter jurisdiction over a "general challenge" to the constitutionality of D.C.'s ABA-approved-law-school-degree requirement, as opposed to the specific challenge to the plaintiffs' waiver denials. The degree requirement, although originally promulgated by D.C.'s high court, was undertaken in its legislative capacity for the bar, not in a judicial one (as was the denial of waivers to the particular applicants). The general challenge to the degree requirement was therefore subject to federal district court jurisdiction, as would any challenge to an unconstitutional piece of legislation. The Supreme Court, however, specifically refused to reach the question whether the litigants might be *precluded* as to that issue because of the prior decision in the D.C. courts. If preclusion was a risk for these litigants, then the decision would caution § 1983 plaintiffs in such situations to proceed immediately to federal court with their "general challenge" to the degree requirement rather than first to try their chances at obtaining a waiver of the requirement in a state judicial proceeding. On the other hand, justiciability problems, primarily in the form of "ripeness," might then attend the general challenge (see Chapter 18), as might arguments for abstention (see Chapter 15).

It is not clear how much is gained by calling the inability of the federal court to hear the waiver-denial challenge "jurisdictional" rather than compelled by preclusion doctrines. *Feldman* based its ruling on an earlier (non-§ 1983) decision in Rooker v. Fidelity Trust Co. (1923) which had indicated that federal district courts did not have the power to sit in review of final state court judicial decision-making. That decision, too, might just as easily have been resolved on preclusion grounds, especially since in *Rooker*, unlike in *Feldman*, the time for review in the U.S. Supreme Court had already come and gone. Unlike preclusion rules, however, the jurisdictional limit on federal district court review of final state court decisionmaking is a principle of federal law that is applicable even if state preclusion rules would somehow not bar the actions. And typically federal courts resolve subject matter jurisdiction questions before getting to nonjurisdictional questions, such as preclusion.

Recently, the Supreme Court reiterated that *Rooker-Feldman* is a relatively limited doctrine, largely confined to cases in which the loser in state court civil litigation seeks to complain in a lower federal court about some injury arising from the state court judgment. *Saudi Basic, supra.* In such cases, direct review in the Supreme Court, not a collateral proceeding in a lower federal court, is the only way to go. To this extent, the provision for direct review under § 1257 is exclusive of other possible grounds of original jurisdiction in the lower federal courts. But even when *Rooker-Feldman* does not apply, preclusion still may. *Id.*

D. Preclusion and the Convicted Criminal

As detailed in Chapter 16 (discussing the relation between § 1983 and habeas corpus), preclusion principles do not fully apply in most federal court habeas corpus actions. Persons in state custody claiming their detention is in violation of the Constitution usually have at least one opportunity to re-raise, in a post-conviction collateral challenge to their detention, federal constitutional issues that they have properly raised and preserved. However, the Court has held that a person who has been convicted may not bring a later § 1983 action if the issues raised in his § 1983 challenge would necessarily call into question the validity of his prior conviction. Heck v. Humphrey (1994). Instead, said the Court, the underlying conviction must first be set aside on direct review, drawn into question on habeas corpus, or otherwise annulled before such a § 1983 action may be prosecuted in federal court.

Although *Heck* is explored in greater depth in Chapter 16, § C, it is important to note here its relationship to preclusion. First, *Heck*'s barrier applies whether or not the particular constitutional issue that is the basis for relief under § 1983 was actually litigated and lost in the state court trial that resulted in conviction. Second, *Heck* also provides a basis for barring federal court relief whether or not the state court system would consider the issue to be precluded in a later action. And third, the *Heck* limitation arguably applies whether or not the § 1983 plaintiff is currently in custody and thus able to bring a state or federal habeas action in which the issue might first be raised and the conviction brought into question. Muhammad v. Close (2004) (noting issue as an open one). Thus, although *Heck* itself is not a rule of preclusion, it poses a substantial barrier to federal court (re)litigation of certain federal questions in § 1983 actions brought by prisoners.

E. Guilty Pleas, Arbitration, and Release–Dismissal Agreements

Other actions by a § 1983 plaintiff have the potential to bar his § 1983 claim as well. For example, a § 1983 plaintiff might contractually agree to dismiss his claim in exchange for the prosecution's dropping of criminal charges arising out of the events giving rise to the § 1983 action. Such agreements are enforceable and are governed by federal, not state, law. Town of Newton v. Rumery (1987). Provided such an agreement is voluntary rather than coerced, and does not suggest prosecutorial overreaching, a § 1983 defendant can seek to have the plaintiff's claim dismissed, perhaps on summary judgment. E.g., Woods v. Rhodes (8th Cir.1993). On the other hand, a guilty plea might not be issue preclusive in a later § 1983 suit as to all underlying constitutional issues, because nothing was actually litigated in such a proceeding. Haring v. Prosise (1983). But there is at least room to argue now that *Heck* should forestall some § 1983 suits following a guilty plea, preclusion problems to one side.

Arbitration is still another means by which a potential § 1983 plaintiff may voluntarily have his claim resolved non-judicially. The Supreme Court has held that a § 1983 plaintiff who has been subject to informal labor arbitration at the state level will not be precluded by the full faith and credit statute in his later § 1983 action, at least so long as the arbitration proceeding is not judicially reviewed. McDonald v. City of West Branch (1984). But it may be possible for certain would-be § 1983 plaintiffs contractually to agree to arbitration whose outcome might thereafter be enforceable to the exclusion of a civil action under § 1983.

CHAPTER 15

ABSTENTION AND RELATED DOCTRINES

Overview

Despite the holding of Monroe v. Pape (1961) that state remedies do not have to be attempted or exhausted before taking advantage of the § 1983 remedy in federal court, there are a number of now well-established doctrines which limit that holding. Some of these doctrines are statutorily created; others are judge-made. The primary statutory restrictions on immediate availability of the federal court § 1983 remedy are directed to constitutional challenges to state and local taxes and rate-making.

The judge-made abstention doctrines are more numerous. As discussed below, a federal court may dismiss a § 1983 action that seeks declaratory or injunctive relief against the enforcement of an unconstitutional law when the § 1983 plaintiff is also the subject of an ongoing state criminal or other coercive proceeding in which his constitutional questions can be raised by defense. In addition, a federal court hearing a § 1983 action seeking equitable or declaratory relief may abstain from immediately deciding federal constitutional questions when underlying unclear questions of state law may moot the need to decide the constitutional questions in a case. More rarely, a federal court may dismiss a § 1983 action when its decision would interfere with state administrative efforts to establish coherent regulatory policy. But it is ordinarily not the case that a federal court can refrain from deciding a § 1983 action simply because there is an ongoing parallel civil action between private litigants in the state courts which happens to involve constitutional questions similar to those at issue in the federal suit.

A. Tax and Rate Injunction Acts: 28 U.S.C.A. §§ 1341 & 1342

There are at least two important statutory barriers to obtaining relief from a federal court under § 1983. During the 1930's, Congress enacted a pair of jurisdictional limitations denying federal courts jurisdiction to "enjoin, suspend or restrain" state and local taxes or rate regulations when there was a "plain, speedy and efficient" remedy in the state courts to redress unlawful taxation or rate making. The tax statute is now embodied in 28 U.S.C.A. § 1341, and the rate statute (the "Johnson Act") is in 28 U.S.C.A. § 1342.

The statutes were part of a New Deal roll-back of federal jurisdiction in the wake of cases such as Ex parte Young (1908), and they gave state courts greater control over the supervision of these areas of economic activity. Any federal questions raised in the state courts could be preserved for eventual review in the Supreme Court after state proceedings were completed. These statutes bar federal interference whether or not there is, at the time the federal suit is brought, any ongoing state proceeding in which the constitutional claim can be raised. In short, these statutes force the filing of an independent action in the state system to obtain relief—something that is ordinarily not required under *Monroe.*

1. The Scope of the Non-interference Rules

Although these statutes were enacted prior to the re-emergence of § 1983 and the modern civil rights era, the Supreme Court has concluded that § 1983 actions are subject to them. Moreover, more than injunctive relief is barred. In California v. Grace Brethren Church (1982), for example, the Court rejected an argument that a First Amendment challenge to the taxation of church property could be maintained in federal court, even though it was only an action for declaratory, not injunctive relief. The Court concluded that the language of § 1341 barred the exercise of federal jurisdiction over declaratory as well as injunctive actions. On the other hand, the Court has also concluded that equitable challenges to certain school vouchers could proceed in federal court because they did not threaten to "enjoin, suspend or restrain tax collection," although it clearly interfered with state tax policy. Hibbs v. Winn (2004).

Damages actions brought under 1983 § that challenge the constitutionality of tax collection fare little better than injunctive actions. In Fair Assessment in Real Estate Ass'n, Inc. v. McNary (1981), the Court upheld dismissal of a federal § 1983 action challenging county and state tax assessments as unconstitutional even though the suit sought damages only. Although the Court did not rest its decision on the Tax Injunction Act per se, it concluded that the principle of "comity" reflected in the Act should bar the damages action. Thus, whether the constitutional challenge to a state or local tax seeks injunctive, declaratory, or monetary relief, the federal court § 1983 action will ordinarily be barred, on one theory or another.

Nevertheless, the Court in *Fair Assessment* held open the possibility that a damages action that challenged unconstitutional state action "on its face" rather than "as applied" might dictate a different result. The notion is that comity concerns surrounding federal court scrutiny of the actual manner of assessment would not be implicated in such a facial challenge. This window for possible federal jurisdiction for such facial challenges to taxes, however, should not be applicable to claims for declaratory or injunctive relief, because those claims (unlike damages claims) are barred by the Tax Injunction Act itself, not just by the principle of comity. The principle of comity also led the Court to conclude that a § 1983 action (with its panoply of remedies, including attorney's fees) challenging an unconstitutional state tax assessment could not be maintained in a state court either, at least where a post-assessment state-law remedy already in place. National Private Truck Council, Inc. v. Oklahoma Tax Comm'n (1995).

2. What Constitutes a "Plain, Speedy and Efficient" State Remedy?

The jurisdictional bar in these statutes is especially powerful because the Supreme Court has given a broad interpretation to what constitutes a plain, speedy, and efficient state court remedy. It is probably not necessary, for example, for a state to provide a pre-deprivation injunctive remedy to enjoin an unconstitutional tax assessment or statute; a post-payment taxpayer remedy will ordinarily do. The Court has also held that the language of the tax injunction statute is procedural only, and that arguable substantive shortcomings in the state remedy (e.g., failure to provide interest on an unconstitutional assessment) are ones that should be raised in the state courts, which can be addressed on direct review in the U.S. Supreme Court, if necessary. That the Supreme Court will address substantive deficiencies on direct review is demonstrated in cases such as McKesson v. Florida Alcoholic Beverages & Tobacco Div. (1990), in which the Court remanded a tax case in which the state courts had denied a refund remedy even though the state courts had held a particular tax unconstitutional. And as for what is a sufficiently "speedy" state court remedy, the Court has bowed to litigational reality and accepted the possibility that a number of years might pass before post-exaction recovery is possible. Rosewell v. LaSalle Nat'l Bank (1981).

Litigation over the Johnson Act's prohibition on challenges to state rate regulations has been less frequent, but it is likely that interpretations of the Act's language will track the interpretations of the similar language in the tax injunction statute. The only significant differences between the two are that the Johnson Act specifically exempts challenges based on claims of federal pre-emption or the Commerce Clause. In other words, if the § 1983 challenge to the state rate regulation is based on its inconsistency with federal law, or that it interferes with interstate commerce, the Johnson Act will not prevent a federal court challenge to the rate (although other, judge-made abstention doctrines could conceivably apply).

In addition, there is authority to the effect that the absence of anticipatory injunctive relief in state court may sometimes run afoul of the rate statute's "plain, speedy and efficient" remedy requirement, although that is apparently not the case with tax assessments. Driscoll v. Edison Light & Power Co. (1939). The difference may be due to the fact that recoupment of rate undercharges as against myriad third-party rate-payers would be difficult to obtain after the fact. Wrongfully assessed taxes, however, may easily be recovered by the taxpayer after the fact and typically require no injunction. Of course, an injunctive remedy may be required even in the tax context if a pay-first, seek-refund-later scheme does not exist under state law.

B. The Anti–Injunction Act: 28 U.S.C.A. § 2283

Another potential barrier to federal relief, even outside of the areas of rates and taxes, is the Anti–

Injunction Act, 28 U.S.C.A. § 2283. This provision, which has antecedents going back to 1793, bars federal courts from issuing injunctive relief against ongoing state court proceedings except in a handful of limited circumstances. Unless an injunction is (1) necessary in aid of a federal court's exercise of its jurisdiction, or (2) is issued to protect or effectuate existing judgments of the federal court, or (3) is "expressly authorized" by congressional statute, state court proceedings at the trial and appellate levels will be allowed to proceed free of federal court interference by way of injunction.

Despite the anything but express language of § 1983, however, the Court determined in Mitchum v. Foster (1972) that § 1983 actions were an express exception to the strictures of the Anti–Injunction Act. The Court concluded that in at least some cases an injunction against state court proceedings might be the only way to give effect to § 1983 which was aimed at unconstitutional state action of all varieties: legislative, law-enforcement, and judicial. To be sure, *Mitchum* gave some good reasons why Congress should make § 1983 an express exception to the Anti–Injunction Act, but it did not do an especially good job of explaining how Congress had done so. As noted below, a narrower ruling might have been more defensible and consistent with the Anti–Injunction Act's terms.

Nevertheless, while the Anti–Injunction Act will not itself be a barrier to injunctions of ongoing state court proceedings under § 1983, other doctrines developed by the Court make such injunctive relief very problematic. Of course, injunctions of merely threatened (as opposed to ongoing) proceedings have never been thought to be forbidden by the Anti–Injunction Act. Dombrowski v. Pfister (1965). But, as noted above, if the § 1983 challenge is to rates or taxes, §§ 1341–1342 will effectively prevent most relief, even prospective injunctive relief.

C. "Our Federalism": The *Younger* Doctrine

1. Ongoing State Criminal Proceedings

(a) Deference to Good Faith State Criminal Process

Despite its holding in *Mitchum* (and despite the rhetoric of immediate federal court access in *Monroe*), the Court has developed a broad set of judge-made abstention rules that take back much of what *Mitchum* might have allowed. In Younger v. Harris (1971), the Court concluded that a federal court could not ordinarily enjoin an ongoing state criminal prosecution, even when it was alleged that the prosecution was based on a statute that violated the free speech guarantees of the First Amendment. If the § 1983 plaintiff could raise that constitutional issue by way of defense in the state court criminal proceeding, principles underlying what the Court dubbed "Our Federalism" required the federal court to defer to the state criminal process. The result of the application of *Younger* is dismissal of the federal proceedings. As in the area of the Tax and Rate Injunction Acts, constitutional questions can be preserved for direct review in the Supreme Court, or, if the proceedings resulted in conviction and custody, in a post-conviction collateral attack on federal habeas corpus.

Younger's deference to state criminal process arguably reinforces a number of parallel doctrines. First, it reinforces the principle of exhaustion of state remedies that is required before relief may be sought on federal habeas corpus to challenge constitutional error in state court criminal proceedings. Second, it reinforces the refusal of Congress to enact any general provision for the removal of criminal cases from state court, even when they raise defenses based on federal law (unless such prosecutions are brought against federal officers). And finally, it reinforces the Supreme Court's refusal to read the civil rights removal statute, 28 U.S.C.A. § 1443, as allowing for removal of a state criminal prosecution simply because it is premised on an unconstitutional statute. Georgia v. Rachel (1966). Instead, to secure removal under this latter (and seldom used) provision, a party must usually show that the very act of being prosecuted will itself deny him rights that are specifically protected by a federal "equal rights" statute. Id.

(b) The Bad–Faith Prosecution "Exception"

(i) Equitable Relief

The *Younger* Court did suggest, however, that there might be "extraordinary circumstances" that would permit a federal court to enjoin ongoing state criminal proceedings. If, for example, the state proceedings had been brought in bad faith or for purposes of harassment, or when there was no genuine expectation of conviction, or when the challenged statute was patently and flagrantly unconstitutional "in every clause, sentence and paragraph" *Younger*'s bar would be inapplicable. Perhaps the bringing or maintenance of such proceedings is an independent constitutional violation that § 1983 by its express terms would allow courts to enjoin. If so, the Court could simply have said that § 1983 was an exception to the Anti–Injunction Act only in those limited circumstances. Instead, the Court chose a more complicated route. It made § 1983 an across-the-board exception to the Act in *Mitchum*, but then added a judge-made abstention doctrine in *Younger* that made injunctive relief against state courts unavailable in most cases, and then added exceptions on top of *Younger* itself.

The Supreme Court, however, has been reluctant to give teeth to the "bad faith" and related exceptions. Nevertheless, lower federal courts have enjoined prosecutions shown to have been brought because of race or for the specific purpose of retaliating against the defendant's exercise of constitutional rights. E.g., Wilson v. Thompson (5th Cir. 1979). Although a "bad faith prosecution" objection might just as easily be made as a defense in the state court proceeding itself, the Court has not insisted that it be made in the very proceeding that is alleged to be tainted. Instead, the federal court is open, *Younger* notwithstanding. In fact, the Supreme Court itself once concluded that manifest state tribunal bias might be sufficient to get around *Younger*. In Gibson v. Berryhill (1973), the Court upheld an injunction against state proceedings to revoke the license of an optometrist when the tribunal was staffed by other optometrists who stood to benefit economically from the license revocation.

Similarly, if the filing or maintenance of state proceedings amounts to an independent constitutional violation (as opposed to the good faith invocation of an unconstitutional statute), then immediate federal court access may be available, *Younger* notwithstanding. For example, a state proceeding brought in violation of the Double Jeopardy Clause presents a prosecution that a litigant has a constitutional right not to endure, in a way that a litigant facing a good faith prosecution under a possibly unconstitutional statute does not. Thus, immediate federal intervention, whether through accelerated direct review of the state court's decision in the U.S. Supreme Court, or preemptively through a § 1983 action in a federal district court may be available. See Smalis v. Pennsylvania (1986) (allowing accelerated direct review); Doe v. Donovan (1st Cir.1984) (allowing § 1983 action under *Younger* exception).

(ii) Damages Actions

Although bad-faith prosecution cases under § 1983 tend to involve injunctive relief, damages have also been recovered for such proceedings after-the-fact, at least as against those who do not enjoy absolute prosecutorial immunity. For example, if the § 1983 plaintiff can show that the filing or maintenance of a prosecution would not have occurred but for a constitutionally impermissible reason—such as race—damages ought to be available. See Stemler v. City of Florence (6th Cir.1997) (concluding in damages action that impermissibly motivated prosecution would be violative of equal protection). "Malicious prosecution" actions under § 1983 to recover damages for prosecutions undertaken without probable cause are more problematic, and are briefly addressed in the next Chapter.

2. Declaratory Relief and Damages

Younger's prohibition on injunctive relief also bars federal court declaratory relief when there is an ongoing state criminal proceeding against the § 1983 plaintiff in which the same issue may be raised. Samuels v. Mackell (1971). The Court in *Samuels* held that declaratory relief in favor of a § 1983 plaintiff who was also a criminal defendant in state court could interfere with the state proceedings through preclusion and similar consequences. In addition, a plaintiff's damages action in federal court will be stayed (but not dismissed), pending the outcome of state criminal proceedings against him. Deakins v. Monaghan (1988). For example, a § 1983 plaintiff may have a Fourth Amendment claim respecting an unconstitutional search and seizure, but the same issues can be litigated in the ongoing criminal proceeding brought against him in a motion to suppress evidence from the search. Dismissal of the § 1983 action is inappropriate, presumably because damages relief cannot be had in the ongoing state court criminal proceeding. But because a first-in-time federal court decision of the Fourth Amendment issue would have a similar potential to interfere with an ongoing state prosecution as would a declaratory judgment, the Court has upheld a stay of the § 1983 damages action. *Deakins, supra.*

The result of a stay of the federal damages action may not be much better than dismissal, however, at least from the perspective of the § 1983 plaintiff. That is because preclusion and related doctrines may prevent an independent determination by the federal court of any underlying constitutional issues in the later-litigated damages action following the state court's prior resolution of those same questions. See Chapter 14.

3. *Younger*, Ex parte Young, and "Anticipatory" Relief

More troubling for the Supreme Court was whether *Younger*'s non-interference principle could be reconciled with the familiar principle of Ex parte Young (1908), allowing for anticipatory injunctive relief from federal courts, including injunctions against threatened state court prosecutions. The most obvious difference is one of timing. *Younger* involved state criminal proceedings that were ongoing; *Young* involved an effort to enjoin state proceedings before they had been filed. But both kinds of relief have the ability to interfere with state court criminal process. Over time, the Court gradually (if haltingly) reaffirmed most of the vitality of *Young* and the availability of equitable relief against state court enforcement actions in the no-pending-prosecution context.

(a) Declaratory Relief

First, *Younger* does not bar a declaratory judgment action by a § 1983 plaintiff who has been threatened with arrest under an unconstitutional statute but who is not being prosecuted. Steffel v. Thompson (1974). In *Steffel*, the § 1983 plaintiff was threatened with arrest for violating a state anti-leafleting statute. The plaintiff was not being prosecuted when he sought federal declaratory relief under § 1983, even though his cohort had been arrested and was undergoing a state criminal prosecution for violating the same ordinance. Although the Court had earlier held (*Samuels, supra*) that declaratory relief was unavailable in the face of an ongoing prosecution because of its similarity to the interference posed by injunctive relief, the Court now concluded that declaratory relief was actually less drastic medicine than an injunction, at least when there was no prosecution pending in state court against the party who was the § 1983 declaratory plaintiff. Thus, the plaintiff who was not being prosecuted could seek declaratory relief, *Younger* notwithstanding; his cohort who was being prosecuted could not.

The showing that the plaintiff in the no-pending-prosecution context had to make was that he faced a "genuine threat of prosecution" even though he was not actually being prosecuted; he did not have to show that the threatened prosecution would have been in bad faith, or any other extraordinary circumstances called for by *Younger*. The ruling reaffirmed the modern reading of *Young* that a party did not have to violate a law (and risk prosecution) to test its constitutionality.

(b) Preliminary and Permanent Injunctions

In addition, prospective injunctive relief is available in the no-pending-prosecution context, without having to show extraordinary circumstances such as bad faith or harassment. In Doran v. Salem Inn, Inc. (1975), the Court upheld an order of preliminary injunctive relief on behalf of two bars against an allegedly unconstitutional topless-dancing ordinance. Although a third bar was being prosecuted for violating the ordinance at the time the preliminary injunction was entered, the other two were not, and they were therefore in a position like that of the § 1983 plaintiff in *Steffel*. Thus, the two bars were able to obtain an injunction pending a final determination on the merits in the federal court, and to carry on in the interim the very activity the ordinance outlawed.

Still later the Court concluded that, in appropriate circumstances, even permanent injunctive relief could be had against the future filing of criminal proceedings, at least when none were ongoing at the time of the request for injunctive relief. Wooley v. Maynard (1977). It was unclear in *Wooley*, however, whether permanent injunctive relief (as opposed to preliminary injunctive relief) would require a showing of extraordinary circumstances such as those required to make out an exception to *Younger*.

Nevertheless, not even purely prospective injunctive relief is available to a plaintiff who is actually being prosecuted. For example, a party being prosecuted under an unconstitutional statute cannot get an injunction against his ongoing prosecution because of *Younger*. But he might nevertheless wish to engage in similar conduct pending the prosecution's outcome, like the successful plaintiffs in *Salem Inn*. The Court has held, however, that a party in such a position cannot seek injunctive relief, even if it would only be against future rather than pending prosecutions. Roe v. Wade (1973). The result was reached although, as in the damages context, there was no available state court remedy in the criminal proceedings to obtain either interim or permanent injunctive relief.

(c) Timing

Timing is critical, but it is not always dispositive. Getting to the federal courthouse first will not always ensure a federal trial forum for § 1983 plaintiffs. Even when a federal § 1983 plaintiff manages to file suit in federal court before any state court criminal proceedings are brought against him, *Younger* will still bar federal injunctive relief if the state proceedings are commenced before there have been "proceedings of substance on the merits" in the federal court. Hicks v. Miranda (1975). And once *Younger* kicks in, it continues to bar federal court interference until state appellate process is concluded. Huffman v. Pursue, Ltd. (1975).

Presumably, if the § 1983 plaintiff had obtained a preliminary injunction from the federal court before the state proceedings were brought against him, such proceedings would be sufficient to prevent a state prosecutor from going forward in violation of the injunction; but what activity short of a preliminary injunction from the federal court would be sufficient to keep the federal action on track is not clear. All that the Court has said on the issue is that a federal court's denial of a temporary restraining order did not amount to "proceedings of substance on the merits" sufficient to prevent the state from gearing up a prosecution after the filing of the § 1983 action, thus triggering *Younger* dismissal. *Hicks, supra.*

The optimal § 1983 plaintiff in such cases, therefore, is someone who has not yet violated the law he seeks to challenge in federal court, and who therefore cannot be prosecuted for past violations moments after filing his federal § 1983 action. Of course, that means he must be able to thread the needle of showing a "genuine threat of prosecution" even when he has not violated the law in the past. Such showings may be difficult, but certainly not impossible, when law enforcement officials have made clear their intent to enforce particular laws against violators, and when a sufficiently strong showing can be made of the plaintiff's future activity. When the threat of prosecution is less than clear, would-be § 1983 plaintiffs sometimes may have to entice the relevant public official to go on record as threatening to enforce particular statutes by announcing their own planned intentions to violate those statutes. The optimal plaintiff must also continue to abide by the law until such time as the preliminary injunction is obtained (or until there have been other proceedings of substance on the merits in the § 1983 action sufficient to avoid the application of *Younger*).

Finally, although the Supreme Court has not resolved the issue, it would undermine the purposes of preliminary injunctive relief in most cases if, after losing on the merits of his § 1983 claim, the § 1983 plaintiff could be prosecuted for acts taken under the protection of a successfully obtained preliminary injunction. Edgar v. MITE Corp. (1982). If the state stands to suffer economic injury while the preliminary injunction is in effect, it can presumably protect itself by insisting on the posting of appropriate security under Rule 65(c), Fed. R. Civ. P.

4. *Younger*'s Application to Civil Actions

(a) Government–Initiated Civil Enforcement Proceedings

Younger was a criminal prosecution. But its rationale of deference to the coercive enforcement of state public law and related norms quickly expanded. The Supreme Court has therefore held *Younger* applicable to nominally civil government-initiated enforcement actions, such as suits to abate a public nuisance. Mitchum v. Foster (1972) (state-initiated enforcement of anti-obscenity provisions). And it has been applied to government-initiated civil actions in aid of enforcement of criminal laws. Huffman v. Pursue, Ltd. (1975). Other government-initiated enforcement actions such as welfare termination proceedings and proceedings to remove children from abusive homes have also been held subject to *Younger*'s strictures.

Even administrative proceedings that are judicial in nature, such as state bar disciplinary hearings, have been held subject to the requirements of *Younger*. Middlesex Cty. Ethics Ctte. v. Garden State Bar Ass'n (1982). Thus, if a § 1983 litigant believes that a state agency is enforcing an unconstitutional law against her, she will typically have to raise that constitutional question in the agency proceedings themselves, or on state court judicial review of those proceedings. Ohio Civ. Rts. Comm'n v. Dayton Christian Schools, Inc. (1986). The principle does not run afoul of the no-administrative-exhaustion rule any more than *Younger* runs afoul of the no-judicial-exhaustion rule. Those rules permit a party to bypass "remedial" administrative and judicial avenues that are capable of being initiated by the would-be § 1983 plaintiff, but not to bypass "coercive" ones initiated by the state or its proxy.

But here, too, *Younger*'s exceptions should be applicable in the proper case. If the administrative proceeding itself amounted to a constitutional injury because, for example, it was undertaken for a constitutionally impermissible motive, then the administrative proceeding should be able to be enjoined. That such a claim should be considered by a federal court on the merits is borne out by the Supreme Court's willingness to consider on the merits—before upholding dismissal on *Younger* grounds—a religious school's claim that a state equal employment agency's exercise of jurisdiction over the school was itself a violation of the First Amendment's Free–Exercise Clause. *Dayton Christian Schools, supra.*

It therefore seems safe to say that when government is in the posture of a good-faith plaintiff in almost any ongoing state enforcement proceeding brought against the would-be § 1983 plaintiff, *Younger* will bar his obtaining federal relief. So long as the state proceedings are judicial in nature and there is a mechanism in them by which to raise the constitutional challenge that would have been the subject of the § 1983 action, it should not matter whether the proceedings are criminal, civil, or administrative. And *Dayton Christian Schools* may suggest that it may be sufficient for *Younger* purposes if such an avenue is available only in state court judicial review of a coercive administrative proceeding.

(b) Private Litigation

More significantly, however, the Court has extended *Younger* to bar federal courts from hearing constitutional challenges in some instances of *pri-*

vate enforcement of "important state interests" such as state court civil contempt proceedings, Juidice v. Vail (1977), or the enforcement of state court civil judgments by private parties pending appeal in the state court system. Pennzoil Co. v. Texaco, Inc. (1987). Constitutional challenges to the statutes pursuant to which such enforcement proceedings are instituted have therefore been dismissed from the federal courts when there was arguably a mechanism in the ongoing state proceedings by which to raise such challenges.

Despite these expansions of *Younger* into the civil arena, the Court has made it clear that the doctrine will not apply to all state court civil proceedings. The mere existence of a pending parallel (nonenforcement) state court civil proceeding (in which the constitutional issues that are the subject of a § 1983 suit can also be raised) should not be a basis for abstention under *Younger*. See NOPSI v. New Orleans Council (1989) (no abstention when the parallel state and federal actions were both brought by § 1983 plaintiff). Obviously, some state interest is at stake even when a state merely provides a forum for the resolution of otherwise private disputes. But that interest alone has never been thought enough to allow federal courts to abstain in other contexts when their jurisdiction has been properly invoked, and it is presumably even less of a reason to allow for abstention in the § 1983 context. Colorado River Water Cons. Dist. v. United States (1976).

D. Unclear Questions of State Law: *Pullman* Abstention and Certification

1. Abstention Theory

A different kind of abstention can take place even when there is no pending state proceeding at all. In Railroad Comm'n of Texas v. Pullman Co. (1941), plaintiffs sought injunctive relief against enforcement of a state agency's order that required a Pullman "conductor" and not just a Pullman "porter" to supervise sleeping cars on interstate trains traveling through Texas. The order was challenged on Commerce Clause and Equal Protection grounds because the jobs were racially segregated and the result of the order was to give greater job responsibilities to the (then) all-white conductors and to take those responsibilities away from African–Americans. The order was also challenged on the basis of Texas law, the plaintiffs arguing that the Railroad Commission, which had issued the order, lacked power to make such employment decisions as a matter of state law.

The Supreme Court upheld a lower federal court's decision to abstain from hearing the constitutional questions until the state courts had resolved an underlying and unclear question of state law, namely whether the state agency that promulgated the order had the power under state statutes to do what it did. If, as a matter of state law, the agency lacked authority to regulate such employment matters, the federal constitutional question would not have to be considered, and the order could be enjoined on state law grounds alone. If, on the other hand, the agency did have such power under state law, the federal constitutional question would have to be decided, and the federal court could then (but only then) proceed to resolve it.

Because of the Court's often-expressed desire to avoid "premature" decisions of constitutional 08 questions, and its federalism-based desire to avoid unnecessary "friction" with state regulatory efforts, the Court upheld the carving off of the potentially dispositive question of state law and required the litigants to get an answer to it from a state court before proceeding further with their federal constitutional challenge. In addition, the Supreme Court, before Brown v. Board of Ed. (1954), may have been reluctant to reach into the area of race relations unless it had to.

Previously, the Court had sanctioned the initial resolution of potentially dispositive questions of state law in constitutional litigation, although resolution of the state-law questions had been left to the federal court itself. Siler v. Louisville & N.R.R. Co. (1908). In the regime prior to Erie v. Tompkins (1938), this made sense because federal courts did not always feel themselves hamstrung by state judicial interpretations of state law, including, on some occasions, state public law. *Erie*, of course, called for greater fidelity to state judicial interpretations of state law. But when federal courts otherwise had jurisdiction of state law questions, nothing (before *Pullman*) prevented federal courts from going forward in the ordinary setting and providing their best assessment of state law. So, this second feature of *Pullman*—carving off unclear questions of state law and sending them to state court—was less readily justifiable. As noted below in the discussion of abstention under Burford v. Sun Oil (1943), however, sending injunctive claims raising unclear questions of state separation-of-powers law may make sense for many of the same reasons that Pennhurst State School & Hosp. v. Halderman (1984) concluded that injunctive claims against state officials under state law should be barred altogether from the federal courts.

Although *Pullman* was not styled as a § 1983 action, it probably would be today. Because of *Pullman*, federal courts routinely stay injunctive proceedings under § 1983 that challenge a statute on federal constitutional grounds when an underlying issue of unclear state law could either moot the constitutional question or put it in a substantially different light. But the federal proceedings are merely postponed under *Pullman*, not dismissed outright as with *Younger*.

It is important to note, however, that subsequent developments in the area of sovereign immunity may have partially curtailed the availability of *Pullman* abstention, although they have not eroded its underlying theory. In Pennhurst State School & Hosp. v. Halderman (1984), discussed in Chapter 7, the Supreme Court concluded that federal courts had no jurisdiction to hear claims against state officials for injunctive relief that were based on state law. Such suits were in reality suits against the state, said the Court, and no fiction of "individual officer liability" could disguise that fact. According to *Pennhurst*, the fiction would be indulged only for claims for relief seeking to vindicate the supremacy of federal law and the Constitution.

Thus, the pendent state-law claim for injunctive relief in *Pullman* (but not the federal claim) would today have to be dismissed outright. The federal court could not retain any jurisdiction over it. No similar dismissal requirement, however, would attend a state-law claim for injunctive relief against local governments or their officials rather than against the state or its officials. Sovereign immunity is not an issue in such suits. Nevertheless, it is still possible that if a state-law claim like that in *Pullman* is dismissed, or never brought in federal court in the first place, a federal court could still order abstention on the federal claim until any unclear question of state law is first resolved in the state courts.

2. *Pullman* Abstention Procedure and Certification

The logistics of *Pullman* abstention can be complex. If the defendant's motion to abstain based on the criteria of *Pullman* is successful, the § 1983 plaintiff is effectively required to file a proceeding in the nature of a declaratory judgment action in state court. *Pullman* assumes, of course, that such procedures will be available; if they are not, its rationale would be inapplicable and abstention should be denied. The entry point within the state judicial system is ordinarily the state trial court, whose decision can be reviewed up the ladder of state appellate process, in the ordinary manner.

Other mechanisms for obtaining state court input on uncertain questions of state law have also been developed, including "certification" of questions from the federal courts directly to the state's highest court. But, as a matter of state law, this procedure is discretionary (that is, a state court could refuse certification). And, in many states, certification is not available for questions from federal district courts (as opposed to higher federal courts). Thus, if a federal court of appeals determines that a district court improperly failed to abstain under *Pullman*, the appellate court might either remand to the federal district court for abstention, or, if the procedure is available in the relevant state court system, it can simply certify the unclear state law question to the appropriate state court and ask for its answer before remanding.

Under *Pullman*, once the state court has the state law question before it, there is no guarantee that it will not reach out and decide the federal constitutional question as well. And if it does, there is a danger that the decision could be preclusive on the federal court. See Chapter 14. The Supreme Court once faced the problem and advised the plaintiffs that they could always preserve their federal forum for the resolution of the federal constitutional questions in their case if they made a reservation on the record of the state court proceedings indicating that they intended to pursue their already-filed federal action depending on the outcome of the state proceedings. England v. Louisiana State Bd. of Medical Examiners (1964).

Indeed, so long as the § 1983 litigant does not voluntarily submit her federal claims for resolution to the state court, she will not be deprived of the opportunity to have a federal court pass on them once the federal court's jurisdiction has already been properly invoked, even if she does not happen to make an express "*England* reservation." The reservation is therefore sufficient, but not necessary. On the other hand, the Court thought it was still appropriate for the federal litigant to "expose" her federal constitutional issues to the state court, even if she should not "submit" them for their decision, so that the state court might have the benefit of understanding the implications of its decision on the unclear questions of state law. Id. If a § 1983 plaintiff does voluntarily submit claims for state court resolution beyond those reserved under *England*, preclusive consequences will likely attach. San Remo Hotel v. San Francisco (2005).

3.   Assessing the Uncertainty of State Law

Pullman spoke of unclear questions of state law whose resolution had the potential to moot the federal constitutional question. Much subsequent litigation has involved the question of "how unclear is unclear enough?" Apparently, the simple fact that the relevant provision has gone uninterpreted by the state judiciary is not enough to trigger *Pullman* abstention, if the statute does not "obviously" admit of an interpretation that could moot the federal constitutional question. Hawaii Housing Auth. v. Midkiff (1984).

Thus, abstention will not be ordered simply on the outside chance that an obliging state court might be willing to give a counterintuitive but narrow construction of the challenged statute that could avoid the federal constitutional question. But cf. Arizonans for Official English v. Arizona (1997) (not indicating clearly whether similar standard would apply on "certification"). Similarly, the Court has suggested that where requesting a state court's interpretation of sufficiently unclear state law would result in irreparable harm pending the outcome of state court proceedings, either preliminary injunctive relief might be granted in the federal court or abstention might appropriately be denied altogether. Babbitt v. UFW (1979); Pike v. Bruce Church, Inc. (1970).

4. Parallel State Constitutional Grounds

Pullman issues often arise when the § 1983 plaintiff has brought two claims for relief—one based on the U.S. Constitution and one grounded in state statutes, as in *Pullman* itself. Sometimes they may arise even when the plaintiff has alleged only a federal claim, when for example, there is an implicit underlying state-law question concerning the applicability of the state statute to the challenged conduct. That was the case in *England, supra,* in which the federal plaintiff had challenged a state statute on constitutional grounds, asserting that if a particular medical degree requirement applied to the licensing of chiropractors it was unconstitutional. Although no separate state-law claim was expressly raised, abstention was ordered on the underlying state-law question as to whether the state statute applied to chiropractors at all. If it did not, there would be no federal constitutional question to answer.

Sometimes, however, the relief sought by the § 1983 plaintiff could have been (or may actually be) based on parallel state and federal constitutional grounds. For example, a plaintiff might seek to remedy public school segregation by raising injunctive claims under both the state and federal constitutions, or she might seek relief only under the federal Constitution. (Of course, after *Pennhurst, supra*, the § 1983 plaintiff could invoke the parallel state law ground only against local governmental entities and their officials—not the state or its officials.) In either case, she may face an argument that interpretation of the parallel "equal protection" provision under state law may provide the relevant relief and could moot the need to decide the federal issues. The Supreme Court once ordered abstention when the plaintiff had invoked both state and federal constitutional provisions in a challenge to a state statute regulating fishing rights. Reetz v. Bozanich (1970). The state constitutional provision specifically related to the problem of fishing rights and had not yet been interpreted by the state judiciary.

Yet in Wisconsin v. Constantineau (1971), the Court concluded that a § 1983 plaintiff would not have to repair to state court to seek an interpretation of the Due Process Clause of the state constitution that largely mirrored the federal constitutional provision on which the plaintiff's claim was exclusively based. Perhaps the state constitutional provisions presented no unclear question of state law because they were a mirror image of federal provisions which were themselves clear. But states can generally interpret their own constitutions in ways that accord greater (but not fewer) rights than similar provisions in the federal Constitution. So, the fact that a state constitution "mirrors" a clear federal constitutional provision does not necessarily mean that the state constitutional provision presents no unclear question of state law.

Even if the state constitution did present an unclear question of state law, the result in *Constantineau* seems right. Many if not most states have a "Bill of Rights" or a provision for equal protection that might mirror federal provisions. And, as noted above, there may often be a genuine lack of clarity in such provisions. Yet regularly ordering abstention when such parallel state constitutional provisions exist would make *Pullman* abstention the rule and not the exception. It would also, given the prevalence of such state constitutional provisions, dramatically curtail federal court jurisdiction over § 1983 suits seeking to enjoin unconstitutional state action on federal constitutional grounds.

In addition, requiring a federal court § 1983 plaintiff who has not sought injunctive relief under state law to first seek such relief in state court may overly compromise the no-exhaustion principle of *Monroe*. To be sure, *Pullman* is already something of a compromise on that principle. But in the typical *Pullman* scenario, resolution of the state-law question can result in a finding that a challenged state statute simply does not apply to the conduct at issue—a finding that genuinely moots the need to resolve any federal constitutional attack on the statute. In such cases, resolution of the federal constitutional issues is logically dependent on the interpretation of state law. On the other hand, requiring resort to injunctive relief based on (possibly uninvoked) state constitutional grounds may moot the need for a federal remedy, but it is not so clear that the question whether there is (or was) a federal constitutional violation has also been mooted in such a case. It is partly for this latter reason that *Pullman* abstention is not applicable to suits for damages brought under § 1983. If it were, then uninvoked state court damages remedies would ordinarily have to be pursued first, which is directly contrary to the teaching of *Monroe*.

E. State Administrative Decisionmaking: *Burford* Abstention

An increasing number of § 1983 challenges brought in federal court are to state agency decisionmaking. As discussed in Chapter 2, parties may bring suit in federal court to enjoin threatened enforcement of state laws or regulations enacted by the legislature, even if there are available state remedies in which to press a similar challenge. Nevertheless, the Court has suggested that some challenges to state agency decisionmaking may have to be dismissed on grounds of what some have dubbed "administrative" abstention. See Burford v. Sun Oil Co. (1943). The consequences of *Burford* abstention (unlike *Pullman*, but like *Younger*) is dismissal of the federal claim.

According to the Court, if adequate state court review is available, federal courts should avoid granting equitable and other discretionary relief that would interfere with orders of state administrative agencies if the "exercise of federal review of the question in a case and in similar cases would be disruptive of state efforts to establish coherent policy with respect to a matter of substantial public concern." NOPSI v. New Orleans Council (1989). Of course, all federal review of state agency decisionmaking is potentially disruptive of state policy, as is § 1983 at a more general level. So, the real question is: Is federal disruption through the vehicle of a § 1983 action qualitatively different in this setting than in others? The Court, however, has never given a clear answer to that question.

Burford abstention has its main application in the § 1983 context to challenges directed at completed administrative decisionmaking. But understand what (if anything) *Burford* adds. Federal court interference with *ongoing* agency decisionmaking will often be barred either because the challenge is not yet ripe (in the case of agency lawmaking), or because of *Younger*'s requirement of non-interference with ongoing state administrative proceedings that are coercive and judicial in nature. Even when state agency proceedings are over and done with, the Supreme Court has gone out of its way to reject abstention simply because the exercise of federal § 1983 jurisdiction may interfere with agency decisionmaking by overturning it. In *NOPSI, supra*, the Court sustained federal court authority over a Commerce Clause and pre-emption challenge to ratemaking orders of a local administrative body. The federal questions could be resolved without having to enmesh the federal courts in underlying factual issues concerning which the state administrative agency and judicial system might be thought to have some particular "local" expertise.

But when that is not possible, abstention may sometimes be in order. *Burford* itself, for example, was a due process challenge to the "reasonableness" of a state agency's issuance of oil-drilling permits in a heavily exploited and highly regulated area of the State of Texas. The issuance of any permit to drill would inevitably impact on the oil reserves available to other nearby property owners. But the "reasonableness" question was inseparable from underlying factual questions regarding which the state agency had admitted expertise, as did the specialized reviewing court in the state which oversaw its decisions and into which all agency appeals were channeled. (Of course, the channeling occurred because of the accident of geography; state agency review went to courts in the particular county in which the state capital and many agencies were located.)

Not long ago, the Supreme Court reiterated the comparative narrowness of the *Burford* doctrine, and reminded litigants that the discretionary power to dismiss under this and other abstention doctrines should rarely if ever be exercised in a case not involving discretionary (i.e., equitable or declaratory) relief. Quackenbush v. Allstate Ins. Co. (1996). And outside of the sort of due process reasonableness challenge implicated in *Burford* itself, the rationale for abstention weakens considerably. See City of Chicago v. Int'l College of Surgeons (1998) (upholding—in non-§ 1983 proceeding—federal removal jurisdiction over a state-law administrative review proceeding attacking a local agency's denial of a demolition permit, in which the plaintiff raised federal and state constitutional challenges to the agency's actions).

In any event, it would be a mistake to assume that federal court "review" of completed state or local administrative decisionmaking somehow runs counter to the traditional role of the federal courts, or that *Burford* routinely requires abstention in such cases. Historically, such review was well settled for many kinds of administrative action. E.g.,

Reagan v. Farmers' Loan & Trust (1894). And decisions of other administrative bodies, such as school boards, are routinely challenged in federal court today without any hint that abstention should pose a barrier. E.g., Brown v. Board of Educ. (1954); Migra v. Warren City Sch. Dist. Bd. of Educ. (1984).

CHAPTER 16

HABEAS CORPUS AND PRISONER LITIGATION

Overview

Habeas corpus provides prisoners a judicial mechanism to challenge the legality of their detention by government officials. Under existing statutes—substantially revised in 1996—state prisoners may seek federal habeas corpus if they are in custody in violation of the Constitution, laws, or treaties of the United States. As currently construed, this habeas mechanism gives prisoners a limited opportunity to re-raise constitutional questions that may already have been decided against them in state courts and to collaterally attack their conviction. Thus, habeas corpus is unlike § 1983 insofar as rules of preclusion are less rigorously enforced than in § 1983 actions. Also, unlike most nonprisoner § 1983 litigation, habeas corpus has an exhaustion-of-state-remedies requirement as a precondition to federal court access. Yet both statutes provide a remedy against governmental illegality, and their remedies have the potential to overlap, at least when the § 1983 plaintiff is a convicted prisoner.

To preserve the independence of each of these statutes, the Court has concluded that when a prisoner challenges the fact of, or duration of, his confinement, he must proceed with a habeas action, and not a suit under § 1983. On the other hand, when a plaintiff challenges the conditions of his confinement—such as the lack of medical care or a beating by a guard—a suit under § 1983 is the normal route. Nevertheless an exhaustion requirement now attaches to prisoner-initiated § 1983 actions challenging conditions of confinement. And other § 1983 actions will be barred if they would undermine or call into question the earlier conviction or the lawfulness of continued confinement.

A. The Habeas Remedy

Since 1867, state prisoners have been able to challenge in federal court the legality of their custody when it is alleged to be in violation of federal law. Although there is considerable doubt whether the 1867 habeas statute was originally designed or employed to permit challenges to jurisdictionally valid albeit erroneous judgments of conviction, the modern judicial history of habeas has allowed for just such a remedy. At least since Brown v. Allen (1953), federal courts have had some ability to reconsider a broad range of federal constitutional issues at the behest of state prisoners, free of the ordinary constraints of preclusion, and to order a new trial or release from custody where rights have been violated. The modern descendant of the 1867 habeas statute is now codified at 28 U.S.C.A. § 2241 and § 2254 et seq.

1. Relitigation and its Limits

Nevertheless, modern decisional law plus congressional reforms of habeas corpus in the Antiterrorism and Effective Death Penalty Act of 1996 (AEDPA), Pub. L. No. 104–132, have cut back on the ready availability of habeas. Federal habeas courts are greatly limited in their ability retroactively to apply "new rules of law" that were not in existence at the time the prisoner's conviction became final. Teague v. Lane (1989). Analogously, in cases to which the AEDPA applies, relief will not be granted unless the state court decision was "contrary to, or involved an unreasonable application of, clearly established Federal law, as determined by the Supreme Court of the United States," or unless the decision was "based on an unreasonable determination of the facts" given the evidence presented. 28 U.S.C.A. § 2254(d). This limitation has the effect of insulating from reconsideration on habeas corpus many erroneous but not unreasonably erroneous decisions of state judges on constitutional issues. Terry Williams v. Taylor (2000). The limitation is therefore somewhat like the qualified good faith immunity normally accorded law enforcement officials in damages actions under § 1983. Although *Teague* and the AEDPA work somewhat similarly, the AEDPA is implicated when the constitutional issue raised on habeas has been adjudicated in the state court proceedings; *Teague* (with its handful of exceptions) applies when it has not. Horn v. Banks (2002).

In addition, the Supreme Court has also concluded that decisions implicating Fourth Amendment exclusionary rule claims cannot be heard on habeas at all, thereby providing one of the few blanket exceptions to the liberal relitigation rule of *Brown*. Stone v. Powell (1976). Thus, litigants are limited to a "full and fair opportunity" to raise such issues in the state courts. This limited protection for exclusionary rule claims results from the Court's debatable conclusion that only a marginal deterrent function is served by the ability to raise such claims on habeas in addition to the trial itself. In short, Fourth Amendment exclusionary rule claims resolved by the state courts, while subject to direct review in the U.S. Supreme Court, will be preclusive in the federal courts on habeas corpus.

2. Defaulted Claims

(a) Non-capital Cases

It is usually not possible for a prisoner to raise constitutional claims on habeas corpus if he has not properly preserved them in his state criminal proceedings. This basic principle of procedural default seems to be unaffected by the AEDPA, at least in non-death-penalty cases. Ordinarily, courts will excuse such procedural defaults only when the prisoner can show "cause" for the default and "prejudice" from the failure to have raised and preserved the issue. Wainwright v. Sykes (1977). "Cause," however, seems to mean something more than that a prisoner's attorney made an error. On the other hand, some attorney errors might be great enough to amount to incompetence of counsel under the Sixth Amendment, thus satisfying the "cause" requirement and allowing the defaulted issue to be considered on federal habeas. "Cause" might also be established by a showing that government officials impeded the raising of a particular issue by withholding exculpatory evidence. Strickler v. Greene (1999); Murray v. Carrier (1986). "Prejudice," meanwhile, may reflect a notion of nonharmless error, and would require a showing (to some degree of likelihood) that the judgment might have come out differently absent the procedural default.

As an alternative to the showing of cause and prejudice to forgive procedural default, the prisoner might attempt to show a miscarriage of justice. Herrera v. Collins (1993). The latter showing, in turn, requires proof that the constitutional violation "probably resulted" in the conviction of someone who was "actually innocent" and that "it is more likely than not that no reasonable juror would have found [the habeas petitioner] guilty beyond a reasonable doubt." Schlup v. Delo (1995).

If, however, cause and prejudice (or a fundamental miscarriage of justice) can be shown, the showing is said to secure only a "gateway" to allow the raising of a defaulted constitutional issue, as opposed to being an independent ground for relief. *Herrera, supra.* Yet it may be possible that a standalone claim of actual innocence, if shown by some sufficient degree of clarity, would suffice for habeas in a capital case in order to avoid a grievous miscarriage of justice. Id. (Opinion of O'Connor & Kennedy, JJ.) (stating that execution of "legally and factually innocent" person would be "constitutionally intolerable"). And if such a showing of actual innocence should operate as a stand-alone ground for habeas in a capital case, it is not clear why it should not be enough in a non-capital case.

(b) Capital Cases

Under the AEDPA, special provisions can apply in capital sentence cases when states have made competent counsel available for state post-conviction proceedings. 28 U.S.C.A. § 2261. Under these provisions, defaulted claims in death penalty cases may be raised only when the default was caused by unconstitutional state action, or was the result of the Supreme Court's recognizing a "new Federal right" that can be retroactively applied to the applicant, or when the factual basis for the claim could not have been discovered with the exercise of due diligence within the time-frame for collateral review. 28 U.S.C.A. § 2264(a)(1)-(3). In short, the new statute seems to slightly re-work the *Sykes* procedural default analysis in death penalty cases in those states conforming to § 2261. Capital defendants in states not providing the protections of § 2261 are presumably still subject to the standards of *Sykes* and its progeny.

3. Timing and Successive Petitions

The AEDPA also severely limits the time within which any habeas petition may be filed in the federal courts, and generally limits applicants to a single bite at the federal habeas apple. Ordinarily, a federal habeas application must be made within a year from the time the state court judgment becomes final (but not counting the time for properly filed state habeas). 28 U.S.C.A. § 2244(d)(2); Pace v. DiGuglielmo (2005). In capital cases in states complying with § 2261, the time for filing federal habeas is 180 days.

A prisoner who wishes to appeal from the denial of a first habeas petition must secure from the district court a certificate of appealability (COA) demonstrating "a substantial showing of a denial of a constitutional right." 28 U.S.C.A. § 2253(c)(2). The Court has held that this standard is met if "reasonable jurists could debate whether ... the petition should have been resolved" differently. Slack v. McDaniel (2000).

After a first federal habeas petition, subsequent federal petitions face an uphill road. Permission to file a second or "successive" petition that raises an issue that was *not* previously raised in an earlier federal habeas petition—whether in a capital or non-capital case—must first be obtained from a panel of the relevant court of appeals before it can be entertained by the district court. And by statute, the court of appeals' decision whether to grant an applicant permission to file a second petition is unappealable. But litigants who are unsuccessful before the court of appeals at this stage may still file an "original" habeas petition directly with the Supreme Court pursuant to its long-standing power to grant such writs in exceptional circumstances as part of its "appellate" jurisdiction. Felker v. Turpin (1996). As a practical matter, however, the chances of success on such original petitions are slim to none. As to issues that were previously raised and resolved in a first habeas petition, preclusion now applies. § 2244(b)(1).

B. The Intersection of Habeas and § 1983

1. Challenges to the Fact of or Duration of Confinement

Although there are aspects of habeas corpus law that could (and do) fill volumes, the sketch above sets the background for the problems arising at the intersection of habeas corpus and § 1983. An early collision at this particular intersection occurred in Preiser v. Rodriguez (1973). A prisoner brought suit for injunctive relief under § 1983 seeking to have certain "good time" credits on his sentence restored to him that he had earned for good behavior in prison. He claimed that the circumstances of their revocation by prison officials amounted to a deprivation of liberty or property without due process of law.

The Court noted that § 1983 might well supply a remedy for the alleged deprivation, but it also noted that the habeas corpus statutes were more specifically addressed to the problem of challenging ongoing unlawful incarceration. The Court therefore held that: "[W]hen a state prisoner is challenging the very fact or duration of his physical confinement, and the relief he seeks is a determination that he is entitled to immediate release or a speedier release from that imprisonment, his sole federal remedy is in habeas corpus." Accordingly, the prisoner was obliged to first exhaust any state remedies available to him as a precondition to seeking federal relief on habeas corpus to have his good time credits restored. Allowing the prisoner the alternative of § 1983 would, thought the Court, undercut the policies that underlay the exhaustion requirement of habeas corpus. As discussed below, *Preiser* has been reinforced by other principles that operate outside of habeas corpus and which limit the ability of a prisoner to maintain § 1983 actions that would undermine the lawfulness of his conviction. Note, however, that although a damages action challenging completed administrative detention might not be subject to habeas corpus, it might sometimes be subject to other doctrines that would limit immediate resort to § 1983. See below § C, subsection 1.

2.   Challenges to Prison Conditions and the PLRA

On the other hand, prisoners have long been able to maintain § 1983 actions for various constitutional harms suffered in prison, other than the harm arising from the simple fact of continued incarceration. For example, as discussed in Chapter 10, prisoners have been able to obtain prospective injunctive relief from federal courts to redress conditions of confinement and to secure a host of other structural reforms, frequently under the Eighth Amendment. For example, in Nelson v. Campbell (2004), the Court treated a challenge to an allegedly unnecessary medical procedure antecedent to lethal injection as a challenge to conditions of confinement actionable under § 1983; but it left open the question of the proper characterization of a possible constitutional challenge to lethal injection itself. So long as the injunctive relief does not affect the duration of the prisoner's sentence, or seek to undo the conviction itself, § 1983 is the appropriate vehicle. Nevertheless, Congress has imposed a number of procedural and remedial limitations on prisoner-initiated structural reform litigation under the Prison Litigation Reform Act of 1995 (PLRA). And unlike most § 1983 actions, suits challenging prison conditions under § 1983 are subject to a non-jurisdictional, prison-remedies exhaustion requirement under the PLRA. 42 U.S.C.A. § 1997e(a).

Damages actions by prisoners are more complicated. Based on the plain language of § 1997e(a), damages actions "brought with respect to prison conditions" are subject to a requirement that "available" prison remedies be exhausted no less than in injunctive actions. The Supreme Court has held, based on the PLRA's language requiring exhaustion of "available" remedies, and based on the PLRA's elimination of exhaustion language in the earlier version of § 1997e that *did* focus on the adequacy of remedies, that prisoners seeking damages under § 1983 must first exhaust available prison remedies, whether or not those remedies provide for damages. Booth v. Churner (2001). The Court rejected the conclusion of some lower courts that administrative remedies that could not supply damages would be futile and therefore did not have to be pursued.

Nevertheless, many lower federal courts once considered certain prisoner suits under § 1983—such as damages actions to redress the use of excessive force in prisons, or the failure to prevent prisoner-on-prisoner violence—not to be suits over "prison conditions" at all (as compared to suits challenging, e.g., the quality of medical care, food, clothing, or shelter). But in Porter v. Nussle (2002), the Court concluded that "all inmate suits about prison life," including an Eighth Amendment claim that a guard severely beat a prisoner, were suits over prison "conditions." Thus, exhaustion is required "regardless of the relief offered through the administrative process." The result probably makes sense and likely comports with Congress's understanding. Thus, all suits challenging the fact or duration of confinement are controlled by habeas corpus and its exhaustion requirement, and all other suits about prison life not making such a challenge are suits regarding prison conditions, and are controlled by the PLRA and its exhaustion requirement.

C. Undermining the Integrity of Underlying Convictions

1. *Heck v. Humphrey*

The Supreme Court has also ruled that an action under § 1983 will be unavailable, even if the prisoner seeks relief unavailable under habeas, if the action would necessarily implicate the integrity of the judgment that sent the party to jail in the first place. Heck v. Humphrey (1994). The § 1983 plaintiff in *Heck* was a prisoner who sought damages for the loss of constitutional rights associated with his criminal prosecution. After being convicted, he filed a § 1983 suit in which he alleged that state officials had engaged in unlawful acts—including destruction of evidence—that led to his conviction. Although the PLRA had not then been enacted, the claim would not have been subject to its exhaustion requirement because it was not a suit about prison conditions. And the damages relief being sought was unavailable in habeas. Nevertheless, the Supreme Court concluded that the claim could not be brought as a § 1983 action unless the underlying judgment was first voided in the state courts, expunged by executive order, or successfully drawn into question in a federal habeas corpus action.

The Court so concluded in part because of its understanding that at common law, malicious prosecution suits could not go forward until there had been a favorable result for the prosecuted party. It also saw the potential for undermining state court criminal process if claims bearing on the events that led to conviction were not first resolved within state processes, or in a more traditional forum for challenging state convictions, such as federal habeas corpus. Thus, *Heck* serves goals similar to those of habeas by requiring resort to state process when the § 1983 litigant's claim would imply the invalidity of his conviction (or, as the court would later hold, if it would implicate the duration of his confinement).

But the *Heck* majority did not, unlike the four concurring justices, simply conclude that *Preiser* was controlling, and that habeas must first be sought by a prisoner because of the impact that a successful § 1983 action would have on the validity of the state conviction (and hence on the fact of incarceration). Rather, the Court's rule was broader, and did not purport to be limited to suits brought by those who were presently in custody when they filed their § 1983 action. Instead, any § 1983 suit that would have the effect of calling into question the lawfulness of a prior conviction in a manner like the suit in *Heck* would be dismissed (not just postponed) unless the § 1983 plaintiff had satisfied one of the prerequisites indicated by the Court.

Obviously, federal habeas is unavailable to someone who is not in custody. Even though custody has been given a broad enough interpretation to cover certain non-physical restraints on liberty, such as being out on parole, Jones v. Cunningham (1963), or being released on personal cognizance, Justices of Boston Municipal Court v. Lydon (1984), it is not an infinitely malleable concept. It does not, for example, include convictions that do not result in the possibility of incarceration but only in monetary fines. Thus, it becomes difficult for those who have served their sentences or who are otherwise not in custody despite being convicted, to bring § 1983 actions that might adversely impact their earlier conviction, because they normally will have no state procedure or habeas remedy available to them. Although *Heck*'s concerns may be well-founded to the extent they are designed to prevent prisoners from using § 1983 to circumvent habeas corpus as the appropriate way to challenge a conviction, *Heck*'s favorable-termination requirement would impose an unfortunate and difficult barrier to relief if it is applied to non-prisoners, i.e., those not in custody. See Spencer v. Kemna (1998) (Opinion of Ginsburg, J.) (arguing that a § 1983 suit by ex-prisoner should not be barred by rationale of *Heck*). But the question is apparently an open one. Muhammad v. Close (2004).

2.　*Heck* versus Preclusion

Even more significantly, *Heck* has the potential to make some preclusion rules superfluous. For example, in Allen v. McCurry (1980), a state prisoner sought to have the issue of an unconstitutional search relitigated in a § 1983 damages action after he had already litigated and lost on the issue in state court. The Court ruled that he would be precluded under the full faith and credit statute from relitigating the issue if state law would have precluded him from relitigating it. But *Heck* might dictate that the prisoner could not bring the § 1983 action at all—whether or not state law would preclude him—until he is first able to get the state system somehow to reconsider its earlier decision. In addition, federal habeas would be unavailable to a § 1983 plaintiff like the prisoner in *Allen*, because of the limitation imposed on the relitigation of Fourth Amendment exclusionary rule claims on habeas set forth in Stone v. Powell (1976).

3.   Assessing *Heck*'s Scope

The standard set by the Court—"necessarily" to "call into question the lawfulness of conviction or confinement"—is less than precise. It suggests that courts must make a potentially difficult inquiry that assesses on a case-by-case basis the prejudice or harmlessness of the federal constitutional question to the judgment of conviction before entertaining a convict's (or ex-convict's) § 1983 claim. Because of this language, *Heck* appears to erode earlier decisions in which the Court allowed a prisoner to seek monetary (as opposed to injunctive) relief for the loss of his "good time" credits without having to exhaust state remedies. Wolff v. McDonnell (1974). The effect of *Wolff* was to allow the federal court in a § 1983 damages action to speak first and potentially preclusively to the constitutional issues surrounding the revocation of good time credits and thereby impact the length of confinement. Although the § 1983 damages suit allowed by *Wolff* would not undermine a prisoner's "conviction," it did have the potential to undermine the "lawfulness of [his] . . . confinement," which *Heck* forbids.

The Court seemed to agree with this conclusion (without discussing *Wolff*) in Edwards v. Balisok (1997). There, it held that *Heck* required dismissal of a § 1983 claim for damages to redress a procedural due process denial associated with the manner in which good-time credits were revoked. Although the validity of the prisoner's conviction was not thereby placed in issue, the federal court's pronouncement as to the validity of the tribunal's proceeding would impact the validity of the deprivation of good time credits, and along with it, said the Court, the length of punishment imposed. The latter, it found, was inconsistent with *Heck*.

Assessing when such impact might occur has not been easy. For example, *Balisok* was distinguished in Wilkinson v. Dotson (2005)—a § 1983 challenge to the manner in which parole eligibility was determined. Although the injunctive relief sought (i.e., the ordering of a new hearing for the prisoner) could conceivably shorten the duration of prison custody, the majority concluded that the relationship between the injunctive relief and speedier release was "too tenuous" and that the "claim would not necessarily spell speedier release." *Wilkinson* distinguished suits for restoration of good-time credits when it stated that such claims were at "the core of habeas corpus" (and presumably, damages claims for their loss were at the "core" of *Heck*).

Heck's favorable-termination requirement was also held not to apply in all prison-discipline cases. Muhammad v. Close (2004). *Muhammad* involved a prisoner's damages action under § 1983 for administrative detention alleged to be the result of retaliation by prison officials. The Court concluded that if the § 1983 suit "threatens no consequences for [the prisoner's] conviction or the duration of his sentence" there was no need to require adherence either to the exhaustion rule associated with habeas corpus or *Heck*'s favorable termination requirement. Nevertheless, if the result of such a § 1983 action would have been expungement of the prisoner's record or other sentence-shortening action (not argued in *Muhammad*), *Heck* could easily have been triggered.

Heck obviously does not put an end to all § 1983 suits by all convicted persons seeking to redress unconstitutional state action. But in combination with the PLRA, it poses a formidable hurdle. If the challenge is to in-prison state action relating to the conditions of (but not the fact of or duration of) confinement, a damages or injunctive action is still available after *Preiser* (subject to exhaustion of prison remedies under § 1997e(a)). And, if the injury claimed is one other than the prisoner's eventual confinement or conviction, and the legal issue is not one that would necessarily call into question the validity of the judgment of conviction, a § 1983 action may still be possible. For example, an unconstitutional search of a convict's home may neither have produced evidence that was admissible against him at trial nor have resulted in his arrest. He could sue over the unconstitutional intrusion, *Heck* (and the PLRA) notwithstanding. As another example, the police may have gratuitously beaten a prisoner while in pre-trial custody for a particular crime and awaiting trial. In this case as well, the constitutional violation that the § 1983 plaintiff sought to address might be sufficiently removed from anything having to do with his ultimate conviction that a successful damages suit would not draw the conviction into question.

On the other hand, consider the facts surrounding the case that began the (re)naissance of § 1983: Monroe v. Pape (1961). Mr. Monroe could bring his § 1983 challenge to the unlawful search of his apartment assuming that he was never prosecuted for anything in connection with that search. But if he had been prosecuted, principles of "Our Federalism" would keep his damages action from going forward until the state proceedings were over. See Chapter 15. If he raised unsuccessfully the search issue in the state proceedings in an effort to suppress evidence from the search, he would likely be precluded from relitigation of that issue in the § 1983 action later. See Chapter 14.

Even if he would not be precluded (because, for example, of a peculiarity of state preclusion law), *Heck* might impose a barrier to the § 1983 action if Monroe was convicted. If a district court were to conclude that Monroe's § 1983 damages action, if successful, would demonstrate the invalidity of his conviction, his § 1983 action would not be immediately allowed. Indeed, *Heck* throws up a barrier even if the issue is *not* brought up in the state court proceeding, and it therefore picks up where issue preclusion leaves off. The one-two punch of preclusion and *Heck* for persons convicted, and other limitations on federal habeas corpus for Fourth Amendment exclusionary rule claims, could therefore combine to make the availability of a federal forum for redressing the unconstitutional state action in Monroe's case less than sure.

D. Damages for Wrongful Imprisonment and § 1983.

Convicted persons sometimes try to bring damages actions for what they claim was their wrongful incarceration. If brought as claims under § 1983, they are, of course, subject to the requirements of *Heck*. But assuming that the conviction has been vacated, reversed, or otherwise drawn in question in a manner that *Heck* requires, would a § 1983 remedy for damages be available? It depends.

First of all, not all erroneous convictions that result in incarceration will be unconstitutional. The conviction might simply be the result of the non-negligent working of the system. And even if negligence were involved, the Constitution might still not be implicated. Daniels v. Williams (1986). Constitutional error made in the course of trial—which might serve as the basis for later overturning of a conviction—might be the result of judicial decision-making only, and judges are absolutely immune. Witnesses also have absolute immunity, as do prosecutors even when they bring criminal proceedings based on unconstitutional motivation. Even if there has been some form of post-trial exoneration of the person convicted, he would still need to point to a non-immune defendant whose constitutional violation was a but-for cause of his wrongful conviction.

Of course, law enforcement officials might be potential targets in such actions insofar as they generally enjoy only qualified immunity. A showing that an officer (or private party working with officers) intentionally destroyed or concealed exculpatory evidence (or fabricated or planted harmful evidence) that helped secure a party's conviction could support an action under § 1983 on a due process/fair trial theory. E.g., Pierce v. Gilchrist (10th Cir. 2004) (fabrication of evidence by lab technician working with officials); Newsome v. McCabe (7th Cir.2001) (withholding of exculpatory evidence by police officer). In addition, an officer's efforts (or a prosecutor's efforts at the investigative stage), to coerce false testimony could conceivably be actionable under § 1983.

Causation, however, is a separate question, even in tainted evidence cases. In suits brought by persons later exonerated, courts would still have to consider whether other, constitutionally untainted evidence pointing to guilt would have resulted in a similar verdict. The fact that the verdict is no longer reliable (because of exoneration) does not mean that it would not have been entered anyway, even absent the constitutional violation. And constitutional violations that would not have changed the result cannot be considered to have caused the wrongful conviction even if the person convicted is "actually innocent."

Finally, statutes of limitation might pose a problem in many cases of pre-trial and trial wrongdoing. Although state limitations periods would apply under § 1983, federal law would govern the question of accrual. See Chapter 12. Ordinarily, accrual occurs at the moment the § 1983 plaintiff knows or had reason to know of the injury that is the basis of the complaint. Chardon v. Fernandez (1981). Absent concealment, the § 1983 suit may come too late, although courts have found that the clock does not begin to run until the conviction is set aside. E.g., *Newsome, supra.* This latter result probably makes sense if *Heck* would have barred the action previously.

None of this is meant to suggest that there will never be an avenue under § 1983 for recovery of damages for wrongful conviction. As noted above, some such suits have been successfully maintained. It is merely to suggest that many of the most obvious avenues will be closed. State law, however, may provide relief where § 1983 cannot.

E. Malicious Prosecution

Closely related to damages actions for wrongful confinement are § 1983 actions for "malicious prosecution" ostensibly complaining that criminal proceedings were undertaken without probable cause. Although brought primarily by persons who were not convicted (but instead who were vindicated) in their criminal proceedings, such an action could also be available to an ex-prisoner whose conviction had eventually been overturned or otherwise favorably resolved. As § 1983 suits, however, such actions can be problematic for some of the same reasons noted above and for other reasons as well. As the plurality stated in Albright v. Oliver (1994), "the extent to which a claim of malicious prosecution is actionable under 1983 is one 'on which there is an embarrassing diversity of judicial opinion.' "

For starters, it is unclear whether proof of a common-law malicious prosecution—an unsuccessful prosecution brought maliciously and without probable cause—would be sufficient to implicate a deprivation of constitutional dimension. See Kerr v. Lyford (5th Cir.1999) (Jones, J., concurring). Nor would proof of the common-law elements seem to be necessary to make out a constitutional violation. In addition, if a tort remedy is available under state law to achieve a similar end, perhaps allegations that amount to little more than a common law tort should be routed to state court consistent with Parratt v. Taylor (1981); *Newsome, supra.* Furthermore, in *Albright, supra,* the Supreme Court concluded that a § 1983 challenge to an arrest without probable cause and a prosecution based on it could not proceed under the rubric of substantive due process. The Court left the door open, however, to a showing that the actions complained of in such a suit might violate the Fourth Amendment.

In the wake of *Albright,* some courts have suggested that a prosecution brought without probable cause would amount to a violation of the Fourth Amendment as an extended unconstitutional "seizure" (e.g., Gallo v. City of Philadelphia (3d Cir. 1998)), even though the protection afforded by the Fourth Amendment has generally been limited to the pre-arraignment setting. Other courts have indicated that a viable claim for an unconstitutional prosecution *must* be predicated on a violation of the

Fourth Amendment. E.g., Lambert v. Williams (4th Cir.2000). But given the possibility that a prosecution might run afoul of Equal Protection or the First Amendment if impermissibly motivated (e.g., Stemler v. City of Florence (6th Cir.1997)), or run afoul of due process if predicated upon the intentional destruction of exculpatory evidence (e.g., *Newsome, supra*), such a blanket limitation seems unsound. Like the common-law tort, however, the § 1983 litigant will have to show that the criminal proceedings ultimately were resolved in their favor or that they were later exonerated. And as with all § 1983 damages actions, someone other than the prosecutor acting in his prosecutorial capacity will have to be available as a suable defendant.

CHAPTER 17

BIVENS AND FEDERAL OFFICER LIABILITY

Overview

Federal officers are not ordinarily suable under § 1983 because they typically do not act under color of state law. But a parallel system of remedies for constitutional violations—not unlike that enforced by the courts under § 1983—applies to federal officers. The right of action is not congressionally created, however. The Supreme Court has instead created an implied right of action for damages directly under the Constitution and the general federal question statute—28 U.S.C.A. § 1331—that can be brought in federal court against the wrongdoing federal officer personally.

The implied constitutional action is nevertheless subject to some degree of congressional displacement—either when Congress has substituted a meaningful statutory mechanism of its own, or when other factors "counsel hesitation" on the part of the courts in implying a constitutional right of action in the particular case. In addition, federal statutes allow for recovery directly against the United States in a variety of circumstances for constitutional as well as non-constitutional claims.

Ordinary (non-constitutional) tort actions, however, are no longer possible against a wrongdoing federal official, at least when the United States properly determines that he has acted in the scope of employment and it substitutes itself as the defendant in place of its officer.

A. Implied Constitutional Rights of Action for Damages

In Bivens v. Six Unknown Fed. Agents (1971), the Supreme Court implied a right of action directly under the Fourth Amendment to allow a victim of an unconstitutional search to sue the offending federal officials personally for damages. No federal statute or comparable version of § 1983 provided for such liability. Indeed, the only statutes that arguably addressed the issue did not cover the injury in question. Under the Federal Tort Claims Act (FTCA), 28 U.S.C.A. § 1346(b), the United States had waived its sovereign immunity from suit for certain torts of its officials, but, as then written, many intentional torts committed by law enforcement officials were excluded.

1. The *Bivens* Action

The facts in *Bivens* were reminiscent of those in Monroe v. Pape (1961). See Chapter 2. The plaintiff claimed that federal narcotics agents entered his apartment, arrested and manacled him in front of his family for supposed narcotics violations. His family was then threatened with arrest and his apartment was searched "from stem to stern." He was later subjected to a visual strip search. Bivens, who was not prosecuted, claimed that the search was warrantless and without probable cause, and that he had been subjected to unreasonable force incident to his arrest, all in violation of the Fourth Amendment. He sought damages against the officers in federal court for his pain and suffering, humiliation, and embarrassment.

The Supreme Court concluded that these allegations stated a cause of action under the Fourth Amendment. "Historically," it stated, "damages have been regarded as the ordinary remedy for an invasion of personal interests in liberty." Although the Fourth Amendment did not itself explicitly provide for its enforcement by a damages action, the Court concluded that when federal rights had been invaded, federal courts had the power to supply a remedy. For authority, the Court relied on its observation in Bell v. Hood (1946), that "where legal rights have been invaded, and a federal statute provides for a general right to sue for such invasion, federal courts may use any remedy available to make good the wrong done." Of course, no federal statute provided for a "general right to sue" in Bivens's case, except for the purely jurisdictional federal question statute, § 1331. Nevertheless, although not cited by the Court, there were also nineteenth-century antecedents to *Bivens* in which the Court had upheld federal question jurisdiction in non–§ 1983 damages actions against non-diverse state officials who had violated the Constitution. E.g., Scott v. Donald (1897).

An important concurrence by Justice Harlan described the issue in separation-of-powers terms: whether the power to provide a damages remedy for a constitutional violation was exclusively congressional. He was persuaded that the judiciary shared such power in part because of a long tradition of judicially fashioned injunctive remedies against officials for their constitutional violations. In addition, the Court had liberally implied private rights of action in the face of congressional silence in the enforcement of federal statutes. For Harlan the power of the judiciary to fashion appropriate remedies was no less in the constitutional area than in the statutory area, and the range of considerations was "at least as broad as" that which Congress would consider in fashioning a legislative remedy. Moreover, for someone like Webster Bivens, said Harlan, "it was damages or nothing" because he would not benefit from injunctive relief given the one-shot nature of the illegal search. Nor was he ever subject to a criminal prosecution in which the legality of the search could be contested.

The Court indicated two possible limitations upon its implied constitutional right of action analysis. First, it stated that the case did not involve "special factors counseling hesitation in the absence of affirmative action by Congress." Second, it noted that there had been "no explicit congressional declaration that persons injured by a federal officer's violation of the Fourth Amendment may not recover money damages from the agents, but must instead be remitted to another remedy, equally effective in the view of Congress." The meaning of those limits would be spelled out in later decisions, as noted below.

2. *Bivens*'s Impact

It is important to see what the decision in *Bivens* accomplished. Prior to that decision, damages suits could be brought against federal officials for their wrongdoing that implicated the Constitution, but the basis of those suits was not federal law. The cause of action was based on state law, or, before Erie R.R. Co. v. Tompkins (1938), "general" common law. Federal law and the Constitution played a role in those lawsuits even though they did not supply the cause of action. If, for example, the officer claimed, in defense to the state-law cause of action, that he had been authorized by federal law to do what he did or that he was otherwise acting pursuant to federal authority, federal questions arose by way of defense to the tort suit. That would allow for removal of such a suit from state court to federal court under the federal officer removal statutes. 28 U.S.C.A. § 1442; Mesa v. California (1989). In response to the defense of valid federal authority the plaintiff might plead or argue that the claimed federal authority was void, because the federal official had acted in violation of the Constitution or otherwise had exceeded his lawful authority. If so, the officer would have been liable like an ordinary citizen for his unjustified tort. Wheeldin v. Wheeler (1963).

What *Bivens* did, therefore, was to federalize the cause of action against the federal officers when the issue was whether they had acted unconstitutionally. Compare Bell v. Hood (1946) (leaving the question open). The officers would now be suable and potentially held liable, not because they had committed a tort, but because they had violated the Constitution. Thus, *Bivens* accomplished much the same thing that *Monroe* did in the state and local officer context. It meant that protection against official illegality would be measured in constitutional terms and not just in terms of ordinary tort law, and the underlying action would be a genuinely federal cause of action. It was not, therefore, a question of a federal court damages remedy "or nothing," as Justice Harlan suggested. As in *Monroe*, it was whether Webster Bivens should have something more than a state-law tort remedy.

The sovereign immunity of the United States is not implicated in *Bivens* actions for damages. The theory of these suits, like the theory of *Monroe*, is individual officer liability. FDIC v. Meyer (1994) (*Bivens* action unavailable against federal agency); cf. Correctional Services Corp. v. Malesko (2001) (*Bivens* action unavailable against private correctional facility operated under contract with federal Bureau of Prisons). In this respect, *Bivens* is like the tort regime that preceded it. Sovereign immunity was not implicated in tort suits properly brought against a federal officer individually, where the suit sought money damages against him personally, or sought injunctive relief that simply required the officer to cease his illegal behavior. E.g., United States v. Lee (1883); see also Chapter 7 (discussing limits on state sovereign immunity in individual officer actions under § 1983).

B.   Expansion of the *Bivens* Action

Following its decision in *Bivens*, the Court expanded the remedy to include Equal Protection violations and violations of the Eighth Amendment's ban against cruel and unusual punishment. These decisions suggested that the scope of the *Bivens* action was as inclusive of constitutional claims as is § 1983, assuming that a particular provision of the Constitution limits federal as well as state action.

For example, several years after *Bivens*, the Court found that a party could state an implied constitutional right of action for damages for gender discrimination. Under the so-called Equal Protection component of the Fifth Amendment's Due Process Clause, a claim for relief was properly stated against a Congressman when he refused to consider the plaintiff for the post of administrative assistant because she was a woman. Davis v. Passman (1979). Although the Court noted that the Congressman might be able to claim some sort of personal immunity as a legislator, it saw the question whether there was a cause of action as separate from whether there might be a good defense to personal liability.

In *Davis*, however, unlike in *Bivens*, there were congressional remedies in the picture. Congress had set up a remedy for employment discrimination under Title VII of the 1964 Civil Rights Act, which allowed persons discriminated against on the basis of gender to sue their employers. And in 1972, the Act had been amended to include suits by federal government employees. But congressional employees were specifically excluded from coverage. Thus, there was some indication that Congress had meant to foreclose sex discrimination litigation by these employees, and therefore some argument that special factors might counsel hesitation in creating a remedy against a Congressperson. Nevertheless, instead of reading this exclusion as indicating Congress's intent to withhold remedies for sex discrimination from its employees, the Court read the exclusion as not implicating the availability of a constitutional remedy at all. The Court therefore strongly suggested the presumptive availability of the *Bivens* action for all constitutional violations by federal officials.

Similarly, the Court concluded that a prisoner could bring a *Bivens* action against a federal official for his infliction of cruel and unusual punishment. In Carlson v. Green (1980), the Court made clear that unless the defendant shows that there are "special factors counseling hesitation" or evidence that Congress has provided an alternative remedy which it "explicitly" declared to be a substitute for recovery directly under the Constitution and which Congress viewed as "equally effective," a *Bivens* action should be allowed for constitutional violations committed by federal agents.

Yet here, too, Congress had been active. In the 1974 amendments to the FTCA, Congress had allowed a tort remedy against the United States for the very sort of harm at issue in *Carlson* (and that had been at issue in *Bivens* itself). In *Carlson*, however, the Court once again was unimpressed by the statutory remedial scheme. It found that the *Bivens* action would be a more effective deterrent to wrongdoing than would an FTCA action: Punitive damages were unavailable in an FTCA action; administrative exhaustion was a prerequisite to an FTCA action; there was no jury trial right in an FTCA action; and state tort law would be the measure of a violation under the FTCA, rather than the Constitution. The Court therefore concluded that the FTCA was not a "sufficient protector" of constitutional rights.

C. Contraction of the *Bivens* Action

1. "Special Factors Counseling Hesitation"

Despite these initial expansions, the Court's later decisions cut back on the ready availability of *Bivens* remedies. One exception commonly invoked is the existence of "special factors," as mentioned in *Carlson* and *Bivens*. As the label suggests, "special factors" cannot be easily defined or predicted, although such factors are apt to be found when serious problems of separation of powers (above and beyond those at issue in a case like *Bivens* itself) are somehow implicated.

For example, the Court once disallowed a *Bivens* action over claims of racial discrimination brought by military enlisted personnel against their superior officers. Chappell v. Wallace (1983). Although it was alleged that discipline was meted out in an unequal fashion, the Court concluded that the "unique disciplinary structure" of the military provided special factors meriting non-recognition of a *Bivens* action. The military justice system might address some aspects of the claimed discrimination through the court-martial process. And in the absence of congressional creation of a remedy against superior naval officers by their subordinates, the Court would not create one on its own.

Another effort by a serviceman to pursue a *Bivens* action was rejected in United States v. Stanley (1987), in which the plaintiff alleged that he had been given the hallucinogenic drug LSD as part of an Army experiment. The Court went further than it had in the subordinate-superior officer context of *Chappell* and concluded that because of "special factors," no *Bivens* action would be available for any damages claim to redress injury "aris[ing] out of or in the course of activity incident to military service."

2. Substitute Congressional Remedies

The *Bivens* remedy is sometimes referred to as an example of "constitutional common law"—a default rule that is not altogether constitutionally compelled. Congress, therefore, has a role in shaping the contours of the remedy. The Court has therefore sometimes denied a *Bivens* remedy when Congress has put in place a set of comprehensive remedies of its own that provide meaningful vindication of the rights in question. In Bush v. Lucas (1983), a *Bivens* action was denied to a whistleblower who claimed that he had been demoted and defamed because of his free speech activities. Although the Court purported to find "special factors counseling hesitation," its decision more likely reflects the Court's approach to allowing displacement of a *Bivens* remedy when Congress has legislated alternative remedies.

The employee in *Bush* had available to him a complex set of remedies under federal civil service statutes—remedies that the employee had tried out, but which offered less complete relief than a *Bivens* action would have. For instance, he had no jury trial right and no opportunity to recover for the loss of dignitary interests and emotional distress for which he could have recovered in a *Bivens* action. On the other hand, the statutory civil service regime provided, in the Court's words, "meaningful remedies," including back pay and reinstatement, and it effectively shifted much of the burden of proof to the government. Given the "elaborate" system of remedies and the fact that the case involved "federal personnel policy," the Court dismissed the implied constitutional claim, even though Congress had not expressly stated that it was substituting the civil service remedy for the constitutional one, and even though the Court expressly acknowledged that the remedy was not "equally effective."

In addition, substitute remedies can apparently displace a *Bivens* remedy, even when there is no separate remediation for the uniquely constitutional component of the injury suffered by a victim of official illegality. In Schweiker v. Chilicky (1988), for example, plaintiffs sued over welfare disability benefits that had been wrongfully denied to them as a result of the government's unconstitutional method of terminating payments. Plaintiffs had been able, because of congressionally enacted administrative and judicial review procedures, to get their payments reinstated and even to recover the interim payments that they had been denied following the termination of benefits but pending judicial review. But no recovery was statutorily available for the interim harms that they suffered as a consequence of being temporarily denied their benefits pending reversal of the decision to terminate.

Alleging that their due process rights had been denied, plaintiffs sought recovery for the emotional distress and other losses they suffered as a consequence of having had their payments unconstitutionally terminated. The Court rejected the claim. Although the Court spoke in terms of "special factors" for denying a *Bivens* remedy (as it had in *Bush*), the primary factor to which the Court looked was the congressional remediation scheme itself. "When the design of a Government program suggests that Congress has provided what it considers adequate remedial mechanisms for constitutional violations" no *Bivens* remedy will be allowed.

Thus, despite language in *Carlson* and in *Bivens* itself, it seems clear that Congress does not have to "expressly" substitute a particular remedy before the Court will find that Congress has displaced the *Bivens* remedy, so long as the substitute remedy offers meaningful relief. And in the true "special factors" contexts such as the military, perhaps even meaningful relief need not be available. This particular approach to displacement of the *Bivens* action clearly shows greater respect for separation of powers concerns than did the early offspring of *Bivens*, and it parallels the Court's retrenchment in the area of implied rights of actions under federal statutes. Nevertheless, it was the earlier free-wheeling regime of implication of federal statutory rights of action—which the Court has since rejected—that itself helped to launch *Bivens* in the first place.

3. Narrowing the Content of "Liberty"

In Siegert v. Gilley (1991), the Court concluded that defamation by a federal official did not constitute a deprivation of "liberty" within the meaning of the Fifth Amendment's Due Process Clause, and therefore could not be the subject of a *Bivens* action. The Court had reached a similar result in the § 1983 context in Paul v. Davis (1976). See Chapter 3. Although the Court did not suggest in *Paul* that the state would be required as a matter of due process to provide a post-deprivation remedy for such an injury, a person defamed ordinarily can bring a tort action in state court to redress such injuries. In *Siegert*, however, no such tort law avenue of redress was possible. Federal officials had previously been held absolutely immune from common-law defamation actions for statements made in the course of employment. Barr v. Matteo (1959). And as noted below, tort actions against federal officials are now largely pre-empted by the FTCA, which does not allow for recovery against the United States for defamation actions. *Siegert*, therefore, is even more troubling than *Paul*, because state tort law—once the only weapon against federal official illegality—has been displaced, and Congress has substituted no civil remedy at all.

D. Remedial Details and Federal Common Law

Bivens actions operate in a manner largely similar to § 1983 actions. Remedies and immunities are governed by federal common law. In fact, the Court has treated immunity decisions for state and federal officers as if they were fungible. The decision that inaugurated the regime of objective good faith immunity, Harlow v. Fitzgerald (1982), was itself a *Bivens* action involving federal executive branch officials.

There are, however, a few differences between § 1983 and *Bivens*. First, some of the remedial or procedural gap filling that goes on in § 1983 litigation is made with reference to 42 U.S.C.A. § 1988. The Court has read § 1988 as requiring courts to look to state law when federal law is silent in such areas as statutes of limitations and the "survival" of a § 1983 claim. See Chapter 12. Section 1988 does not govern *Bivens* actions, however, and the Court has rather consistently applied uniform federal common law to fill such silences. Thus, in a *Bivens* action, survival of the claim is governed by a federal judge-made rule in favor of survival, state law to the contrary notwithstanding. *Carlson, supra*. By contrast, as discussed in Chapter 12, the rule for survival of § 1983 cases is presumptively grounded in state law. Federal common law also supplies missing statutes of limitations for *Bivens* actions, but here, it usually adopts the relevant limitations period of the relevant state. Section 1983 reaches a similar result, but through the apparent command of § 1988.

In addition, although state governors are entitled only to a qualified immunity from civil damages liability under § 1983, Scheuer v. Rhodes (1974), the President is entitled to absolute immunity from civil damages liability at least for actions taken as President and within the "outer perimeter" of his duties. Nixon v. Fitzgerald (1982). The Court so concluded based in part on the "unique status" of the President under the Constitution, the concern that Presidents would be distracted from their duties with any lesser immunity, and because judicial interference at that level of the executive branch would be intolerable. Nevertheless, an immunity for unconstitutional acts performed as President did not answer the separate question whether a sitting President may be sued civilly for actions prior to taking office. Despite the predictable distraction from duties, the Court held a sitting President lacks even a "temporary" immunity from lawsuits for acts taken outside his duties as President. Clinton v. Jones (1997). Other federal executive branch officials, however, including cabinet-level officers, receive only a qualified immunity for their unconstitutional acts. *Harlow, supra.*

Whether the President himself is suable for injunctive relief for his unconstitutional acts is unresolved. Franklin v. Massachusetts (1992); Mississippi v. Johnson (1867). But the issue may have little practical importance because a litigant may be able to sue an appropriate cabinet-level official for injunctive relief, as, for example, when steel producers enjoined the President's unconstitutional seizure of the steel mills. Youngstown Sheet & Tube v. Sawyer (1952). Acts merely in excess of the President's delegated authority, however, will generally not give rise to a constitutional claim at all. Dalton v. Specter (1994).

In addition, attorney's fees are probably not available in *Bivens* actions, although they would be in § 1983 suits. In federal courts, fee shifting is ordinarily unavailable in the absence of a statute, or unless the losing party litigated in bad faith. No statute allows for fee shifting against the individual officer against whom the *Bivens* action is brought. Under the Equal Access to Justice Act (EAJA), however, fees are available against the United States when a plaintiff has prevailed in litigation in any action brought against the United States "not sounding in tort," and when its defense was not "substantially justified." 28 U.S.C.A. § 2412(d)(1)(A). The EAJA further defines suits against the United States as including suits against federal officers in their "official capacity." Id. at § 2412(d)(2) But given the individual liability theory of *Bivens* actions, it is difficult to see how the EAJA would allow fee shifting against the United States, which is not a party to the action. Although the Supreme Court may have left the question open, lower courts have rightly been reluctant to award fees in *Bivens* suits. E.g., Kreines v. United States (9th Cir.1994).

Bivens actions are not subject to an-exhaustion-of-administrative remedies requirement, unless specifically required by a relevant federal statute. For example, prior to the Prison Litigation Reform Act of 1995 (PLRA), the Supreme Court had held that *Bivens* actions brought by prisoners against federal prison officials were not subject to an exhaustion requirement because no statute then required exhaustion for federal prisoners (unlike for state prisoners). McCarthy v. Madigan (1992). But courts have read the PLRA as imposing a new exhaustion requirement for federal prisoners as well as state prisoners in suits "brought with respect to prison conditions." 42 U.S.C.A. § 1997e(a); Ghana v. Holland (3d Cir.2000). They have done so by reading the language of the PLRA which refers to suits brought by "a prisoner" under § 1983 "or any other Federal law" as including suits by federal prisoners grounded on a *Bivens* theory. See Garrett

v. Hawk (10th Cir.1997). As a result, the limits on the exhaustion requirement applicable in the state prisoner context should be applicable in the federal prisoner context as well. In addition, suits by federal prisoners for prospective relief seeking to reform prison conditions are subject to the same remedial limits as § 1983 suits now are under the PLRA. 18 U.S.C.A. § 3626(g)(5); see Chapter 10.

E.   Federal Tort Claims and The Westfall Act

As noted above, a potential parallel remedy to the *Bivens* claim, both for constitutional and for non-constitutional injuries, lies with the FTCA. Suits under the FTCA are brought not against the wrong-doing officer, but against the United States, which has waived its immunity for certain sorts of injuries inflicted by its officers. 28 U.S.C.A. §§ 1346(b), 2671–2680. Liability under the FTCA is statutorily defined, but it is not uniform. Rather, liability is based on the tort law of the state in which the injury complained of took place. If someone in the position of the United States would be liable as a private person for the tort of its agent under the law of the relevant state, the United States will be liable. The FTCA requires exhaustion of administrative remedies and does not allow for the recovery of punitive damages or a jury trial, but it will allow for compensatory damages, including for loss of life. Molzof v. United States (1992). It also substitutes a solvent defendant for a potentially insolvent or immune one, and a plaintiff may take advantage of liberal state tort rules respecting respondeat superior in some cases.

There are some important exceptions to the FTCA's waiver of immunity. Most significant are the several exceptions from intentional tort liability. For example, "assault, battery, false imprisonment ... abuse of process, or malicious prosecution" are actionable under the FTCA, but only if committed by an "investigative or law enforcement officer." Id. § 2680(h). Other intentional torts, including defamation and misrepresentation, are not actionable at all under the FTCA. Id. There is also an important exception for discretionary functions, § 2680(a), and for claims "arising in" a foreign country, § 2680(k). In Sosa v. Alvarez–Machain (2004), the Court held that under the foreign-country exception, the FTCA was unavailable to remedy an injury occurring in a foreign country (in that case, the abduction of plaintiff in Mexico) even if the injury was caused by federal officials' tortuous acts or omissions in the U.S. Finally, the Court has concluded that the FTCA cannot be used to remedy injuries to service personnel that "arise out of or are in the course of activity incident to service" in the military. Feres v. United States (1950). As noted above, the Court has fashioned a similar limitation on *Bivens* actions where constitutional violations are concerned. *Stanley, supra.*

More recent amendments to the FTCA have substituted the FTCA remedy for the tort action that previously would have existed against the federal officer individually. The Westfall Act, 28 U.S.C.A.

§ 2679, was enacted to ensure that federal officials would be absolutely immune from common-law actions brought against them, whether or not their acts involved the exercise of discretion. Compare Westfall v. Erwin (1988) (finding no immunity from damages in common law tort claim arising from officer's nondiscretionary acts). So long as the United States determines that the officer acted in the scope of employment, it may (subject to judicial review of that determination) substitute itself as the party defendant in place of the officer. Gutierrez de Martinez v. Lamagno (1995).

Accordingly, if a party now sues a federal official for an on-the-job tort that he committed, the United States may substitute itself as the defendant, remove the case to federal court if it has been filed in state court, and force the plaintiff to proceed against the United States alone, subject to the strictures of the FTCA. If a plaintiff sues a federal official individually for a tort for which the officer would have been personally liable, but the tort is *not* covered by the FTCA, the action may then be *dismissed* after the United States substitutes itself. United States v. Smith (1991). Thus, if a plaintiff sued a federal official (other than an investigative or law enforcement officer) under state law for battery, the United States could substitute itself as the defendant if it concluded the battery was inflicted in the course of employment and remove the case to federal court. It could then move to dismiss, because the suit now fails to state a claim for which the United States has waived its immunity under

CHAPTER 18

JURISDICTION AND PROCEDURE

Overview

Section 1983 suits arise under federal law and therefore implicate a number of run-of-the-mill concerns common to all federal question litigation, including subject matter jurisdiction, venue, removal from state to federal court, and the bringing of pendent state-law claims and other supplemental actions. Section 1983 actions also require some attention to the niceties of pleading, especially with respect to "individual" versus "official capacity" suits. Finally, as with all suits brought in federal court, there are concerns of justiciability that must be satisfied—including the familiar requirements of standing to sue, ripeness, and mootness.

A. Subject Matter Jurisdiction

Suits under § 1983 arise under federal law. Plaintiffs may therefore bring them in federal court under the general federal question statute, 28 U.S.C.A. § 1331, without regard to the amount in controversy. Section 1983 also has its own specialized jurisdictional provision, 28 U.S.C.A. § 1343(3). Section 1343(3) allows for federal court jurisdiction over any claim alleging a deprivation of rights secured by the Constitution, and for violations (by state and local actors) of federal statutes, but only if the statute is one providing for "equal rights." The federal question statute (§ 1331) is the broader of the two jurisdictional provisions and would therefore encompass any suit that fits within the contours of § 1983: all constitutional violations and violations of federal statutes, whether or not they relate to equal rights. Thus, there is no § 1983 case in which it is necessary to invoke § 1343(3), although litigants tend to invoke it when they can, along with § 1331, more out of habit than anything else. Neither statute now has an amount-in-controversy requirement.

Things were not always so tidy. When § 1331 did have an amount-in-controversy requirement (before 1980), § 1343(3) mattered quite a lot. If, for example, a party had a § 1983 claim for less than the requisite amount in controversy under § 1331, her only possible ticket into federal court was § 1343(3) (which has never had an amount-in-controversy requirement). Resort to § 1343(3) was necessary when the constitutional violation could produce only minimal provable damages, or when the § 1983 claims involved injunctive relief of uncertain valuation. But notably, § 1343(3) did not, and still does not, reach all § 1983 claims. While § 1343(3) would reach all constitutional claims, it did not reach all claims based on officials' violations of federal statutes. That is because the Court has read § 1983 (but not § 1343(3)) as encompassing claims for violations of federal statutes without regard to whether the federal statute relates to equal rights.

Accordingly, as discussed in Chapter 5, a party can bring a § 1983 suit for a state official's violations of a federal welfare statute—a non-equal-rights statute. Maine v. Thiboutot (1980). Section 1343(3), however, would not support federal jurisdiction, because it was and is limited to violations of "equal rights" statutes (in addition to covering all constitutional violations). And, once upon a time, § 1331 was unavailable if the claim fell below the then-requisite amount in controversy. Somewhat dubiously, therefore, the Court in *Thiboutot* concluded that there were some § 1983 claims—those for violations of non-equal-rights statutes—that, at the time, could only be brought in state court but not federal court.

Now, of course, that oddity no longer exists, because § 1331 will always do the job of securing jurisdiction in all § 1983 claims. If a litigant feels compelled to invoke § 1343 (which she clearly no longer needs to do) in addition to § 1331, she should do so only for constitutional violations or for violations of federal equal-rights statutes.

B. Supplemental Jurisdiction over Pendent Claims and Parties

1. Judicial Power

Under 28 U.S.C.A. § 1367(a), if a party has a claim over which a federal court has subject matter jurisdiction, he may append transactionally related contests, even if those additional contests would not satisfy federal subject matter jurisdiction on their own. The statute provides supplemental jurisdiction over additional contests that are sufficiently related to the jurisdictionally valid claim that they can be said to form part of the "same [constitutional] case." At a minimum, therefore, § 1367(a) seems to allow for supplemental jurisdiction over all additional claims that arise out of a "common nucleus of operative fact" with the jurisdictionally valid claim arising under federal law. United Mine Workers v. Gibbs (1966). Supplemental jurisdiction extends both to additional claims against a party already in the lawsuit, as well as to additional claims brought against new parties.

In the § 1983 context this means that it is permissible to bring a § 1983 claim and a pendent state claim against an officer sued in his individual capacity for particular activity that is illegal under both federal and state law. In addition, a § 1983 plaintiff may bring a "pendent party" state-law claim against a municipality on a respondeat superior theory, if the state jurisdiction recognizes such liability for the torts of their officers as a matter of state law. Because pendent party jurisdiction is allowed in federal question actions under § 1367(a), it is not necessary that the city itself be suable under § 1983 in accordance with the more restrictive doctrine of Monell v. New York Dept. of Soc. Servs. (1978); the plaintiff may append her state-law respondeat superior claim against the city to her § 1983 suit against its officer.

Of course, it may be possible to allege both theories of recovery against a municipality in a particular case—one under § 1983's standard that requires a showing of action undertaken pursuant to official policy and one under a potentially more liberal state tort law that allows for respondeat superior liability for official torts as a matter of state law. The option of pendent-party suits against cities was not always available, however. Prior to the advent of § 1367 and the decision in *Monell*, cities could not be joined on such state-law pendent-party claims in § 1983 suits. Aldinger v. Howard (1976). Section 1367, however, appears to have legislatively overruled *Aldinger*. See Exxon Mobil Corp. v. Allapattah Servs. (2005) (discussing purposes of § 1367 in non-§ 1983 setting).

Pendent state-law claims against *the state*, however, are highly problematic. Because states are not suable "persons," no claim is possible against them under § 1983. See Chapter 7. And a pendent state-law claim against the state would ordinarily be subject to a defense of sovereign immunity. Id. Even assuming that a state has waived its sovereign immunity from some suits brought against it on the basis of state law, courts are apt to interpret the waiver as a waiver of immunity from such suits in state court only. Only in the unlikely event that there is the clearest of expressions that the state has waived its immunity from suit in federal court for suits grounded in state law will a state-law action against a state be maintainable in federal court as a pendent claim. Otherwise, damages claims against states on state-law grounds will be barred on sovereign immunity grounds, as are state-law claims for injunctive relief against states or their officers.

2. Judicial Discretion

In addition, § 1367(c) indicates that there may be circumstances in which the district court can exercise its discretion to dismiss a supplemental claim. First, if the state-law claim presents "novel or complex issues" of state law, the district court may dismiss the state-law claim (but not the § 1983 claim). Second, when the pendent state-law claim "substantially predominates" over the § 1983 claim, a federal court may decline jurisdiction over the state-law claim. Third, if the § 1983 claim is dismissed pre-trial, a federal court may decline to exercise supplemental jurisdiction over any remaining state-law claims. Although the federal court still has jurisdiction (in the sense of judicial power) to continue to hear the supplemental state-law claims at that point, the earlier the § 1983 claim is dismissed, the more likely the state claims will be dismissed.

Absent one of these three possibilities, however, there must be a showing of "exceptional circumstances" and "compelling reasons" before a district court may dismiss the supplemental state-law claims. Arguably, the regime set up by § 1367 restricts the ability of a district court to refuse to exercise supplemental jurisdiction compared to what it was prior to § 1367's enactment in 1990. In addition, abstention doctrines (see Chapter 15) give the federal courts authority in some circumstances to postpone or dismiss the state and sometimes the federal law claims as well.

C. Venue

Under the current venue statute, 28 U.S.C.A. § 1391(b), the proper federal judicial district in which to bring a § 1983 suit is the one in which the defendant resides, or, if there is more than one defendant and they reside in the same state, in the district in which any defendant resides. In addition, or alternatively, venue lies in any district in which substantial events giving rise to the cause of action took place. If there are multiple defendants and they do not all reside in the same state, the latter option is the exclusive one.

There is also a fall-back provision under the current venue statute, which is triggered only if there is no federal district at all in which venue may be laid under the first two options. That would seem to be possible only when defendants did not all reside in the same state (or when one or more defendants is an alien), *plus* the cause of action arose outside of any federal judicial district. The chances for this happening in a § 1983 suit are almost nil. But if these unlikely circumstances are met, then venue will lie in any district "in which any defendant may be found" (§ 1391(b)(3))—which effectively means that the plaintiff may sue in any district in which she can obtain personal jurisdiction over all of the defendants (not just "any" defendant).

In Leroy v. Great Western United Corp. (1979), the Court seemed to suggest that venue in a § 1983 action might not lie outside of the state in which state officials have engaged in unconstitutional activity—i.e., their home state. *Leroy* was a suit to enjoin the operation of an Idaho corporate-takeover statute on the ground that it violated the "dormant" Commerce Clause and federal statutes regulating corporate takeovers. Suit was brought in Texas against Idaho officials charged with enforcing the statute, because that was the situs of the corporation that was injured as a consequence of not being able to take over an Idaho corporation. The old venue statute, at issue in *Leroy*, allowed venue "where the cause of action arose." The Court read this venue provision narrowly, to protect the defendant officials, and concluded that the action arose elsewhere than in Texas. But the upshot of the opinion is that state officials may be able to be sued only in their own backyard in the typical case.

D. Removal

Civil actions arising under federal law that could have been originally filed in federal court may be removed by the defendant if they are filed in state court. Thus, in a § 1983 suit against a single defendant filed in state court, the defendant may remove it if he wishes to, because the plaintiff could have filed it as an original matter in federal court. Thus, most such § 1983 claims will be heard in state court only when both the plaintiff and defendant in effect agree to have it heard there—the plaintiff by choosing the state forum, and the defendant by failing to remove. As noted below, however, if there are multiple defendants, there is authority that removal can be thwarted if all defendants do not agree to removal.

Removal ought to encompass all pendent contests filed in state court along with the § 1983 claim, assuming that they are sufficiently related to the § 1983 claim that they form part of the same constitutional case under § 1367(a). 28 U.S.C.A. § 1441(a)–(b). The reason is that the entire set of contests could have been filed as an original matter as a single civil action in the federal courts under § 1331 and the supplemental jurisdiction statute, § 1367. City of Chicago v. Int'l College of Surgeons (1997) (non-§ 1983 case). If the other contests are *not* sufficiently related to the § 1983 action to satisfy § 1367, it may still be theoretically possible to remove the entire lawsuit from state to federal court under the current version of 28 U.S.C.A. § 1441(c)—a seldom relevant provision that allows removal of lawsuits when there is a federal claim and a transactionally *un*related state claim. The federal court can (and presumably then must) remand to state court all contests that are so transactionally unrelated as to fail to satisfy § 1367—"must" because it is doubtful whether such unrelated claims, over which there is no independent or even supplemental jurisdictional basis, can be included under Article III's jurisdictional umbrella. Although the current removal statutes do not appear to allow for piecemeal removal of parts of a state court lawsuit (stray language about 1441(a)-

(b) in *Exxon, supra*, notwithstanding), removal under § 1441(c) and remand of the unrelated state claim might effectively accomplish such a result.

There are also timeliness requirements for removal that are applicable to all removable cases. A "notice of removal" must typically be filed by the defendant with the federal court within 30 days of defendant's receipt of formal service of the summons and complaint, or 30 days from the time an amended complaint first shows that the suit is within the original jurisdiction of the federal courts. Murphy Bros. v. Michetti Pipe Stringing, Inc. (1999). There is decisional authority that, even in cases arising under federal law, all defendants must join in removal if there are multiple defendants, and that the 30–day period begins to run from receipt by the first of multiple defendants.

Failure to remove in a timely manner waives the right to remove. If a party believes that a removed case is not within the subject matter jurisdiction of the federal courts or that removal was untimely or otherwise procedurally flawed, she may make a motion to remand the case to state court. The motion must ordinarily be made within 30 days from filing of the notice of removal, but a subject matter jurisdictional error may be raised at any time. Thus, a motion to remand for jurisdictional reasons is not subject to time limits. Objections to removal procedure or timeliness are lost, however, if the motion to remand itself is not made in a timely fashion. In short, the right to remove is waivable if a notice of removal is not filed in a timely manner. But an objection to untimely removal is itself waivable if a motion to remand is not brought in a timely manner. Appeals of remand orders for jurisdictional or procedural error are ordinarily not available. 28 U.S.C.A. § 1447(d); Things Remembered, Inc. v. Petrarca (1995). But remands based on abstention grounds are. Quackenbush v. Allstate Ins. Co. (1996).

E. Pleading

1. Liberal or Strict Pleading?

Despite the efforts of lower courts, the Supreme Court has thus far resisted imposing a strict pleading requirement for § 1983 complaints. Under Rule 8 of the Federal Rules of Civil Procedure, a scheme of notice pleading is set up in which the complaint need only supply a "short and plain statement of the claim showing that the pleader is entitled to relief." That phrase was interpreted in Conley v. Gibson (1957), to require not the pleading of specific facts in some degree of particularized detail, but the providing of notice sufficient to apprise the defendant of the legal and factual basis of the suit. See also Swierkiewicz v. Sorema, N.A. (2002). As stated in *Conley*:

> The Federal Rules ... do not require a claimant to set out in detail the facts upon which he bases his claim. To the contrary, all the Rules require is a "short and plain statement of the claim" that will give the defendant fair notice of what the plaintiff's claim is and the grounds upon which it rests.

The Supreme Court expressly invoked the *Conley* standard in Leatherman v. Tarrant County Narcotics Intelligence and Coordination Unit (1993), when it concluded that § 1983 plaintiffs were not generally held to heightened pleading standards when suing local governmental entities (and in which they had to establish "custom or policy"—see Chapter 6). Greater particularity, said the Court, is required in Rule 9 only for certain claims—such as "fraud" or "mistake"—and the expression of such a standard in those cases should be taken to imply the exclusion of it otherwise.

The *Leatherman* Court stated, however, that it was not answering the question whether heightened pleading requirements might be applicable to issues of individual officer immunity—i.e., when defendants sued in their personal capacities claim that their conduct does not violate "clearly established" constitutional norms. Seizing on this language, some courts held that § 1983 plaintiffs were subject to a kind of heightened pleading standard in such cases, *Leatherman* notwithstanding. See. e.g., Schultea v. Wood (5th Cir.1995). These courts concluded that the § 1983 plaintiff must "engage" the immunity defense by pleading—in a "reply" (under Rule 7, Fed. R. Civ. P.) to the defendant's answer raising a defense of official immunity—sufficient facts which, if true, would overcome the defense. The purported concern was that anything less would force a defendant to endure potentially substantial discovery when he might have a right to avoid trial altogether.

Consistent with some of these suggestions, the Supreme Court in Crawford–El v. Britton (1998), indicated that if, for example, immunity is raised as a defense, the district court may order the plaintiff to file a reply under Rule 7. As with *Shultea*, the practical effect of such an order is to compel a greater degree of specificity in connection with the pleading of qualified immunity than would otherwise be required, while still honoring the basic import of decisions such as *Conley* and *Leatherman*. But, as noted further below, *Crawford-El* also went out of its way to reject lower court suggestions that, when constitutionally impermissible motive was at issue, the plaintiff was required to come forward with "clear and convincing" evidence of such motive in order to survive a motion for summary judgment under Rule 56, Fed. R. Civ. P. Instead, all that was needed was evidence from which a rational finder of fact could find that the defendant was unconstitutionally motivated. *Crawford-El*, when taken in conjunction with more recent decisions such as *Swierkiewicz, supra*—which rejected heightened pleading in a case of impermissible motive under Title VII of the 1964 Civil Rights Act—should effectively spell the end of heightened pleading in the impermissible motive context. See Educadores Puertorriquenos En Accion v. Hernandez (1st Cir. 2004).

2. Burdens of Pleading (and Proof)

The § 1983 plaintiff has the burden of pleading and proving the elements of his claim, including the deprivation of a constitutional right, and that it was undertaken under color of law. He also bears the burden of showing that the defendant is a suable "person" under § 1983. In the context of municipal liability, this means that the plaintiff may be required to plead and prove that the constitutional harm suffered was undertaken pursuant to the official policy of the entity. The defendant, however, bears the burden of pleading (and probably proving) personal immunities from liability, such as good faith or absolute immunity. Gomez v. Toledo (1980). In short, a defense of qualified immunity is an affirmative defense and must be pleaded as such. *Crawford-El, supra.* The defendants must also raise by affirmative defense any statute of limitations or res judicata objections. Subject matter jurisdiction and Eleventh Amendment issues may be raised by defense or by the court on its own motion, as can the decision to abstain. After trial, however, nonjurisdictional objections not raised below should probably be considered waived.

When the issue raised by the § 1983 plaintiff involves a question of unconstitutional motive, the issues of burden of proof become more complicated. If improper motive is a prerequisite to making out a constitutional violation, then it is ordinarily the plaintiff who must show that the defendant was motivated by a constitutionally impermissible reason. For example, in a case alleging a violation of the Equal Protection Clause, the plaintiff would have the burden of pleading and proving that the defendant was motivated by unlawful discriminatory intent. A similar burden would be placed upon a plaintiff who alleged, for example, that her discharge was taken in retaliation for her free speech activities in violation of the First Amendment. In such a case it is incumbent upon the plaintiff at trial to produce evidence sufficient for a rational factfinder to find unconstitutional motivation by a preponderance of the evidence, and for the factfinder to so find if the plaintiff is to prevail.

That these ordinary burdens of production and proof applicable elsewhere in civil litigation are equally applicable to constitutional tort litigation is borne out by *Crawford-El, supra*, in which the Court rejected any higher showing when unconstitutional motivation is at issue. The defendant bears no burden of proof in such a case, but he may (and as a practical matter he will) produce evidence suggesting a legitimate reason for his action in an effort to have the factfinder disbelieve any claim of unconstitutional motivation.

But if the factfinder should conclude that the defendant has acted with mixed motives—one that was constitutionally impermissible, and one that was legitimate—the burden of persuasion, not just the burden of production, may then actually shift to the defendant. Assuming that the plaintiff produces evidence from which a factfinder could and does find unconstitutional motivation, the plaintiff will recover unless the defendant can persuade the factfinder by a preponderance of the evidence that he would have done what he did anyway, even absent his unconstitutional motivation. Thus, if the plaintiff would not have suffered injury "but for" the unconstitutional considerations, she will be able to recover against the defendant. Mount Healthy City School Dist. Bd. of Ed. v. Doyle (1977).

F. Individual versus Official Capacity Suits

As described elsewhere at greater length (Chapter 7), care must be taken when alleging the appropriate capacity in which a particular § 1983 defendant is being sued. Suits against officers to recover against them personally are brought against them in their individual capacities. To make out a claim under § 1983, the plaintiff must allege that the officer acted "under color of" law (for example, that he was engaged in the performance of his job as a police officer). Nevertheless, the fact that someone has acted "officially" in this color-of-law sense does not make the suit one against the officer in his official as opposed to his individual capacity. In addition, for an officer to be liable in his individual or personal capacity, there is no need to show that he acted pursuant to the custom or policy of the entity for which he worked, as long as he acted "under color of" law. Individual capacity allegations against officers are typical in the damages context.

A suit against an officer in his official capacity is a suit, not against the officer, but a suit against the entity for which he works. Thus, a suit seeking injunctive relief against local or state officials in their official capacity is a suit for injunctive relief against the local entity or the state for which the officials work. Of course, injunctive relief against a local government may be brought against the entity itself (or against the relevant officer in his official capacity—it makes no difference), because such entities are suable persons. See Chapter 6. But injunctive relief that effectively runs against the state under § 1983 must still be pleaded against the officer, not the state. States themselves cannot be made defendants in federal court § 1983 actions because they are not suable "persons" and because of sovereign immunity concerns. See Chapter 7. When a state or local officer has been properly sued for injunctive relief and is replaced in office or dies, the succeeding officer may be substituted under Rule 25, Fed. R. Civ. P. (By contrast, in an individual-capacity action against an officer, the officer's death means that the § 1983 plaintiff must now pursue his claim against the defendant's estate, which should be substituted under Rule 25.)

A suit for damages against an official in his official capacity is therefore a suit for damages only against the entity for which he works. Accordingly, if the officer is a city or county employee, the plaintiff must plead and prove that the officer was acting pursuant to custom or policy because those are prerequisites for holding local governments liable in damages. A damages suit against a state official in his official capacity, however, is a suit against the state for damages and such suits are forbidden. It is therefore a gross pleading error to seek damages against state officials sued only in their official capacities.

G. Justiciability

As with any suit brought in federal court, certain requirements relating to justiciability must be satisfied. Although these issues are dealt with in detail in treatments of Constitutional Law, Administrative Law, and Federal Courts, they merit at least brief attention here.

Some of these requirements are generated by Article III of the Constitution and its insistence that the judicial branch exercise "judicial power" and resolve only "cases" or "controversies." This means that an actual dispute must be presented to the federal courts that is adversarial in nature and susceptible of judicial resolution. Flast v. Cohen (1968). For example, the Supreme Court has held that the judicial role of federal courts in the scheme of American separation of powers prevents them from rendering advisory opinions, and allows them only to resolve concrete cases. Muskrat v. United States (1911).

Other requirements are said to be merely "prudential"—i.e., not required by the Constitution but imposed because of other, policy-based concerns. For example, the Court has repeatedly stated that it will not resolve constitutional questions unless it is necessary to do so, and will instead resolve cases on non-constitutional grounds whenever possible. Ashwander v. Tennessee Valley Authority (1936). In addition, the Court has been reluctant to allow third parties to raise constitutional claims that more immediately affect others. The Court has also

not allowed parties to raise "generalized grievances," i.e., complaints that are shared equally by
the public at large (although it is not always clear
whether this is a "prudential" or a "constitutional"
limitation). Rather, such complaints are better han-
dled through the political process, or perhaps by a
suit in which the government itself is the plaintiff.
These and other prudential requirements are said
to be self-imposed limitations undertaken in fur-
therance of the Court's professed goal of institutional restraint. But as in the case of the prohibition on
generalized grievances, the prudential requirements
often border on constitutional concerns.

The main considerations taken up here are standing, ripeness, and mootness. Standing deals with
the question of "who" may sue; ripeness and mootness both deal with the question of "when" a party
may sue. As indicated below, however, there are
rarely problems of justiciability when a plaintiff
brings a § 1983 action for damages for past injury
she has suffered because of alleged unconstitutional
action on the part of a public official. Instead, it is
in the context of injunctive or declaratory relief that
most justiciability problems arise. Moreover, application of standing requirements is notoriously difficult to predict, because it sometimes happens that a
court's view of the merits may color its view of the
justiciability of particular cases.

1. Standing to Sue

Standing to sue has to do with the question of
whether a party has suffered an injury that entitles

her to seek judicial relief. The Supreme Court has identified a number of Article III prerequisites to standing. First, the Court has insisted that the plaintiff must allege that she has suffered "injury in fact" or is imminently threatened with such injury. Second, the plaintiff must be able to allege that the injury is "fairly traceable to" the defendant's violation of some legal norm. And third, the plaintiff must be able to show that the harm she has alleged will be "redressable" by the relief that she has sought. Elk Grove Unified Sch. Dist. v. Newdow (2004). Absent a sufficient personal stake in the outcome of the litigation as indicated by these three inquiries, standing to sue will be denied. Standing requirements, moreover, are jurisdictional and are therefore non-waivable, and they may be addressed by a federal court on its own motion. Steel Co. v. Citizens for a Better Environment (1998); United States v. Hays (1995).

(a) *Injury in Fact*

Allegations of injury in fact help to ensure that the plaintiff's concerns are not merely hypothetical, and that there will be a genuinely adversarial presentation of the issues. Economic injury, even in small amounts, is the classic sort of injury to which a plaintiff might try to point. But the requisite injury need not be economic injury. Bennett v. Spear (1997). The requisite injury may, if "distinct and palpable," include less tangible harms such as injury to the plaintiff's appreciation of the environment at a particular locale frequented by the plaintiff, Sierra Club v. Morton (1972), or inability to live in a racially integrated community, Trafficante v. Metropolitan Life Ins. Co. (1972).

(i) Generalized Grievances

By contrast, a citizen's generalized interest in seeing the government act lawfully—an interest that all citizens might share—will ordinarily not be enough to satisfy the injury requirement, at least in the absence of the plaintiff's being able to allege particularized injury to herself apart from the interest in governmental regularity. Valley Forge Christian College v. Americans United (1982). Generalized grievances are off-limits to federal courts because it is thought—given the widely shared nature of such grievances—that the political process provides the appropriate avenue for their resolution. Lujan v. Defenders of Wildlife (1992).

Nevertheless, some § 1983 plaintiffs have succeeded in making out claims of injury even when their grievances seem to be widely shared or generalized. For example, persons offended by a publicly sponsored religious display have been able to sue to enjoin the display, despite the widely shared nature of their experience. Similarly, in a series of Equal Protection cases, the Court has upheld standing on behalf of voters residing in and challenging the constitutionality of voting districts that have been redrawn as "majority-minority" districts to enhance minority voter representation. Shaw v. Reno (1993); United States v. Hays (1995). In those cases the Court has effectively concluded that the constitutional right is an individual right to vote in a non-racially-gerrymandered district. Thus, depending on how broadly or narrowly the Court is prepared to define the constitutional right of which the plaintiffs have been deprived, injury may be a more or less easy matter to establish.

(ii) Taxpayer Standing

The injury requirement plays a dominant role in the context of taxpayer standing. In the non–§ 1983 context, for example, the injury requirement has been used to limit taxpayer standing when plaintiffs have challenged federal spending programs as beyond Congress's powers. Frothingham v. Mellon (1923). In *Frothingham*, it was less than clear that success would have reduced the plaintiff's tax bill. And although a structural guarantee can create individual rights, the plaintiff's injury was diffuse at best. In addition, the Court rejected as a generalized grievance the effort of plaintiff taxpayers to demand that the federal government provide an accounting by the C.I.A. of its expenditures, as arguably required by Article I, § 9. United States v. Richardson (1974).

Nevertheless, state and federal taxpayers will have standing to challenge expenditures by their state or federal governments that are alleged to be in violation of the First Amendment's Establishment Clause. Flast v. Cohen (1968). Thus, for example, state taxpayers had standing to challenge state expenditures for religious schools. Everson v. Board of Education (1947). And state taxpayers who challenge the constitutionality of a tax that is imposed on them will typically have standing to do so if the federal courts are otherwise open to them. Of course, many, if not most, challenges to state or local taxes will have to go forward in state court, not federal court, because of the Tax Injunction Act, 28 U.S.C.A. § 1341. See Chapter 15. And state courts, unconstrained by Article III, may accord broader standing than federal courts. ASARCO Inc. v. Kadish (1989). But the Supreme Court seems to have concluded that it has Article III power to review, at the behest of defendant state officials, a successful state court challenge to a state tax, even when the suit would have flunked standing requirements if it had been brought as an original matter in federal court. On the other hand, the Court has also concluded that it lacked Article III power to review a similar state court lawsuit at the behest of the unsuccessful plaintiffs. Doremus v. Board of Ed. (1952).

(b) Causation/Traceability

The requirement that the injury alleged be "fairly traceable" to the conduct of the defendant means that the plaintiff must allege facts indicating that his injury was or would be caused by the defendant's challenged actions. In Warth v. Seldin (1975), for example, various plaintiffs attacked a restrictive zoning ordinance that prevented low-income and minority plaintiffs from moving into a city. But allegations by contractors and builders that they were prevented from constructing low-cost housing were insufficient to give them standing to attack the ordinance insofar as they did not allege that they had been denied any "current" project because of the ordinance. And allegations by prospective tenants were insufficient to confer standing on them because they failed to show that, absent the zoning ordinance, they would have been able to purchase or lease property. If plaintiffs could have identified a "specific" building project that the zoning ordinance blocked, however, both the contractors and the prospective tenants presumably could have established their standing to sue. See Arlington Heights v. Metropolitan Housing Dev. Corp. (1977).

But here too, it might be possible to recast the relevant constitutional injury so that the causation requirement, and therefore standing, can be met. For example, the Court has upheld the standing of an association of non-minority contractors to bring a § 1983 challenge to a city's minority set-aside program—jobs on which only minority-owned firms could bid. Northeastern Fla. Chapter of Assoc. Gen'l Contractors v. Jacksonville (1993). Although perhaps many non-minority contractors may have suffered no injury in the sense called for by *Warth* (since they might not be able to point to a specific contract that they had lost because of the set-aside), they successfully argued that their constitutional harm was the more individualized harm of being excluded from individual consideration on all contracts without regard to race. Cf. Gratz v. Bollinger

(2003) (challenge to use of race in undergraduate admissions to promote diversity).

(c) Redressability

The "redressability" requirement means that plaintiffs must be able to allege that relief will benefit *them.* In the injunctive context, this means that changing the defendant's behavior in the manner requested will remedy the injury that the plaintiff has suffered or is threatened with. The redressability requirement shades into (and is often indistinguishable from) the "causation" requirement, because a change in the defendant's behavior—for example, ceasing particular activity—will redress the plaintiff's injury only if the defendant caused the injury in the first place.

For example, in a non–§ 1983 case, the Court held that African–American parents of school children lacked standing to challenge the legality of tax exemptions for racially discriminatory private schools, because, although the plaintiffs may have suffered "injury in fact," they could not show that, if the exemption were lifted, their children would be any more likely to be able to attend desegregated schools. Allen v. Wright (1984). And the Court denied standing to indigent would-be hospital patients who attacked a tax-exempt hospital's unlawful refusal to admit such patients because the plaintiffs could not show that lifting the tax exemption would necessarily result in the admission of a greater number of indigent patients. Simon v. Eastern Ky. Welfare Rights Org. (1976). For similar reasons, in part, suits to compel prosecutors to enforce particular laws against others are routinely denied on standing grounds. Doubts about whether prosecution of third parties will necessarily redress a victim's injuries reinforce the traditional reluctance to allow private parties to second-guess governmental decisions not to prosecute. Linda R.S. v. Richard D. (1973).

(d) Associational and Third–Party Standing

An association or organization may be able to bring constitutional challenges to state action under § 1983 because of injuries suffered ostensibly by its members, provided the association satisfies three requirements. First, individual members of the association would have to have had standing to bring their own individual actions; second, the interests that the association is seeking to protect must be germane to the organization's purpose; and third, the relief sought by the association must be such that presence of individual members would not be required. Sierra Club v. Morton (1972). Thus, for example, an association of Washington State apple growers was able to challenge a North Carolina labeling regulation that was argued to be an interference with interstate commerce. Hunt v. Washington State Apple Advertising Comm'n (1977). And more recently, although in a non–§ 1983 suit, a Union was accorded standing to sue for damages on behalf of its members for a violation of a federal statute regulating plant closings. United Food & Commercial Workers Union v. Brown Group, Inc.

(1996). Of course, if the association were itself somehow injured—for example, if it were subject to an unconstitutional ban on its advertising—it would have standing to sue under § 1983 in its own right. *Warth, supra.*

Securing standing is more difficult, however, if the party seeking to assert the rights of others is an individual. As a prudential matter, third-party standing is ordinarily not allowed; parties must instead assert their own rights. This helps to assure adversarial presentation by finding the preferred plaintiff. Kowalski v. Tesmer (2004). In *Kowalski*, for example, the Court denied third-party standing to attorneys who brought a constitutional challenge to a state law that denied indigent criminal defendants (who had pled guilty or nolo contendere) an automatic right to state-provided counsel on appeal. The Court found that the relationship between the lawyers and their hypothetical clients was insufficiently close, and that there was little hindrance to the assertion of the constitutional claim by defendants in their ongoing criminal cases.

But the Supreme Court has upheld, for example, the right of a doctor to assert the constitutional rights of his patient to obtain an abortion, at least when some direct interest of the doctor was implicated—e.g., the possibility of criminal penalties for performing an abortion. Doe v. Bolton (1973). And a seller of beer was allowed to assert the Equal Protection rights of male customers to challenge a state's drinking-age statute that allowed women but not men to drink at age 18. Craig v. Boren (1976).

Similarly, the Court has upheld the right of a white seller of property to assert the rights of a black purchaser to invalidate a racially restrictive covenant. Barrows v. Jackson (1953). These examples arguably suggest the existence of constitutional rights in these plaintiffs themselves to be free from the challenged regulation. But the Court's decisions still enable these parties to make a broader challenge than their own injuries might seem to warrant.

2. Ripeness

Sometimes litigation comes too soon. The Court has considered as part of Article III's case-or-controversy requirement that a case be "ripe" for judicial consideration before it can be heard. Ripeness is not typically a problem when a litigant seeks to redress past illegality under § 1983 in a damages action. Instead, ripeness tends to be a problem in the context of injunctive or declaratory relief. If, for example, matters have not come to the point that there is a live dispute between two parties, there may be no need for the judiciary to act. In addition, it may be harder to tell whether a plaintiff's not-yet-ripe injury is sufficiently nongeneralized. To be sure, anticipatory § 1983 actions, whether for injunctive or declaratory relief, always involve some uncertainties—uncertainty about what the plaintiff's future actions will be and uncertainty about what the official's future actions will be. But some such uncertainty will have to be tolerated, unless § 1983 is to be available only to redress past harms (i.e., damages actions) and be unavailable for prospective relief (i.e., injunctive and declaratory actions).

Accordingly, the Court has stated that when a party is making a prospective challenge to a state or local statute on constitutional grounds, she must show a "sufficiently genuine threat of enforcement" of the statute against her. Steffel v. Thompson (1974). Thus, the litigant is not forced to choose between violating a statute to test it, or forgoing protected activity out of fear of prosecution. In *Steffel*, for example, an anti-war protester was permitted to seek declaratory relief against enforcement of a no-leafleting ordinance when he could demonstrate that his friend had already been arrested for leafleting, and the plaintiff himself had been threatened with arrest if he returned. And in Roe v. Wade (1973), a woman who was pregnant was able to challenge a statute banning abortions even though she had not yet obtained or arranged for one.

But not all allegations will necessarily be taken at face value. The Supreme Court, for example, has refused to allow prospective constitutional challenges to statutes when there was a history of prosecutorial refusal to enforce them. Poe v. Ullman (1961). And, in contrast to the pregnant woman in *Roe, supra*, a non-pregnant woman was held unable to challenge the same abortion statute because her dispute was not yet ripe, even though she alleged that the uncertainty over her rights had adversely affected her marriage. Id.

A particular concern in the area of ripeness involves injunctions against unconstitutional law enforcement practices. As discussed in Chapter 10, the fact that a person has been previously subject to particular unconstitutional action does not necessarily mean that he will have standing to enjoin that same action for the future. Thus, the victim of an unlawful choke-hold by the Los Angeles Police Department was able to sue only for damages under § 1983. Because of the uncertainty whether the plaintiff would be arrested again, and whether the police would unlawfully use the choke-hold again, the Court denied him the opportunity to sue for injunctive relief against future use of the choke-hold. Los Angeles v. Lyons (1983). Although couched in terms of standing to seek equitable relief, the opinion also presents the classic concerns of ripeness.

3. Mootness

(a) Individual Litigation

Sometimes litigation comes too late. If, after the bringing of a lawsuit, the controversy is resolved or settled, there may be no need to adjudicate an underlying dispute. In this sense, mootness relates to the Court's concern that the plaintiff be able to show that the wrongs he faces will be redressed by judicial relief. It is also related to the Court's concern that it not decide questions that are (or, by the passage of time, have become) hypothetical. Arizonans for Official English v. Arizona (1997).

Thus, for example, a law student's injunctive challenge to a state university's affirmative action admissions program was held to be moot when the student, who had been admitted under a trial court injunction, was in his last semester of law school by the time the case reached the Supreme Court. De-Funis v. Odegaard (1974). At that point, the student would suffer no adverse consequences if he lost the case and the program were upheld; and if he won, he could obtain nothing beyond what he had already obtained. Mootness was found even though both parties argued that the case was not moot. Similarly, a prisoner seeking to correct unconstitutional prison conditions may find his case moot if prison officials go ahead and correct the problem, or an offending statute is changed while litigation is pending, or the prisoner is released. But if he also has a § 1983 claim for damages for past injury arising from the unconstitutional conditions, that will ordinarily keep the action from becoming moot altogether.

Nevertheless, just because the defendant halts his challenged conduct does not automatically mean that the plaintiff's challenge to it has become moot, at least if there is a "reasonable likelihood" that the behavior would be renewed against the plaintiff. Honig v. Doe (1988). Otherwise, defendants would have it in their power to thwart review of their repeated unconstitutional action. City of Erie v. Pap's A.M. (2000). And if particular behavior is "capable of repetition yet evading review," judicial review may still be possible even when the case between the parties is otherwise moot. Thus, although the pregnant woman who challenged an abortion statute in *Roe, supra*, was no longer pregnant by the time her case went to the Supreme Court, the Court held that her case was not moot. Otherwise, given the length of the human gestation period and the predictable pace of the justice system, the particular plaintiff would have been unable, then or in the future, to obtain a ruling on her challenge.

(b) Class Action Litigation

A somewhat similar rationale allowed a named plaintiff in a § 1983 class action to continue a challenge to a one-year residency requirement for divorces even after the year was up. Although she was subject to the requirement when suit was filed, by the time of trial, she no longer was (and, unlike the plaintiff in *Roe*, would not in the future be subject to it). *Her* claim, therefore, was moot. But her action on behalf of the members of the class, which had been certified under Rule 23 of the Federal Rules of Civil Procedure while the named plaintiff's claim was still live, was not moot. Sosna v. Iowa (1975).

Perhaps, therefore, *DeFunis, supra*, might have come out differently if it had been brought as a class suit on behalf of current and prospective nonminority law school applicants. Class certification of a § 1983 claim also has the advantage of stopping the clock on the statute of limitations for the claims of those who are within the definition of the class and whose claims would have been timely at the time of the filing of the class action. And merely bringing a suit as a class action allows a named plaintiff whose individual case later becomes moot to appeal the denial of class certification. United States Parole Comm'n v. Geraghty (1980). Furthermore, class action treatment in the injunctive relief context allows for enforcement of the court's decree by a larger group of persons than might otherwise be possible in an individual § 1983 action. But unless suit is brought as a class action, the above-noted "capable of repetition yet evading review" exception to mootness will work only if a particular issue is "capable of repetition" as respects the particular plaintiff.

H.   "Facial" versus "As Applied" Challenges

Finally, a distinction between two types of challenges, typically to legislation, should be noted: challenges "on their face" and challenges "as applied." Facial challenges seek to invalidate or enjoin a statute altogether so that it cannot be enforced at all, in any manner, to any conduct. "As-applied" challenges seek only to invalidate or enjoin a statute as it bears upon specific activities of the challenger. The former type of challenge may proceed largely without factual development; the latter ordinarily may not. The consequences are also different. A statute struck down as applied to particular conduct may lawfully be applied to other conduct. A statute struck down on its face may not.

The main difficulty with facial challenges, however, is one that is closely related to standing. A party seeking to strike down a statute on facial grounds is arguing, in effect, not only that the statute might be unconstitutional as applied to her own conduct, but as applied to the conduct of others as well. Thus, such challenges implicate concerns similar to those associated with third-party standing. The Supreme Court therefore once stated (in a non-First Amendment case) that a facial challenge may only be brought when a statute is susceptible of no constitutional application at all. United States v. Salerno (1987).

Elsewhere, however, the Court has concluded that a facial challenge may be brought when a statute is unconstitutional in many of its applications but not all. The latter formulation appears to have developed from the Court's standing rules in First Amendment cases involving the unconstitutional "overbreadth" of statutes that are alleged to chill the exercise of free speech. Overbreadth challenges argue that a statute, although perhaps constitutional in some of its applications, is unconstitutional in a substantial number of them. Broadrick v. Oklahoma (1973). It allows someone to whom a statute may or may not be constitutionally applied, to seek its judicial invalidation if it is illegal as to others, and if the overbreadth is "real" and "substantial." New York v. Ferber (1982). The First Amendment rationale is that, taking the time to hammer out the myriad legal applications on a case-by-case basis will not eliminate the substantial chill to protected speech posed by the statute. If the particular constitutional right at issue presents similar time-is-of-the-essence qualities (as, for example, in challenges to abortion restrictions) then perhaps a "substantial" overbreadth argument should suffice instead of having to show that there could be "no constitutional application" of the statute. Nevertheless, to the extent that the alleged chill is to the conduct of others and not to the plaintiff, such standing still reflects the problems of third-party standing and plaintiffs who seek to enforce more generalized grievances, not necessarily their own.

I. Jury Trial Rights

Under the Seventh Amendment, in "suits at common law, where the value in controversy shall exceed twenty dollars, the right of trial by jury shall be preserved." U.S. Const. amend. VII. Insofar as congressionally created causes of action are concerned, the Amendment has been read as requiring a jury trial in federal court when the statutory action is sufficiently analogous to suits that would have been tried by courts of common law in 1791, as distinguished from courts of equity. While many differences mark out the ancient opposition of courts of law and equity, the primary ones had to do with matters of procedure and remedy. Generally speaking, common law suits would be tried before a jury with money damages as the typical relief, while equitable matters would be tried before the judge with injunctive or other coercive relief being customary. Although § 1983 does not itself provide for jury trials, it does specifically refer to the ability of a plaintiff to bring an "action at law [or] suit in equity." And insofar as the Court has elsewhere characterized the remedy under § 1983 as "a species of tort liability," Heck v. Humphrey (1994), one might suppose that whenever damages relief was sought under § 1983 a jury trial would be available; similarly, if injunctive relief were requested, the matter would appear to be appropriate for equity.

Things seem to have proved more complicated. Instead of characterizing all § 1983 damages actions as akin to a tort or trespass action (which surely would have been triable by jury at common law), the Court recently indicated it would inquire into whether the claim underlying the § 1983 action would itself present a historically legal or equitable analogy. In City of Monterey v. Del Monte Dunes (1999), the Court split closely on the question of whether a § 1983 claim for damages against a municipality for a regulatory taking of property without just compensation should be tried to a jury. A plurality expressly rejected an analogy to inverse condemnation—a proceeding that would not have traditionally been a jury triable matter. And a narrow majority concluded that the claim for just compensation "sounded basically in tort," in part because the property owner "sought not just compensation per se but rather damages for the unconstitutional denial of such compensation." Only Justice Scalia would have made all damages claims under § 1983 jury triable, without regard to the underlying claim.

Even when a jury trial is appropriate, however, there remains the difficult question of what the jury is to resolve, and what the judge. It is easy to state the general principle that issues of disputed fact are for the jury, and questions of law for the judge. But juries are also involved in the application of law to fact, at least when the underlying facts are in dispute. To this end, they will be instructed by the court as to the law that they must apply to the facts as they happen to find. Sometimes, of course, the law-fact divide is not always so neat. For example, the Court has tended to treat the question of qualified immunity as one of law, but as noted elsewhere, jury decisionmaking may be required when the underlying factual issues surrounding immunity are disputed. See Chapter 8. Cf. Willingham v. Crooke (4th Cir.2005) (indicating that qualified immunity question should be resolved by district judge even when case goes to trial). In addition, although the Court has stated that the task of identifying "policymakers" for purposes of local governmental liability is a question of law and not one for the jury, see Jett v. Dallas Indep. Sch. Dist. (1989), factual disputes over such matters as "custom or policy" have been submitted to juries.

In *Del Monte Dunes* the Court concluded that a jury ought to decide not only whether the plaintiff property owner had been deprived of all economically viable use of his property, but that the jury should also decide whether the city's property regulations were reasonably related to the achievement of a legitimate public interest. It is hard to know what purpose is served by having a jury decide the rationality of governmental regulations in constitu-

INDEX

References are to Pages

---

†